S0-ARX-853

FLORIDA STATE
UNIVERSITY LIBRARIES

JUL 13 1998

TALLAHASSEE, FLORIDA

LABOR AND DEMOCRACY IN NAMIBIA, 1971–1996

Labor and Democracy in Namibia, 1971–1996

Gretchen Bauer

OHIO UNIVERSITY PRESS
ATHENS

JAMES CURREY PUBLISHERS
LONDON

HD
8808
,B38
1998

Ohio University Press, Athens, Ohio 45701
© 1998 by Gretchen Bauer

James Currey Ltd.
73 Botley Road
Oxford
OX2 OBS

Printed in the United States of America
All rights reserved

Ohio University Press books
are printed on acid-free paper ⊖™

02 01 00 99 98 5 4 3 2 1

Library of Congress Cataloging-in-Publication Data
Bauer, Gretchen
   Labor and democracy in Namibia, 1971–1996 / Gretchen Bauer.
      p.   cm.
   Includes bibliographical references (p.) and index.
   ISBN 0-8214-1216-7 (alk. paper). — ISBN 0-8214-1217-5 (pbk. :
alk. paper)
      1. Trade-unions—Namibia—History—20th century.
   2. Democracy—Namibia—History—20th century. 3. Namibia—
   Politics and government—1946–1990. 4. Namibia—Politics and
   government—1990–
   I. Title.
   HD8808.B38   1998
   331.88′096881—dc21   97-49202
                                             CIP

British Library Cataloguing in Publication Data
Bauer, Gretchen
   Labor and democracy in Namibia, 1971–1996
   1. Labor movement—Namibia 2. Industrial relations—Namibia
   3. Democracy—Namibia 4. Namibia—Politics and government—
   1946–1990 5. Namibia—Politics and government—1990–
   I. Title
   331.8′096881′09045

ISBN 0-85255-753-1 (cloth)
ISBN 0-85255-752-3 (pbk.)

CONTENTS

ACKNOWLEDGMENTS

Conducting the research for and writing this book have taken me several years—nearly the time that Namibia has been independent from South African rule. During these years the assistance of many people and institutions has contributed much to the final product.

I am very grateful for comments on earlier drafts of this book and for continued mentoring and support from Crawford Young, Michael Schatzberg, and Aili Mari Tripp. In addition, Gay Seidman, Ben Ulenga, Pekka Peltola, and Jeremy Baskin read earlier versions and offered insightful comments, for which I am grateful.

I would like to thank the Social Science Research Council, Fulbright, the MacArthur Scholars Program at the University of Wisconsin, and the University of Delaware General University Research grants program for funding support during various phases of this project.

I am also grateful for the untiring assistance of the staff at several libraries in Namibia, including the National Library, the National Archives, and the libraries of the Namibia Institute for Social and Economic Research (NISER) and the Namibia Economic Policy Research Unit (NEPRU). In addition, I would like to thank organizations in Windhoek such as the Namibia Peace Plan, the Namibia Institute for Economic Affairs, the Private Sector Foundation, and the Chamber of Mines that made their special collections available to me.

I have benefited very much from the encouragement and support of colleagues and friends at the Namibia Institute for Social and Economic Research at the University of Namibia (UNAM), now the Social Sciences Division of the Multidisciplinary Research Centre at UNAM, where I was based from late 1991 to late 1993. NISER was a wonderful place from which to operate; it provided a stimulating environment and generous facilities without which this project would have been much less successful. I also thank the Friedrich Ebert Stiftung, the Legal Assistance Centre, and the Ford Foundation in Windhoek for including me in some of their labor-related activities and availing me of their facilities.

I am especially indebted to the many friends I made in the labor movement in Namibia. What began as distant relations between a foreign researcher and local informants ended, in many cases, in closer friendships. In particular, I came to work frequently with the unions of the National Union of Namibian Workers, ultimately participating, as a researcher, in several of its conferences and symposia. This interaction afforded me a unique vantage point from which to investigate labor and democracy in Namibia.

Many others in Namibia, including politicians, government and party leaders and officials, journalists, scholars and other researchers, businesspeople, community activists, and ordinary citizens have helped me enormously over the years. They have taken me into their confidence and shared with me their experiences; they have revealed to me the errors of my own analysis and interpretation and tried to steer me along what seemed the right path. Some have been formal informants and others more casual acquaintances, and I am very grateful to them all.

I would like to express my ongoing appreciation to friends who nurtured and sustained me during long periods of work in Namibia. These include Nepeti Nicanor, Rosa Nakale, Kandali Nghidengua, Ben and Nambata Ulenga, Doufi Namalambo, Meriam Haimbodi, and Franna Kavari.

I would also like to thank the editors and staff at Ohio University Press for their very professional work and pleasant demeanor.

Finally, I would like to mention my husband, Moses Haimbodi, and my daughter, Mavetjiua, for whom, as for all other Namibians, the future of Namibia's nascent democracy is crucial.

LIST OF ABBREVIATIONS

ACN	Action Christian National
CCN	Council of Churches of Namibia
CDM	Consolidated Diamond Mines
COSATU	Congress of South African Trade Unions
DTA	Democratic Turnhalle Alliance
ELCIN	Evangelical Lutheran Church in Namibia
FOSATU	Federation of South African Trade Unions
FWEP	Farmworkers Education Project
GRN	Government of the Republic of Namibia
GSSA	Government Service Staff Association
ICFTU	International Confederation of Free Trade Unions
ICJ	International Court of Justice
IG	Interessengemeinschaft
ILO	International Labour Organisation
IMLT	Institute for Management and Leadership Training
JUC	Joint Union Committee
LAC	Legal Assistance Centre
LAUN	Local Authorities Union of Namibia
MANWU	Metal and Allied Namibian Workers Union
MAWARD	Ministry of Agriculture, Water and Rural Development
MLMD	Ministry of Labour and Manpower Development
MUN	Mineworkers Union of Namibia
NAFAU	Namibia Food and Allied Workers Union
NAFWU	Namibia Farmworkers Union
NAMSA	Namibia Municipal Staff Association
NANAU	Namibia National Allied Unions
NANSO	Namibia National Students Organisation
NANTU	Namibia National Teachers Union
NAPWU	Namibia Public Workers Union
NATAU	Namibia Transport and Allied Union
NAU	Namibia Agricultural Union
NAWU	Namibian Workers Union
NBWU	Namibia Building Workers Union
NCSTU	Namibian Christian Social Trade Unions

NDAWU	Namibia Domestic and Allied Workers Union
NEF	Namibia Employers Federation
NEPRU	Namibia Economic Policy Research Unit
NIEA	Namibia Institute for Economic Affairs
NISER	Namibia Institute for Social and Economic Research
NNCCI	Namibia National Chamber of Commerce and Industry
NNFU	Namibia National Farmers Union
NNTU	Namibia National Trade Union
NPF	National Patriotic Front
NPP 435	Namibia Peace Plan Study and Contact Group
NPSM	Namibian People's Social Movement
NTU	Namibia Trade Union
NUM	National Union of Mineworkers (South Africa)
NUNW	National Union of Namibian Workers
NWRWU	Namibia Wholesale and Retail Workers Union
NWV	Namibian Women's Voice
OPC	Ovamboland People's Congress
OPO	Ovamboland People's Organisation
PLAN	People's Liberation Army of Namibia
PSF	Private Sector Foundation
PSUN	Public Service Union of Namibia
RMU	Rossing Mineworkers Union
RSA	Republic of South Africa
SWA	South West Africa
SWAAU	South West Africa Agricultural Union
SWACOL	South West Africa Confederation of Labour
SWAMSA	South West Africa Municipal Staff Association
SWAMU	South West Africa Mineworkers Union
SWANLA	South West Africa Native Labour Association
SWANU	South West Africa National Union
SWAPO	South West Africa People's Organisation
SWAPO-D	South West Africa People's Organisation—Democrats
SYL	SWAPO Youth League
TCL	Tsumeb Corporation Ltd
TGNU	Transitional Government of National Unity
TUN	Teachers Union of Namibia
UDF	United Democratic Front
WAC	Workers Action Committee
WFTU	World Federation of Trade Unions
WOSC	Workers Steering Committee

One

INTRODUCTION

The late 1980s and early 1990s were a period of considerable optimism in Africa and elsewhere in the world, as efforts at the transition from authoritarian to more democratic rule seemed to be succeeding in one country after another. In Africa, these attempts at political liberalization took myriad forms, from the convening of national conferences and the holding of national elections to promises by military regimes of guided transitions to democracy. Indeed, a 1996 issue of *Africa Demos* lists sixteen African countries as "democratic," six countries as "directed democracies," seven as experiencing "contested sovereignty," and six more as still "authoritarian." The remaining countries were listed as regimes in transition with either a moderate or ambiguous commitment to democracy. Of the democratic countries, newly independent Namibia is ranked as one of the very few to be only one step away from the "consolidation" of democracy.[1]

But by the mid- to late 1990s, participants and observers alike had become much less sanguine about the long-term prospects for rapid transitions to democracy. Recent work raises the concern that around the world the "third wave" of democracy may be over, that democratic reversals may be on the horizon, all the more so as democratization promotes heightened competition and unleashes latent conflict.[2] Recent analyses have called for a more critical evaluation of prodemocracy movements and political liberalization in Africa. For example, while acknowledging that "the political landscape has significantly changed in the last half decade," Julius Nyang'oro cautions that tremendous problems remain: continued one-party dominance despite multiparty elections, the recycling and reinvention of once authoritarian leaders, continuing efforts by states to undermine the forces of civil society, and vicious conflicts usually

1

portrayed in ethnic or regional terms.[3] Similarly, Julius Ihonvbere concedes that the "'aura of invincibility' of political strongmen in Africa" has been shattered but warns that "elections by themselves will not redeem Africa." The great concern for Ihonvbere in Africa today is prodemocracy movements that have no alternative agendas or, when they do, are not wedded to them. Just as disappointing, in his view, have been the "new oppositions" that are merely reconstituted parties of past authoritarian rulers: "The current 'transitions' in Africa are largely dominated, influenced, conditioned and operated by the very same elites who subverted the early democratic experiments, collaborated with military juntas, and ruined African economies."[4]

Many scholars and activists who are concerned about democratic prospects in Africa believe there is an alternative to the recently formed or newly reconfigured political parties and prodemocracy movements. For them, the concept of civil society promises the strongest hopes for the future of democracy in Africa.[5] As Celestin Monga notes, in the face of "the risk of being deprived of their democratisation, society has had to invent alternative structures to manage and express its dissatisfaction"; these are the organizations of civil society. Four groups in civil society stand out so far, according to Monga: students, the clergy, lawyers, and intellectuals and journalists.[6] This civil society and its organizations and movements are variously expected to articulate alternatives to existing one-party states, represent society's fight for resources and power, redefine politics and provide the basis for institutional reform, constitute a potentially subversive space from which new structures and norms may take hold to challenge existing state orders, become an arena for dissent and opposition, hold government accountable, provide a counterweight to state power, facilitate the new alliances and coalitions necessary for the functioning of a viable democracy, be part of a larger, more sustained effort to create a plural society, and more.[7]

Then again, argue others such as E. Gyimah-Boadi, civil society's record in Africa has been one of disappointment, "most glaring[ly] in the crucial area of ensuring public accountability," because civil society is too weak to tip the balance in favor of social forces. Moreover, "civil society has also failed to transcend ethnoregional, religious, and other cleavages in any lasting way," according to Gyimah-Boadi. Further, it has made no contributions to economic reform and development. These deficiencies stem from a variety of sources, according to Gyimah-Boadi: vulnerability to state repression and co-optation, lack of organizational and financial resources, continuing economic crisis and the patrimonialization of political power, and a political culture of incivility.[8]

Michael Bratton and Nicolas van de Walle, in their comprehensive study of democratic experiments in Africa, conclude that though civic groups have been instrumental in democratic transitions, they have performed less well during the early stages of democratic consolidation. In general, Bratton and van de Walle caution against positing a simple positive correlation "between the strength of associational life and the success of democratic government."[9] This book provides an additional case study of the relationship between civil society and democratization in Africa. It examines newly independent Namibia, where by all accounts the prospects for the consolidation of democracy are more favorable than elsewhere in Africa, and seeks to determine what role civil society, as represented by the organized labor movement, will play in the democratization process.

Organized Labor and Democratization

Numerous accounts from outside Africa indicate that labor movements can have a significant effect on efforts at democratization. For example, in their examination of the emergence of worker protest and organized labor movements in eight Latin American countries in the early twentieth century, Ruth Berins Collier and David Collier explain the strategies of control and mobilization different states used in response. Collier and Collier believe that the legacies of these strategies have been important influences in "shaping the political arena," including patterns of regime change and the authoritarian or democratic paths taken in the 1960s and 1970s. Gay Seidman, in her comparison of South African and Brazilian labor movements, shows how these remarkably similar movements challenged authoritarian rule in their respective countries. Margaret Keck and Leigh Payne, in their separate treatments of Brazil, have elaborated the discussion of labor and the transition to democracy there. Dietrich Rueschemeyer, Evelyne Huber Stephens, and John Stephens, in their comparative study of democracy and capitalist development in Latin America and Europe, argue that the growth of a working class—developed and sustained by trade unions, political parties, and similar groups—is critical for the promotion of democracy. And for South Korea, Frederic Deyo has shown how a weakly organized labor force initially facilitated continued authoritarian rule, yet more recently, as the labor movement became more mobilized, has been able to challenge that same authoritarian rule.[10]

Samuel Valenzuela has observed that labor movements are often particularly well placed to influence efforts at democratization. Labor "occupies a special place among the forces of civil society" during the transition from authoritarian rule because a labor movement "generally has a greater capacity for extensive and effective mobilization at critical moments than other social groups" if it has a mass base (an organized network in the form of already established unions) and an ability to disrupt the economy.[11] Collier and Collier also attribute the political importance of labor movements, in part, to their capacity for collective action. More important, an organized working class, they believe, can be "one of the most important 'bearers' of the mediations and political symbols relevant to the problem of legitimacy." In other words, labor movements can confer legitimacy upon a regime. They can also serve as the principal vehicle for protest against state policy. Thus for a state or, indeed, for a political party, the capacity to control a labor movement or to mobilize its support is a significant political asset.[12]

Even though most of Africa is made up of largely underindustrialized economies and huge informal sectors, workers and their organizations have, at times, played a pivotal role in politics. In the aftermath of World War II, trade unions emerged in significant numbers and strength throughout the continent. In many colonies, unions joined with (even spawned) nascent nationalist movements to lead the struggle for political independence.[13] Prolonged worker protest formed an integral part of the fight against continued colonial domination. And in most cases, small African working classes were not only articulating their own specific grievances but were demanding an agenda of relevance to wider urban populations (with ramifications for even larger rural populations).[14]

For many organized labor movements, however, independence was no boon but often led to the rapid demobilization of trade unions. Thus by the mid-1970s, one observer wrote: "It is widely believed that African trade unions have nothing to lose but their subordination to the state, are weak, inactive, ineffective in behalf of members, their leaders coopted by the state, while rank and file members are seen to have little consciousness of their interests but, nonetheless, to have benefitted disproportionately in income relative to other wage workers and peasant farmers."[15] Indeed, the charge that since independence organized labor has been subordinated to the state has been difficult to counter. As early as 1966, one writer found that almost nowhere in Africa were trade union–sponsored governments in power. In many other cases (for example, Ghana, Guinea, Tanzania, Tunisia, Egypt, Algeria, Ivory Coast, Senegal, and Kenya), trade unions had been quickly absorbed into "party machines."[16] Where unions were not directly integrated into party structures, governments frequently moved to impose trade union unity through the creation of single "national labor centers" or trade union federations, as in Nigeria and Zimbabwe. In some cases, such as Ghana, trade unions were initially prohibited from engaging in political activities, and their leaders were to be hired, not elected, according to criteria specified by government. In other cases, the most militant trade union leaders were offered positions in government and, as in Tanzania and Kenya, trade union federation general secretaries were appointed by government and made to serve as ministers of labor as well. State of emergency regulations were often used against trade unionists and, in general, labor laws that restricted the right to strike, proclaimed minimum wages in certain sectors, established liaison or workers' committees at the workplace, or imposed onerous registration requirements rendered already struggling trade unions powerless or redundant.[17]

Although one-party states proved particularly adept at extinguishing independent trade union movements in the early years of independence, evidence from several African countries suggests that trade unions have begun to reassert themselves and in some cases have played significant roles in recent democratization efforts. In his work on recent regime changes in Africa, Bratton has found the number of trade unions to be the best predictor of the frequency of political protest in the prelude to a democratic opening.[18] More often than not, trade unions have challenged existing political parties.[19] For example, although it is not clear that the new regime is very different from the old, in 1989 the Zambia Congress of Trade Unions (ZCTU) spearheaded a campaign for the creation of a new political party in Zambia—the Movement for Multiparty Democracy (MMD)—and in late 1991 MMD leader Frederick Chiluba defeated Kenneth Kaunda, who had been president since independence, in national elections. In Senegal, according to Babacar Kante, disaffection among the population following the 1993 elections has manifested itself in a "quest for autonomy on the part of party-dominated organizations such as trade unions." In future, Kante continues, Senegalese leaders will have to worry less about opposition political parties and more about "the rising trade unions [that] will be challenging their social and economic agenda and their capacity to manage the country." In Zimbabwe, the Zimbabwe Congress of Trade Unions, further weakened by the effects of the Economic Structural Adjustment Program, revealed its dissatisfaction with operating within the confines of the Zimbabwe African National Union (Patriotic Front) and its intention to explore the possibility of forming an opposition political party.[20] Further examples of trade unions that have become actively involved in democratization efforts are evident in Nigeria and Malawi.

Trade Unions and Democracy in Namibia

In Namibia, however, the nascent organized labor movement emerged from colonialism and the struggle for independence in a weak condition. Namibia's most recent census estimates an economically active population of about 500,000, of which about 270,000 are assumed to be in subsistence agriculture in the rural areas, in the informal sector in the urban areas, or unemployed. The remainder work in the formal sector.[21] Of these approximately 230,000 formal sector workers, just over half are estimated to be members of one of more than fifteen trade unions aligned to one of two trade union federations—the National Union of Namibian Workers (NUNW) and the Namibian People's Social Movement (NPSM).[22] But the organized labor movement's weakness is indicated by more than simply its small absolute numbers. Most trade unions in Namibia are experiencing a serious lack of capacity in organizational, administrative, financial, leadership, research, and policy matters. Only some unions are effectively servicing their members and redressing in any way the continuing apartheid legacy in the workplace. As a whole, unions have not succeeded in articulating a clear socioeconomic and political vision to work to enhance their members' living and working conditions and to guide their interactions with employers and the state.

For the organized labor movement, Namibia's colonial experience and struggle for independence—an oppressive colonial rule for much longer than other African states endured and a harsh guerrilla war waged by the South West Africa People's Organisation (SWAPO) in exile against the South African forces of occupation—threaten a lasting and potentially debilitating legacy. Neither the repressive apartheid rule of the South Africans nor the nature of the armed liberation struggle, led by one nationalist organization (SWAPO) deemed by the United Nations to be the "sole and authentic representative of the Namibian people," has been conducive to the development of strong social movements in Namibia. As Colin Leys and John Saul have written, "While a formally democratic system has indeed emerged in Namibia, it seems fair to say that little popular empowerment has been realized."[23] Indeed, it appears that in Namibia after independence, the "organizations of civil society" are in disarray. Herein lies the potentially debilitating legacy: a civil society so weak that the successful consolidation of democracy is threatened.

The political space to organize in Namibia became somewhat available only in the last five (preindependence) years of "interim government" rule. Still, many of these efforts at community-based organization were, to a certain extent, hampered by the interim government and the externally based nationalist liberation movement, both of which recognized the subversive nature of such activity and were therefore (initially at least) hostile to it. In addition, differences in political orientation and strategy—in particular over the question of participation in the interim governments—tended to divide sharply the emerging organizations of civil society and continue to do so today. For example, even after independence, the women's movement remains divided largely along party political lines; nearly half of the major women's organizations in Namibia today are the women's league or women's council of a political party.[24] Before independence, organizers of one women's group, Namibian Women's Voice (NWV), were suspended from SWAPO (and the organization eventually disbanded) for working with women outside of the SWAPO Women's Council, and these tensions continue as well.[25] Since independence, the student movement has also been rent by a split in its ranks—to the point of the formation of a second student organization—over the issue of formal affiliation to SWAPO. The split has badly weakened the young student organization.[26] The churches, meanwhile, have emerged tainted from the liberation struggle after their failure to investigate allegations from 1984 that SWAPO was detaining its own cadres in exile. The major church federation, the Council of Churches of Namibia (CCN), suffers from the loss of its most competent people to government after independence, decreased unity among member churches, and a lack of vision concerning the church's role now that the liberation struggle is over.[27] Meanwhile, in the rural areas, according to some observers, the basis for community development work and organization continues to be mired in "a web of political tensions, suspicious motives, and identities along party lines that persist today."[28]

Of all of the groups in Namibian civil society, the ones with the greatest potential for strong and autonomous organization seem to be the many trade unions. The labor movement is well positioned because the country has a relatively highly wage-dependent population and trade unions claim to represent just over one-half of this wage-earning workforce. Unions are strongest in the crucial revenue-generating mining sector and are rapidly building strength in the government, which is the single largest employer in the country.[29] Moreover, workers in Namibia, in particular contract migrant workers, figure prominently in the historiography of the ruling political party SWAPO (and indeed of Namibia); they are credited with starting the Ovamboland People's Organisation (OPO), SWAPO's predecessor, in Cape Town in the late 1950s and with providing the bulwark of SWAPO's support throughout the liberation struggle. Indeed, at least in its rhetoric, SWAPO always privileged the concerns of Namibian workers and their families during the nationalist struggle. In addition, since independence the political and legal environment facing organized workers has improved markedly: not only does the constitution guarantee important rights, but new labor legislation, implemented in late 1992, represents a dramatic gain for Namibian workers and offers a framework for collective labor relations, among other things. Finally, in the new international context, trade union organizations in Africa should be less prey to the foreign policy connivances and ideological struggles of East and West and therefore better able to address national and regional concerns.

Many observers have argued that contemporary analyses of democratization in Africa must focus not only on the formal aspects of political democracy—free and fair elections and multipartyism—but also on the vibrancy of associational life, on the strength of social movements and independent organizations that can potentially check the excesses of government and give voice to the underrepresented. For Namibia, however, such argument does not augur well for the successful consolidation of democracy. Indeed, the labor movement, which is better situated than other sectors of society (women, churches, students, rural dwellers) to spawn strong and autonomous organizations in the form of trade unions, appears in the first years of independence to be in a precarious position. As I will elaborate in the concluding chapter, the reasons for this weakness lie, first, in the structural characteristics of the Namibian economy, that is, a primary export-dominated economy with an insignificant manufacturing sector and a large segment of the population reliant on subsistence agriculture or the informal sector for its livelihood. Second, labor's weakness lies in both the restrictions and later reforms of an oppressive colonial rule and its enduring legacy, especially in the workplace. Finally, the National Union of Namibian Workers—the major trade union federation in Namibia—and affiliated unions are weak because they emerged and evolved in the context of an externally based nationalist movement, now the ruling party in government (SWAPO), anxious to consolidate its position in postindependence Namibia.

More specifically, in the years before the general strike of 1971–72 in Namibia, a heavily regulated contract labor system, held in place by an authoritarian colonial state in collaboration with employers, precluded the organization of black trade unions. Still, both covert and overt forms of resistance abounded among workers, culminating in a general strike in the early 1970s that prompted the state and employers to reappraise their strategy of repression. From the late 1970s the colonial state and some of the larger employers began to consider an alternative strategy of co-optation and incorporation in which a reform process would be set in motion eventually legalizing black trade unions but requiring them to be nonpolitical. Among other things, this strategy resulted in a highly fractured labor movement in a country with few formal sector workers.

The origins of the unions of the NUNW within the nationalist movement have had an even more profound effect, blurring completely the distinction between trade union and political party and hindering the postindependence transition from a struggle for political independence to one for economic emancipation. Part of the political struggle of this nationalist movement was to mobilize workers' economic grievances, but it was, initially at least, reluctant to countenance the separate organization of workers because it feared rival leaders and organizations. Since independence the nationalist movement, now the ruling political party, desperate to maintain peace and stability and to attract much needed foreign investment, has exhibited little commitment to the workers of Namibia, let alone to the notion of strong and autonomous trade unions. For all intents and purposes, the party has sought to weaken the unions or at least to maintain them securely within the party fold. For example, trade union leaders have been taken into government, attempts to disaffiliate the unions from the party have been actively discouraged, and unions have been mobilized in support of SWAPO electoral campaigns and dissuaded from fielding their own candidates. Thus the nature of the Namibian economy and the legacies of colonial rule and the nationalist struggle (and association with the nationalist movement cum political party) have weakened trade unions in Namibia, diminishing the prospects for the successful consolidation of democracy in that country.

LITERATURE ON LABOR IN NAMIBIA

Despite Namibia's position as one of the few democracies in Africa, very little scholarly research had been undertaken on the country until recently. Indeed, the trade union movement and labor relations in Namibia warrant closer examination, in part, because they have been so little investigated or so inaccurately portrayed in the past. A fair amount of work—historical treatises, autobiographical and fictional accounts, and scholarly analyses— does exist on the early contract migrant labor system, most of it dealing with the period up to the general strike of 1971-72. In addition, within the large body of "solidarity literature"—that literature used for mobilizational purposes during the course of the liberation struggle—there is some work that deals with workers and even trade unions in Namibia, although this is highly rhetorical in form and content. Thus a more balanced account, particularly of the years following the general strike during which trade unions and labor relations actually emerged in Namibia, is needed.

A great deal of work, relatively speaking, has been carried out on the contract migrant labor system in Namibia, some of which touches on issues of organized labor and labor relations. Several published histories of Namibia by Namibian academics (and onetime exiled SWAPO activists) have dealt with the class position of workers in Namibia and their role in resistance to colonialism and capitalism.[30] Numerous theses and dissertations have been written over the years by younger Namibian scholars touching on migrant workers' relationship to nationalist organizations and political parties, their relations with management, and the wider legal and labor relations frameworks.[31] Most of these authors were exiled SWAPO or South West Africa National Union members who had little or no access to primary material inside Namibia on which to base their work.

Many autobiographical and fictional accounts also have dealt with the life of migrant laborers in Namibia; in addition, other Namibians have published their personal observations and experiences of the contract labor system in nonfiction form.[32] Although all of these works are enormously useful as firsthand accounts, they are, for the most part, not scholarly analyses and, in any case, depict only conditions during the 1950s, 1960s, and early 1970s in Namibia. Accounts by foreigners who lived and worked in Namibia, though extremely helpful and insightful, suffer from some of the same limitations of the firsthand accounts by Namibians.[33] In addition, there are theses and dissertations by other non-Namibians who had access to primary material in Namibia and South Africa (and elsewhere); these touch on such aspects of migrant labor as its effect on "Ovambo tribal life" and early incarnation in Ovamboland to the plight of particular workers such as farmworkers, labor control strategies by management and the colonial state, workers' relationship to nationalist organizations, and their consciousness as members of a working class.[34]

The migrant labor system has been the subject of academic study. Keith Gottschalk, in a 1978 article, details South African labor policy in Namibia from 1915 to 1975, outlining the reserves policy, the regulatory legislation, methods of discrimination against workers, examples of worker resistance, and the general strike of 1971–72. Robert Gordon provides evidence that collective labor resistance did not begin with the general strike but dates back to the late nineteenth century in Namibia; in another article he analyzes the stimuli on the part of the colonial state and those in the sending areas that contributed to the migration of Ovambo laborers. In other work, including an article and a book, Gordon notes the lack of organizations such as trade unions among workers in Namibia and describes what he calls an ethos or system of "brotherhood" operating among migrant workers; the brotherhood, delineating "a distinct moral universe which specifically excludes all whites," provided the main organizational framework, according to Gordon, for an underground or "private" resistance network among migrant workers. Richard Moorsom has written about the level of class consciousness and collective labor action among migrant workers in Namibia and the general strike of 1971–72; he has contributed much to our understanding of the origins of the contract labor system in Namibia, of aspects of that system such as the recruiting agency, the

South West Africa Native Labour Association (SWANLA), and of early patterns of class formation and differentiation in the migrant labor sending area of Ovamboland.[35]

SWAPO has published books and booklets dealing largely or exclusively with the situation of migrant workers in Namibia and their organizations. In addition, numerous papers for solidarity conferences as well as studies have been produced by organizations and institutions in support of SWAPO. All of these, however, including the SWAPO publications, have been written by foreign academics (or journalists) often with little access to what was happening inside Namibia and with a clear mission to support with the written word the SWAPO-led liberation struggle.[36]

In the mid-1980s two important edited volumes were published in Namibia which augment nicely the earlier literature on the contract migrant labor system. Both Christine Von Garnier's *Katutura Revisited: Essays on a Black Namibian Apartheid Suburb* and Gerhard Toetemeyer, Vezera Kandetu, and Wolfgang Werner's *Namibia in Perspective* provide numerous firsthand accounts by community activists and others of their work with the nascent trade union movement and other community-based organizations during those years. In addition, Tessa Cleaver and Marion Wallace provide some observations on the emerging trade union movement in their book on the women's movement in Namibia in the late 1980s. Also during the 1980s, South African journals such as the *South African Labour Bulletin* and *Work in Progress* began to provide brief but informative accounts of the new labor movement in Namibia, as did the *Review of African Political Economy*. Since independence other significant volumes have been published. Leys and Saul's *Namibia's Liberation Struggle: The Two-Edged Sword* provides an in-depth and critical examination of SWAPO politics inside and outside Namibia during the liberation struggle, as well as insightful accounts of emerging social movements inside Namibia during the 1980s such as those involving the students and churches. Heike Becker's *Namibian Women's Movement, 1980 to 1992*, documents the emergence of disparate women's movements in Namibia and the relationship of women's groups to political parties and other community-based groups. Finally, Pekka Peltola's *The Lost May Day: Namibian Workers Struggle for Independence* provides a short account of the many obstacles Namibian workers faced as they sought to organize and assert their position over the last two decades. In particular, Peltola's work focuses on the labor-related activities of SWAPO in exile, of which he had personal experience.[37]

All these works offer important insights into the contract labor system and labor migrancy in Namibia, but they have largely not dealt with most of the issues raised in this book. For the most part, this is because these works were written before 1975 and deal with the contract migrant labor system before the onset of the reform following the general strike of 1971–72 and before the first attempts to organize trade unions in Namibia. Moreover, exile made primary research impossible for Namibian students and academics, and those researchers who were able to gain access to primary material in Namibia and elsewhere were hampered in their efforts by the climate of war and suspicion or were interested in other aspects such as international diplomatic developments or internal political party maneuverings. In addition, labor was a highly politicized and contentious issue in colonial Namibia, all the more so because workers, in particular contract migrant workers, played such a pivotal role in the original organization of SWAPO and in SWAPO's liberation mythology. Thus much of the literature that has been published has been of a highly partisan nature—either for mobilizational purposes in support of the SWAPO-led liberation movement or in the service of the colonial state. Hence much research remains to be done on the trade union movement and labor relations in Namibia—from their origins in the two decades before independence and into the postindependence period—and from a perspective that locates them as participants in a broader civil society.

In many ways, independence has provided new opportunities and a new impetus for reexamining Namibia's past. With the end of the war, the return of the exiles, the withdrawal of South African civilian and military forces, and the implementation of a policy of national reconciliation, the atmosphere is more conducive to research, and the people and materials that constitute the important sources are more readily available. In some respects, these issues are less politicized and less contentious than in the past, and the absence of a "sole and authentic representative of the Namibian people" has broadened the scope for interpretation.

RESEARCH FOR AND ORGANIZATION OF THE BOOK

The research for this book was conducted during two years in Namibia and southern Africa, from late 1991 to late 1993, and during subsequent trips to Namibia in 1994, 1995, and 1996. In the course of my research, I used three methods of data collection: interviews, documentary analysis, and observation. First, during 1992 and 1993, I conducted more than one hundred interviews with past and present trade unionists, government officials, representatives of business and business organizations, community and student activists, political party officeholders, and members of nongovernmental organizations. These were mostly semistructured, in-depth interviews with respondents who were chosen for specific reasons. Almost all of the interviews were tape-recorded and transcribed. The interviews were conducted over the course of eighteen months, and some people were interviewed more than once. For a separate study on the consolidation of democracy in Namibia in July 1994, I conducted or participated in an additional fifty interviews with similar informants. In summer 1995 I conducted still more interviews, primarily with political party leaders and officials. The various interviews took me to several sites outside of Windhoek, including the Tsumeb Corporation mines in Tsumeb and Otjihase, the Consolidated Diamond Mines in Oranjemund, commercial farms in central and eastern Namibia, and to Oshakati, Ongwediva, Rundu, Otjiwarongo, Swakopmund, and Walvis Bay.

I have relied fairly heavily on interviews in this study because events are so recent, because there is so little documentary evidence for much of what is described here, in particular the emergence of trade unions, and because I made a conscious effort to use Namibian voices. At the same time, I have taken care to protect the identity of some of my informants, especially those who are not "public figures" or whose views are not necessarily known. Consequently, I have not included a list of informants although a list of interviews with the identifying numbers given in the text is available.

As a second method of data collection I gathered documentary evidence in the form of written material from libraries and collections in Namibia and South Africa.[38] This primary material includes government documents from before and after independence such as reports of commissions of inquiry, economic reports, legislation, and parliamentary debates; proceedings from conferences; publications of SWAPO of Namibia from 1960 onward; twenty years of selected Namibian newspapers and magazines; United Nations agency publications; internal documents from various trade unions and trade union federations, including their own newspapers and other publications; company annual reports and newsletters; and public speeches and published interviews. Secondary sources include unpublished theses, dissertations, and other manuscripts, many by Namibian students, and numerous books and articles.

Finally, I engaged in participant observation, in the sense of living and working in the region for an extensive period and participating in trade union and labor-related activities. For example, I was able to take part in several tripartite fora on labor law and labor relations in Windhoek,[39] and I worked with the National Union of Namibian Workers and member unions as a resource person, focusing on the unions' research capacity.[40] I also participated informally in numerous seminars and workshops of the NUNW and affiliated unions on, for example, basic trade unionism, economics, and an evaluation of May Day activities. Finally, I attended the First Congress of the Namibian

Christian Social Trade Unions, the other trade union federation in Namibia, in October 1992. All of these activities were carefully recorded in daily field notes.

This book is organized as follows: after this introductory chapter, Chapters 2, 3, 4, and 5 provide a descriptive narrative of the emergence and evolution of the trade union movement and of labor relations in Namibia. This narrative is placed in the context in Namibia of, first, primitive labor relations and a repressive colonial rule and, later, a reform of labor relations and the political process. At the same time, the emergence of trade unions is framed by the larger nationalist struggle for independence and the relationship between the two. The presentation is largely chronological, following stages in the organization of trade unions in Namibia, but also corresponds to significant events in the political history of Namibia. Chapter 6 concludes the book.

Chapter 2 begins with a cursory overview of South West Africa from 1915, when the Germans lost the territory, until the early 1970s, when the South Africans began to reconsider their political strategy in Namibia; this section focuses on the establishment and operation of the contract migrant labor system and outlines the political, economic, and social conditions in Namibia at the time of the 1971–72 general strike. The bulk of the chapter, however, treats the origins and aftermath of the general strike. I argue that the strike resulted in the amelioration of some of the worst features of the contract labor system, including a rise in wages, and that by the late 1970s the first suggestions of the need for a reform of labor relations were put forth by some employers. At about the same time, as colonial authorities began to reconsider their political strategy in Namibia, many petty apartheid laws were abolished, further eroding the contract labor system.

More important, however, in Chapter 2 I review the origins of SWAPO and show the movement's strong early nationalist, rather than worker, influences. I argue that the general strike, while relying on the accumulated grievances of thousands of migrant workers, was primarily a political event organized initially by SWAPO secondary school students hoping to rejuvenate the internal political struggle following the arrest or forced exile of most of the older generation of internal SWAPO leaders in the late 1960s. Indeed, the strike resulted in a heightened politicization and conscientization among both migrants and the Namibian population at large and set off an unrest in northern Namibia that would continue with the intensification of the war and the mass exodus of Namibian youth into exile from 1974. Contrary to popular belief, there were no trade unions in Namibia at the time of the strike, although the National Union of Namibian Workers was established, on paper, by SWAPO in exile in April 1970; the chapter deals briefly with the activities of the SWAPO Department of Labour in exile in the 1970s, of which the NUNW formed a small component.

In Chapter 3 I pursue further the relationship between the externally based nationalist movement and efforts to organize workers inside Namibia. The chapter treats the labor activity of SWAPO in exile; more important, it reveals the early negative attitude in external SWAPO toward any organized activity, even within the larger nationalist effort. The fear of the SWAPO leadership of the potential threat posed by mass-based organizations such as trade unions is made clear; participants in the NUNW and SWAPO Department of Labour projects in exile were among those arrested, accused of being spies, tortured, and imprisoned by SWAPO from the early 1980s until independence. In particular, some of those involved in labor activities in exile were accused of attempting to form a party within a party, to conduct a revolution within a revolution.

In addition, Chapter 3 describes the larger reform strategy (incorporation and depoliticization) of the colonial state and some employers toward workers in Namibia; it covers the further tentative steps toward reform of labor relations, including a change to labor law in 1978 allowing for the first time the formation and organization of black trade unions (while at the same time imposing a ban on party political affiliation for unions). Still more legislative reform was advocated by the Chamber of Mines; some members of the business community, inspired by similar groups in South Africa, formed organizations such as the Private Sector Foundation and the Namibian Institute for Economic Affairs, which held as one aspect of their mandate to sensitize employers to the need for trade unions and employers' organizations. The first attempt inside Namibia to form a black trade union, based initially among workers at the Rossing uranium mine, was relatively quickly crushed by the colonial authorities as part of a wider repression of political activity inside the territory around 1980. In the early 1980s other trade unions, perceived to be less political, were established.

Chapter 4 treats the last years of colonial rule, under the Transitional Government of National Unity (TGNU), which in some senses may be seen as a period of transition to independence and, perhaps, to democracy. In an effort to garner political support, the transitional government intensified the labor relations reform effort with new labor legislation and the introduction of May Day as a national holiday. In 1987, following two years of heightened industrial unrest, most notably a rash of strikes, the TGNU appointed the Commission of Inquiry into Labour Matters in Namibia, many of whose recommendations were incorporated into the postindependence labor relations dispensation.

This chapter also describes meetings between Namibian businesspeople and professionals with SWAPO in exile, at which the basis for a postindependence compromise was forged.

Further, Chapter 4 documents the final successful emergence of black trade unions in Namibia during the late 1980s. I argue that, contrary to popular belief, the original impetus for these unions came not solely from returned Robben Island prisoners but from among community workers in the Windhoek townships and from mine workers at the Rossing uranium mine and the Consolidated Diamond Mines. These two separate efforts were, however, quickly subsumed under a largely SWAPO initiative led by the returned Robben Islanders. The formation of the trade unions, as of other community-based organizations, was initially viewed with suspicion, even with hostility, by external SWAPO and by some in SWAPO inside Namibia as a threat to the control of the SWAPO leadership—that is, until the mobilizational value of the trade unions became clear. The NUNW unions played a key role in the final years of the liberation struggle inside Namibia as "the fighting arm of SWAPO." Finally, the chapter examines the emerging tension over whether development at the community level could take place before independence or only after and, indeed, whether community-based activity outside of SWAPO structures could be tolerated at all.

The last of the four historical chapters, Chapter 5, explores labor relations in the early years of independence in Namibia, elaborating the new SWAPO government's commitment to a policy of national reconciliation and to a private sector–led "mixed economy." I argue that, in many respects, the postindependence labor relations dispensation is merely the culmination of the reform process already under way before independence and shows the government's overweening concern to preserve peace and stability and to attract foreign investment. The chapter addresses the continued reluctance of employers to organize themselves and documents the deteriorating labor relations environment in the first few years of independence as the apartheid legacy continues to endure in the workplace.

Further, Chapter 5 describes in detail the weak condition of the trade union movement in Namibia, in particular those unions affiliated to the National Union of Namibian Workers. The chapter outlines the favorable political and legal framework facing organized labor, showing, however, the unions' difficulties in taking advantage of the opportunities presented by the new labor relations dispensation. Indeed, in Chapter 5 I analyze the self-acknowledged transition the NUNW unions are experiencing—from their political role before independence to a more economistic role after independence—and document the difficulty the unions are having in the transition process because of their weak organizational, administrative, financial, leadership, and research and policy capacity. Finally, I raise the issue of the unions' affiliation to the ruling political party SWAPO and highlight some of the more recent tensions between the unions and the party, for example, in the establishment of export processing zones in Namibia.

Two

The General Strike and Its Aftermath, 1971–1977

In the historiography of labor in Namibia the general strike of 1971–72 holds a prominent position. Although the first recorded strike in Namibia took place at Gross Otavi in 1893 and dozens of strikes occurred in the intervening years, the 1971–72 strike was unique: more than thirteen thousand contract workers participated in the strike, which effectively shut down twenty-three workplaces and eleven mines during its first month. Also within the first month, most of the striking workers were returned to their place of origin, Ovamboland in the North, where protest then commenced on an even wider scale. This resistance was met with military intervention on the part of the South African colonial authorities, escalating a spiral of violence that would end only with independence in 1990.

For the South African colonial authorities and some political groups inside Namibia, the strike and its aftermath were clear signals that they would have to amend their policies. For employers, the power of an organized labor force was revealed and, for the first time, they began to consider the need to reform labor relations. For workers, a slow and gradual amelioration of the worst features of the contract labor system began: in the immediate aftermath of the strike, some changes in the contract labor system were initiated (though the continuation of the existing pass laws tended to mitigate the effects) and wage increases were granted in several industries. By the end of the decade, changes in labor legislation allowed the qualified participation of black workers in trade unions, and petty apartheid was being abolished on paper throughout the land, further eroding the contract labor system. At a political level, steps toward an "internal settlement" of the South West Africa problem were being taken. Thus the general strike was an important impetus in beginning the reform of labor relations (and political relations) in Namibia during the 1970s.

Though there is no question that the strike was a seminal event with far-reaching consequences, I will argue that it was in large part a politically motivated and inspired action that relied on the long-standing grievances of the workers for its success. As with the earlier formation of the Ovamboland People's Organisation and then the South West Africa People's Organisation, during the general strike workers' demands were harnessed in the interest of the broader nationalist political struggle. Similarly, when SWAPO was in exile, the workers' struggle and trade unionism were used to elicit support from international labor and solidarity organizations for the national liberation struggle. For the workers of Namibia, however, the birth of the labor movement within the confines of the nationalist movement threatens to have a lasting and deleterious effect.

Context for the Strike

The Political Status of the Territory

By 1971 Namibia had been, for all practical purposes, a colony of South Africa for more than fifty years. Before that, the territory had been under German rule for thirty years until South African and British forces defeated German forces in then South West Africa (SWA) in July 1915. At the end of World War I, the territory's political status was decided by the 1919 Treaty of Versailles, which allowed the Allied Powers to take over all former German colonies.[1] A Mandate system was devised whereby the former German colonies (and other conquered territories) would be allocated among the members of the Supreme Council of the Allied and Associated Powers, to be administered under the supervision of the League of Nations.

South West Africa was entrusted as a "C" Mandate to the Union of South Africa on 17 December 1920; the few "C" Mandates (South West Africa and some South Pacific islands) "were to be administered under the laws of the Mandatory Powers as integral parts of their own territories."[2] Annual reports for all Mandates were to be submitted by the Mandatory power to the Permanent Mandates Commission of the League of Nations, and concern for the well-being and development of the people of the Mandate, "as a sacred trust of civilization," was to guide the actions of the Mandatory power.

From 1915 an administrator directly responsible to the South African prime minister was put in charge of South West Africa. The first administrator headed a military government until the Mandate agreement was signed in December 1920; after January 1921 the administrator was assisted by a nominated Advisory Council of six white members (later nine), one of whom was supposed to have a "special knowledge of the indigenous people."[3] In 1925, the South West Africa Constitution Act provided for a Legislative Assembly with eighteen members, twelve elected by the white electorate and six (also white) appointed by the administrator. In addition, a four-member Executive Committee, chaired by the administrator, was to handle daily matters (at this point the Advisory Council was reduced to seven members, including the four Executive Committee members). Of course, the areas over which the Legislative Assembly had any control were limited; "native affairs," external affairs, defense, justice, police, and transport and communications were the province of the South African government and its representative, the administrator.

During the interwar period, rebellions and uprisings among the indigenous population occurred among the Bondelswarts in 1922, the Basters in 1925, and the Ovambo in 1917 and 1933. "Native reserves" were established and "native commissioners" appointed, including in the far northern Ovambo area, which had not fallen under direct German administrative rule before World War I. Walvis Bay, which in 1884 had been incorporated with the guano islands into the Cape Colony, was administered as an integral part of the Mandated territory from 1922 until 1977, at which time it was again placed under the jurisdiction of the Cape Province.[4] The Caprivi Strip, which had been captured by Rhodesian soldiers during World War I, was initially administered by the British high commissioner in South Africa as part of Bechuanaland, placed under the jurisdiction of the SWA administrator in 1929, and ruled directly from Pretoria from 1939.

The (formal) dissolution of the League of Nations in April 1946 and the creation of the United Nations (October 1945) at the end of World War II further changed South West Africa's political status. All of the Mandatory powers holding Mandates under the League of Nations were expected to transfer their Mandates to the Trusteeship Council of the United Nations (UN). The United Party government in South Africa, however, did not regard the United Nations as the successor to the League of Nations and therefore felt it had no supervisory powers over the administration of South West Africa. The South African government further insisted that with the demise of the League of Nations the Mandate itself had lapsed. The government favored direct incorporation of the territory into South Africa; a "white referendum" in 1946 showed the white electorate in favor of incorporation, and native commissioners reported that "tribal leaders" were in agreement. The United Nations General Assembly, however, rejected incorporation in December 1946 and called upon South Africa to continue to accept UN supervision of its administration of the territory.

In 1948, elections in South Africa brought the National Party to power; this government too favored incorporation but in the first instance succeeded only in rejecting UN supervision by, for example, ceasing to submit annual reports on the territory to the United Nations. Instead, the strategy employed for the next twenty-five years was to make South West Africa a de facto, but not de jure, fifth province of South Africa. From 1949, the South West Africa Affairs Act gave white voters in SWA direct representation in the South African Parliament—four seats in the Senate and six in the Assembly; in addition, all eighteen members of the Legislative Assembly were to be elected by the white electorate in SWA and the Advisory Council was abolished. Also from 1949, the South African Citizenship Act extended South African citizenship to all people born in South West Africa. The same legislation that began to formalize apartheid and the policy of separate development in South Africa was extended to the "fifth province." From 1955 "native affairs" were transferred from the administrator to the South African minister of Bantu administration and development.[5]

In 1958 the South African prime minister appointed a Commission of Enquiry into South West Africa Affairs under the chairmanship of F. H. Oderdaal, administrator of the Transvaal.[6] The commission's brief was to make recommendations on the establishment and development of ethnic homelands in SWA and on the integration of the territory's administration into that of South Africa. In the late 1960s the South African government began to implement the proposals made in the Odendaal Commission report of 1964, eventually creating ethnic homelands largely based on the previously existing "native reserves." From 1968, the initial moves toward self-government of the ethnic homelands were taken, followed by the first steps toward the administrative integration of South West Africa into South Africa in 1969. A large number of the functions that had previously been the responsibility of the South West African authorities reverted to different South African government departments.[7] Affairs of the Coloured, Rehoboth, and Nama groups, who did not belong to ethnic homelands, were administered by the South African Department of Coloured, Nama, and Rehoboth Relations.[8] Meanwhile, the affairs of blacks resident in the urban areas (including migrant workers) continued to be largely regulated by the Natives (Urban Areas) Proclamation of 1951.[9]

The course followed by the South Africans in Namibia regarding the territory's political status was not readily accepted by much of the territory's population or of the international community, and the early battleground was the United Nations system itself. From the 1940s and 1950s leaders such as Chief Hosea Kutako of the Herero Chiefs' Council, Chief David Witbooi of the Nama, and others began petitioning the United Nations for an end to South

African rule in the territory.[10] At the same time, the United Nations General Assembly began to appeal to the International Court of Justice (ICJ) for advisory opinions on the status of South West Africa. Early opinions, in 1950, 1955, and 1956, ruled that the Mandate still existed and that South Africa was indeed obliged to submit reports to the UN. Advisory opinions are not binding, however, and the dispute was still not resolved. In 1960 Ethiopia and Liberia initiated legal proceedings in the World Court against South Africa, insisting that it was administering SWA in a manner contrary to the Mandate of the League of Nations, the United Nations Charter, the Universal Declaration of Human Rights, and opinions of the ICJ. In 1966 the ICJ dismissed the case of Ethiopia and Liberia on the grounds that they had no legal standing (locus standi)—rights or interests—in the case and that the court could not pronounce on the merits of South Africa's administration of SWA. The UN General Assembly responded by terminating the Mandate (Resolution 2145) and declaring the territory a direct responsibility of the United Nations. One year later the General Assembly decided to establish a United Nations Council for South West Africa consisting of eleven member states and charged with administering the territory until independence.[11] South Africa rejected this proposal and, in practice, nullified both decisions. Such was the political status of the territory in the year of the general strike, 1971.

Economic Conditions in South West Africa

Since colonial times (and even before) the economy of Namibia has been dominated by its primary sectors—mining, fishing, and commercial agriculture—with the weight of these sectors changing over time. An almost exclusive reliance on black migrant labor has been common to all three sectors. Fishing (in Walvis Bay) is largely a post–World War II development, and over the same years, the balance between mining and commercial agriculture changed. Immediately following World War I efforts were made to restore farming, commerce, and industry, and mining was resumed on a limited scale.[12] These few years were marked by a boom in commercial agriculture, prompted by robust markets and high prices at home, in South Africa and overseas. But by 1922 agriculture was affected by a general postwar recession, exacerbated by the withdrawal of South African forces, the contraction of South African and overseas markets, and a severe drought across the land, followed by heavy flooding and more drought. Similarly, the mining industry, in particular diamond mining, responded to a fall in prices by reducing production. The administrator in 1922 described the situation of the mining industry as "disastrous."[13]

At the same time, despite the poor conditions, the South African authorities initiated policies (including remission of rent, generous provisions for loans, low capital requirements, and payment of transport costs for the move from South Africa) actively encouraging settlers from South Africa to take up farming in South West.[14] In a related move, a "native reserves" policy was undertaken; the active settlement policy meant that land for and of the indigenous population had to be regulated but also that an adequate labor force for the newly created farms had to be assured. Drawing the link between the two, the administrator made the oft-cited observation that the "native question" was "synonymous" with the "labour question" and the "land question."[15] Further legislation to control the livelihood of the indigenous population was introduced, such as the Vagrancy Law (Proclamation 25 of 1920), which prohibited anyone from being in the Police Zone without employment or other obvious means of support, and the Native Administration Proclamation (Proclamation 11 of 1922), which required permits for travel within and outside of the territory and also forbade squatting on private property (unless one was employed on a commercial farm). In addition, curfew regulations and regulations to control urban "locations" were also implemented.[16]

These policies of the early interwar years were geared almost exclusively toward control of the Police Zone, so designated during the German colonial era to indicate the part of the territory south of an imaginary "Red Line," north of which the Ovambo and Kavango people lived, relatively removed from the influx of German and South African settlers. South African authorities further reinforced this distinction by promoting a segmentation of the black labor force, reserving Ovambo and other migrant labor for the mines and designating Police Zone labor for the white commercial farms.[17] The settler farms, because of their weak financial situation, could afford only the lowest wages or none at all (payment was often made in kind), while the mining companies, in a stronger economic position, paid more competitive wages and could make improvements to living conditions if their labor supply was threatened or if the government pressured them to do so.[18] They could also afford to import more expensive labor from South Africa, which was not an option for the settler farmers, or simply to reduce production (an option facilitated by a migrant labor force) during hard economic times, again an option not available to farmers with large stock herds.

With reference to the migrant labor system, Anthony Emmett describes a process by which, in the very early years of the century, drought, famine, and other natural disasters in the sending areas (of the North) facilitated the creation by the colonial authorities of a "comprehensive system of labour control and exploitation."[19] This system included indirect rule, which involved incorporating the Ovambo kings and headmen into the colonial administration and using military force. But migrant laborers from Ovambo preferred not to go to the farms of the Police Zone because of the poor wages, small rations, ill treatment of workers, isolation of the farms, and small number of workers.[20] During much of the colonial history of Namibia farming and mining interests competed for labor and for the implementation of policies to assure a labor supply.

At a conference in Windhoek in 1925 two labor recruiting organizations were created—the Southern Labour Organization (SLO) to provide workers for the diamond mines and the Northern Labour Organization (NLO) to provide laborers for the northern mines and the farms; the SLO would recruit from Ovamboland and the NLO from the Okavango. Workers in the Police Zone were to be channeled to the farms rather than the mines. This attempt to regularize the labor flow followed on years of severe labor shortage in the diamond mines, prompted, in part, by high death and disease rates on the mines and workers' dissatisfaction with the colonial authorities' recruitment policies.[21]

Still, labor shortages continued and economic activity in the territory was further constrained by the late 1920s by more drought and worldwide depression. By the late 1920s the diamond mines were particularly affected by the discovery of similar quality diamonds in South Africa and by the depression. Sharp price drops affected northern copper, tin, and vanadium mines, causing falling wages, cutbacks in labor, and significant drops in exports and thus revenue for the colonial administration all across the mining industry.

There followed a reversal in the relationship between agriculture and mining in the territory that would continue beyond World War II. Whereas in 1925 minerals accounted for 80 percent of Namibia's exports and agricultural products for only 15 percent, by 1933 agricultural products were 82 percent of the total exports and minerals only 6 percent.[22] This trend continued through the war years, when shipping difficulties affected the base metal mines and high demand for agricultural products in South Africa and overseas (and a nascent but successful karakul industry) boosted agricultural revenues. Not until the early 1950s was the mining industry once again in a position to challenge agriculture's dominance of the territory's economy; by the mid-1950s mining accounted for 43 percent of gross domestic product (GDP) and agriculture 23 percent.[23] In addition, after World War II secondary and tertiary industries expanded rapidly in Namibia, and a fishing industry centered at Luderitz and Walvis Bay began to expand rapidly. This postwar balance continued largely unchanged so that by 1970 mining accounted for 30 percent of GDP and agriculture (and fishing) for 14 percent.[24]

The changing weight of agriculture and mining helped shape the contract labor system. A decade after the establishment of the SLO and the NLO in 1925, further measures were introduced to control the flow of labor, which showed the dominance at that time of agriculture: Proclamation 29 of 1935 provided for control of the movement and employment of migrant laborers outside the Police Zone (including other territories) and introduction of a pass system and the registration of all "northern and extra-territorial Natives."[25] Workers without passes could not be employed, and workers in violation of the proclamation could be repatriated to their place of origin (with the cost deducted from their wages). Among other things, this law was an attempt to keep northern migrants from flocking to the territory's urban areas in search of work, thus reserving them for work on the mines, but especially the farms. By 1948 another regulation was introduced which stipulated that all contract laborers going on contract for the first time had to spend at least one period working on a farm. In 1943 the two labor recruitment organizations, the SLO and the NLO, were merged to form the South West Africa Native Labour Association (SWANLA). SWANLA was run by a council made up of two members chosen by the two major shareholders (at its inception, Consolidated Diamond Mines [CDM] and the NLO); several years later a representative of agricultural interests was appointed to the council. By 1952 farmers were appointing two of the five directors of a "new SWANLA."[26]

During the 1930s and 1940s, the flow of migrant labor shifted from the mines to the farms. This was a remarkable achievement, especially given the long-standing resistance on the part of the labor force to work on the white settler farms because of the low wages, poor living and working conditions, and ill treatment of the workers. Emmett contends that the introduction of this formal contract labor system through new legislation in the 1930s and 1940s provided, for the first time, an abundant and cheap supply of labor to the farms, still further enhancing their position.[27]

After World War II the Namibian economy experienced rapid growth, in marked contrast to the interwar years. This growth is evident in the GDP figures: in 1942, GDP (£6.1 million) was slightly less than in 1926 (£6.2 million). After 1943, however, GDP grew steadily, reaching £72.3 million by 1956.[28] This period was marked by rapid growth in the fishing industry and in manufacturing, as well as a steady increase in the settler population and land occupied by white settlers. Not only did the mining industry recover, but new mines and other industries were established. By the postwar years the final reversal of the dominance of agriculture had taken place and mining houses were once again able to privilege their needs and interests.

The Social Situation Inside Namibia

According to the 1970 census, Namibia had a total population of 761,562, categorized by the South African Department of Statistics as 570,696, or 75 percent, "black" (Ovambo, Damara, Herero, Kavango, East Caprivi, Kaokoland, Tswana, other); 78,163, or 10 percent, "brown" (Nama, Coloured, Rehoboth Baster); 89,917, or 12 percent, "white" (Afrikaans, German, English, other); and 22,786, or 3 percent, Bushmen.[29] Of the total, 186,108, or 25 percent, were in urban areas (73,181 black, 37,685 brown, 777 Bushmen, and 67,099 white) and 560,310, or 75 percent, were in rural areas (468,222 black, 39,917 brown, 21,132 Bushmen, and 23,559 white). The largest single concentration of people, 295,508, was in the Ovambo homeland; Windhoek, the capital and largest town, had a population of 75,026 (31,301 black, 11,992 brown, and 29,789 white).[30]

According to the South African Department of Statistics, the economically active population in 1970 was 260,800, of which 196,300 were black or Bushmen, 28,800 brown, and 36,700 white.[31] Wolfgang Thomas gives the distribution of the economically active population in Namibia at the time as follows: 87,500, or 34 percent, in subsistence agriculture; 36,500, or 14 percent, in commercial agriculture; 7,500, or 3 percent, in fish and fish processing; 18,000, or 7 percent, in mining; 12,000, or 4.5 percent, in manufacturing, electricity, and water; 12,000, or 4.5 percent, in construction; 11,500, or 4.5 percent, in transport and communication; 19,500, or 7.5 percent, in commerce and finance; 33,000, or 13 percent, in government and domestic service; and another 20,500, or 7.9 percent, unemployed or unspecified.[32]

Some indications of wage rates among the territory's population at the turn of the decade can be gathered from disparate sources. An official South African publication stated that in 1966 contract workers from the North, with no previous experience, working on commercial farms in central and southern Namibia, started at R7.50 per month, and were raised to R8.25 per month after twelve months, to R9.00 six months later, and to R9.75 another six months later.[33] Prescribed minimum rates for shepherds started at R9.00 per month, rising to R11.25 and R12.00 per month at six-month intervals. According to this source, however, agricultural employers paid "considerably higher than the prescribed minima" (set by SWANLA) because of labor shortages, in addition to providing food and accommodation. By contrast, Jo Morris reports that a white assistant farm manager at Tsumeb received about R450 per month plus such benefits as annual leave, accommodation, medical care, and transport and education subsidies.[34]

The *Financial Mail* cites the findings of researcher Bettina Gebhardt, who surveyed more than one hundred farms in the territory.[35] She found the

lowest cash wage of R4.50 for a "young Ovambo shepherd" on a two-thou-
sand-hectare farm in the South. Ovambo contract workers on the farms earned
between R6 and R10 per month, while black foremen, acting on behalf of
absentee landlords, earned between R20 and R30 a month with food, accommodation, overalls, and boots. Indeed, the *Financial Mail* reports that the
1970–71 agricultural census in SWA found the average cash wage, based on
information supplied by employers, to be R10.25 per month.

The *South West Africa Survey, 1967* gives the following average
monthly wage figures for "Native" mine workers: skilled, R45.34; semiskilled,
R23.07; clerks, R31.14; unskilled, R17.58. The *Survey* notes that mine workers
could earn good wages and adds that wages varied considerably among mines
with an unskilled worker at CDM earning R23.78 per month. In addition to
these cash wages, "all workers receive free medical care and hospitalisation, free
food, housing, transport, clothing, recreation, etc.," the monthly average value
of which was estimated at R15.25. According to Des Matthews of the SWA
Association of Mining Companies, cited in the *Financial Mail,* most mines
paid well above the minimum; a black bulldozer operator at Tsumeb could
earn up to R100 per month. At the same time, a white shift boss at the Tsumeb
mine earned R375 per month plus a R10 safety bonus and a varying production bonus; a mine captain on the same mine earned R435 per month.[36]
Positions for white mechanics, boilermakers, and fitters at CDM in 1973 were
advertised at R285 per month plus benefits.[37]

Rauha Voipio's survey of thirty-six domestic workers in Windhoek in
1971 and 1972 found minimum monthly wages of R6 and R7.50. Maximum
wages were R36 and R44 (R10 of the latter was for ironing); the average in
1971 was R17.62 and in 1972, R22.17. Cash wages in the hotel and catering
industry varied between R15 and R30 per month depending on whether accommodation was provided.[38] The *South West Africa Survey* contends that
"Bantu recruited from the northern territories" were earning average monthly
wages of R30 in the manufacturing, construction, and fishing industries. Laborers employed by the South African Railways started at R26 per month,
rising to R39 after five years.[39] In general, according to one 1968 sample survey
of urban workers in Namibia, 80 percent of "African" men earned between R20
and R49 per month, while 7 percent earned less than R20 per month and 5
percent earned more than R20 per month.[40]

Education levels at the time influenced the social condition of the
majority of Namibians. Simple statistics of school attendance provide some
indication of the situation. According to the South African Department of
Statistics, out of a total primary school population of 123,110 in 1970, 90,282,
or 73 percent, were "black" and Bushmen; 17,785, or 14 percent, were

"brown," and 15,043, or 12 percent, were "white."[41] At the secondary school level, out of a total number of 9,789 students, 1,943, or 20 percent, were black and Bushman; 1,195, or 12 percent, were brown; and 6,651, or 68 percent, were white. Although the numbers for primary school corresponded roughly to the different groups' overall representation in the population, the numbers for secondary school attendance were seriously skewed even in 1970. Some calculations of the data reveal the following total teacher-pupil ratios: black and Bushmen 1:45, brown 1:28, white 1:19. Ten years later, in 1981–82, government expenditure on education was R232 per black pupil, R300 per coloured pupil, and R1210 per white pupil.[42]

Like other facilities, educational institutions were segregated by race and different authorities controlled the various education systems: the education of whites was controlled by the SWA administration, that of coloureds (and Nama and Rehoboth Basters) by the relevant department in South Africa, and that of blacks, according to the Bantu Education Act, by the South African Ministry of Bantu Education.[43] Similarly, there were separate syllabi, separate admission and promotion policies, separate training and wage scales for teachers (grossly inferior for blacks), and so on.

Social conditions were also reflected in opportunities for employment and for mobility. By the start of the 1970s a battery of legislation regulated almost every move of black residents of the territory, with the ultimate objectives of supplying adequate labor to the farms, mines, and factories and keeping the number of blacks in the "white areas" at a minimum. In contrast to South Africa, however, in Namibia job reservation was never enshrined in law except in the case of the mining industry. The Mines, Works, and Minerals Regulations of 1968 provided that whenever the manager of a mine was "European," those holding the jobs of mine overseer, shift boss, ganger, engineer, surveyor, hoist driver, bankman, and onsetter had also to be white.[44]

Regardless of whether a color bar existed legally in the territory, the recruitment of labor and thus work opportunities were controlled by the contract system, especially for workers from the North, as embodied in the SWANLA apparatus. SWANLA had headquarters in Grootfontein and offices in Ondangua (Ovamboland) and Rundu (Okavango). Any employer in the South, except for farmers, who required labor had first to obtain a permit from the local magistrate.[45] If the permit was granted, the employer then forwarded it to SWANLA with a requisition for labor indicating the type of work, the duration of work (twelve to eighteen months, depending on the type of work), and the wages offered. After undergoing a humiliating physical ("medical") examination, potential SWANLA recruits were classified into categories of A,

B, or C, which ostensibly determined the type of work they were capable of doing. Recruits were, in theory, then given the choice of vacancies suitable to their category. Minimum wages for different job categories were prescribed, and free food, accommodation, and medical care, if required, were to be provided.[46] Transport costs were usually covered by the employer, who also paid a recruitment fee to SWANLA. "Breaking contract"—"Okuteya Odalate" as the term was widely known in Oshivambo—was a criminal offense; workers could not change jobs at will, and upon completion of their contract they were to return home for at least one month before reapplying to SWANLA. Workers were not allowed to bring their families with them on contract, and families were only rarely allowed to visit the workers.

The pass laws further regulated and controlled the movement, employment, and place of residence of black Namibians. In 1971 these laws existed in various amended versions (and associated regulations) of the Native Labour Proclamation of 1919, the Vagrancy Proclamation of 1920, the Native Administration Proclamation of 1922, the Native Passes (Rehoboth Gebiet) Proclamation of 1930, the Extra-Territorial and Northern Natives Proclamation of 1935, the Natives (Urban Areas) Proclamation of 1951, and the Aliens Control Act of 1963.[47]

The essence of the pass system was embodied in two pieces of legislation: the Native Administration Proclamation of 1922, which required black people, with a few exceptions, to have a pass to leave their place of residence or employment (outside of the reserves or homelands),[48] and the Natives (Urban Areas) Proclamation of 1951, which prohibited a black person from remaining in an urban or "proclaimed" area (any area where large numbers of black people were gathered for the purposes of mining or industry) for more than seventy-two hours unless he or she met one of four very special conditions.[49] As a rule, women were not allowed to leave the reserves to live or seek work elsewhere. The Natives (Urban Areas) Proclamation further made provision for avoiding "vagrancy," in other words, for the arrest without warrant of any black person deemed to be "idle" or "undesirable."[50] Such was the social situation in Namibia on the eve of the general strike.

Origins of the Strike

The origins of the strike must be placed in the context of some of the early political organization in the territory,[51] in particular, of the Ovamboland People's Congress (OPC) and the Ovamboland People's Organisation, first established in Cape Town in the late 1950s.[52] The OPC and the OPO are important as the predecessor organizations to the South West Africa People's Organisation and are usually portrayed as organizations of and for the contract workers of Namibia. For example, most accounts of their origins say that a group of two hundred Ovambo laborers, many of whom had deserted from contracts on mines in South Africa, were gathered in Cape Town under the leadership of Andimba Toivo ya Toivo.[53] Other accounts, by contrast, describe the group gathered in Cape Town as consisting of workers and "students and other intellectuals," the latter of whom dominated the leadership.[54] Toivo ya Toivo and Andreas Shipanga were both trained as teachers, Ottilie Schimming Abrahams and her husband, Kenneth Abrahams, were students, Fanuel Kozonguizi was a student, and Emil Appolus was an aspiring journalist who had just finished his studies. Jacob Kuhangua was also trained as a teacher and, like Toivo ya Toivo, had worked as a clerk in a mine in South Africa.[55]

Peltola maintains that though the OPC is sometimes called a trade union, because of its focus on the contract labor system it should more accurately "be described as a nationalist political movement." Peltola cites his interview with Sam Nujoma, in the late 1950s a railway worker inside Namibia and eventual leader of the organization, in which Nujoma says: "OPO was not a trade union, it was a political party. OPO was never a trade union, but it worked for the interests of the workers." Revealing a tension that remains until this day, Toivo ya Toivo admitted in an interview with Peltola that, at the time, the distinction between political party, trade union, or liberation movement "was still weak for us, because we were politically immature."[56]

The OPO was a thoroughly nationalist organization, not unlike others emerging in Africa at the time. Its constitution "was modelled on that of Kwame Nkrumah's Convention People's Party . . . [and] Nkrumah's nationalist aims of 'freedom and independence' were made the aims of OPO."[57] Emmett contends that from the start its leaders meant the organization to be a nationalist one, based on regional congresses along the lines of the African National Congress model of provincial congresses. Indeed, just as the founders of the OPO were not "only" workers, they were also not "only" Oshivambo-speaking. But the name—Ovamboland People's Congress/Organisation—was chosen, at least initially, quite purposefully, according to Shipanga: "We said let us give the name which will attract those who are, you know, affected by the contract system and these are the Ovambos. Let us create something which they can say is their own and hence OPC and then OPO."[58]

According to Toivo ya Toivo, the Ovamboland People's Congress was established in 1957 with the dual aim of forcing South Africa, via the United Nations, to entrust South West Africa to the UN Trusteeship Council and of abolishing the contract labor system.[59] Toivo ya Toivo was deported from Cape Town in December 1958 after it was discovered that he had smuggled a tape-recorded petition, in a copy of *Treasure Island*, to another student, Mburumba Kerina, at the United Nations in New York. Toivo ya Toivo left Cape Town with Fanuel Kozonguizi with the intention of consulting leaders inside Namibia about establishing a broader nationalist organization. Toivo ya Toivo planned to act as an organizer in Ovamboland but was arrested by the colonial authorities in Tsumeb—with the help of managers from the Tsumeb copper mine—on his way north and placed under house arrest in Ondangua. Inside Namibia, meanwhile, Sam Nujoma was busy establishing a political base among contract workers, especially in Windhoek. There, by 1959, he had "without the benefit of a formal organization, already organized the Windhoek based contract workers into a significant political force" by "holding regular meetings in the Windhoek compound (where grievances against the contract system were expressed and the contract workers politicized), collecting money for a fund to assist contract workers, and encouraging labourers to attend night school."[60]

In April 1959 the OPO was officially launched inside Namibia by Sam Nujoma and Jacob Kuhangua. Membership cards, printed in Cape Town, were distributed and efforts were made to extend the organization beyond Windhoek. Helao Shityuwete, then a contract worker in Walvis Bay, describes how in 1959 Vinnia Ndadi returned to Walvis Bay from a meeting with Sam Nujoma in Windhoek at which Nujoma told of the formation of the OPO, "an organisation to represent the workers, especially those suffering under the contract labor system," and urged workers in Walvis Bay to join and establish an OPO branch there. According to Shityuwete, however, the OPO had other priorities: "OPO, which was formed to be the voice of the workers, never took their problems to the management of firms and companies. No meetings were arranged between workers' representatives and employers. The emphasis was placed on the country's status as a mandate rather than on the inhuman conditions."[61]

While the organization of OPO continued, events on 10 December 1959 provided a significant turning point in the history of resistance in Namibia. On that day eleven residents of the Old Location in Windhoek were killed and forty-four others wounded in a confrontation with the police, following a meeting with municipal authorities who were attempting to break the long-standing boycott of the bus service, municipal beer halls, and cinema mounted by residents in protest over their imminent forced removal from the Main Location to a new site much farther from Windhoek. In the new location—Katutura—people would be housed in ethnic neighborhoods, face much higher rent and transport costs, lose precious gardens, and be required to hold residence permits.[62] The protest against the forced removal was significant because it was the first time an issue was taken up by the recently formed nationalist organizations, and it served to politicize and mobilize a large segment of the Namibian people. The Old Location shootings became a symbol of Namibian resistance to colonial rule—Namibia's Sharpeville. In the aftermath of the shootings, however, much of the nationalist leadership was imprisoned, banned, or restricted by the South African colonial authorities, with the result that many opted for exile.

The activities of the OPO essentially ground to a halt; Toivo ya Toivo was under house arrest in Ovamboland, where he would remain (opening the first black-owned shop as part of a concerted effort to break the monopoly of SWANLA) until his arrest in 1966. Nathaniel Maxuilili, a strong organizer and OPO leader in Walvis Bay, was restricted to that enclave. Sam Nujoma, who in 1959 had been elected president of the OPO, left for exile in March 1960, not to return to Namibia until 14 September 1989. Many of the remaining activists went into exile as well. On 19 April 1960 in New York, the OPO was officially transformed into the South West Africa People's Organisation with Nujoma as president. According to Kozonguizi, "Organization at home was rather on a low ebb due to lack of funds, transport and fulltime organizers, and also lack of propaganda medium, e.g., newspaper."[63]

For the next several years resistance would center around the nationalist movements based outside the country. Indeed, a second nationalist organization, the South West Africa National Union, formed before SWAPO in 1959, was also operating from exile. There had been early unsuccessful attempts to merge the two organizations; in the event, SWAPO soon became the much more significant of the two groups. Meanwhile, inside the territory during these years, according to accounts by John Ya Otto and Ndadi, SWAPO cadres (fresh from OPO) worked diligently to build support among a wide range of Namibians, a task made difficult by constant harassment and arrest by Special Branch police and a lack of resources (bail costs continually depleted the organization's already limited funds).[64] SWAPO activists drove back and forth from Windhoek to Walvis Bay, to Otjiwarongo, Tsumeb, Grootfontein, and the far North, holding public meetings and speaking at rallies, seeking to raise funds and support for the young movement, and always trying to elude the police. In the early years there was still a faith in the efforts at the United Nations, but by the time of the 1966 ICJ ruling this hope was fading.

Armed struggle commenced in 1966 (although SWAPO had already decided to engage South Africa militarily and had begun training combatants in Egypt in 1962).[65] Indeed, in August 1966, SWAPO's military base at Ongulumbashe in the North was discovered and destroyed by the South African police. More than two hundred activists, most of the remaining internal SWAPO leaders, were arrested or fled into exile. In Namibia's "treason trial" in Pretoria in 1967 thirty-seven Namibians (twenty-seven guerrilla fighters and ten of SWAPO's internal leaders) were charged with treason.[66] After sitting in detention while waiting for the Terrorism Act (of 1967) to be made retroactive, thirty of the accused, including Toivo ya Toivo, were found guilty of violating the Terrorism Act and sentenced to up to twenty years on Robben Island. John Ya Otto, Nathaniel Maxuilili, and Jason Mutumbulua were found guilty of violating the Suppression of Communism Act and received suspended sentences of just a couple of years. Upon their release in 1968, Ya Otto and Maxuilili were restricted to Ondangua and Walvis Bay, respectively, and Mutumbulua returned to Katutura. According to Leys and Saul, during these years, "the scale of activity remained modest . . . being at first largely confined to house meetings" among SWAPO supporters in urban locations.[67]

Like the formation of the OPC/OPO, the origins of the 1971–72 strike are "subject to confusion and controversy."[68] There is considerable disagreement over whether the strike was organized or spontaneous and, if organized, by whom. Many people recall the strike as largely spontaneous, although they grant that SWAPO members must have played a role, especially since "maybe 99 percent of the workers were SWAPO supporters," even though in those days it "was very difficult to be openly a card carrying SWAPO member."[69] Zedekia Ngavirue argues in his 1972 thesis that the organizers of the strike "operated independently of SWAPO and SWANU, and without a formal organisational structure."[70] Ya Otto indicates that shortly after the ICJ ruling, while still confined to Ovamboland, he got word of a planned strike from SWAPO leaders in Windhoek.[71] Official SWAPO texts attribute the strike to months of careful and secret preparation by its branches and rank-and-file activists, particularly from the SWAPO Youth League (SYL).[72] A *SWAPO Information Bulletin* published in Luanda in 1987 goes so far as to say that the National Union of Namibian Workers "was strongly involved in the general strike of 1971/72, through its workers' committees which were particularly well organised at the fish and meat processing factories in Walvis Bay and Windhoek, respectively."[73]

Meanwhile, Andreas Shipanga, acting secretary for information and publicity at SWAPO's exile base in Tanzania at the time, says the strike "took us by surprise, honestly." As SWAPO's "chief propagandist" at the time, he should have known about the strike if the group was involved.[74] According to an article in the *Windhoek Advertiser,* SWAPO issued a statement, signed by London representative Peter Katjavivi, denying that SWAPO engineered or perpetrated any of the strike actions and viewing it instead as "a form of protest appropriate to the situation." Rather than seeing the strike as against only the contract labor situation, the statement described it as "part of the general Namibian protest against South Africa's occupation." In his much more recent history of Namibia, Katjavivi insists that the strike was organized by ordinary workers ("most of whom had little formal education"), although "many of the strikers were SWAPO members or supporters, and SWAPO was clearly involved in the strike."[75]

Three related events, all of which took place in the latter half of 1971, are usually considered to be the immediate precipitators of the strike: the 21 June International Court of Justice ruling that called on South Africa to withdraw from Namibia;[76] the 30 June Open Letter to the South African prime minister in which leaders of two of the largest churches in SWA, asked by the colonial authorities to comment on the ruling, said that South Africa had failed "to take cognisance" of human rights as declared by the United Nations in 1948;[77] and the attempt in November by commissioner general of the indigenous peoples of South West Africa (otherwise known as "Bantu Commissioner") Jannie De Wet to deny the church leaders' assertion that the contract labor system was a form of slavery. Rather, De Wet described the system as purely voluntary.[78] Observers at the time believed this statement to be particularly infuriating to workers and students and, therefore, a key catalyst in the strike. The statement was widely used to mobilize Namibian workers.

More generally, however, the strike was in large part a politically inspired event, organized, or at least initiated, by SWAPO secondary school students but made possible by the workers' long-standing grievances against the contract labor system. Indeed, hatred of the contract labor system had been brewing for decades. Pastor Gerson Max, who ministered among contract workers in industrial centers throughout Namibia, relates, as do many, that the word "contract" had become known as "Ondarate" [Odalate] in Oshivambo from the Afrikaans word "draad," meaning "wire." In brief, "many men felt that they were slaves of the SWANLA system."[79] SWANLA was seen to be trafficking in human cargo. Helao Shityuwete, himself a contract worker in the late 1950s, relates that SWANLA "used to collect laborers and then sell these laborers to the respective employers, whatever, mining, the farms and any other respective employers."[80]

Two firsthand written accounts of the strike and the preparations leading up to it are given by Hinananje Shafodino "Kandy" Nehova and John Ya Otto.[81] Nehova provides much more detail and seems the more accurate of the two; few other contemporary reports of the strike devote much, if any, attention to how it was organized, but those that do corroborate Nehova's account. Nehova's account also supports the common perception that the strike was somehow facilitated by the SWAPO Youth League, although this is not entirely accurate because the SWAPO Youth League had not yet been formally organized in Namibia at the time.[82] But the strike could still have been the initial work of SWAPO youth and students.[83] In any case, the strike was not the work of the National Union of Namibian Workers. The NUNW barely existed in exile in late 1971, and there is no evidence to suggest that it, or any other black trade union, operated (even underground) inside Namibia at the time of the general strike.[84]

According to Kandy Nehova, a secondary school student at the time and one of the organizers of the strike, it "was not an isolated labor activity, it was part of the overall strategy for national liberation."[85] More specifically, it was an action taken by the youth and student movements because the "leadership of the mother body [SWAPO] was nonexistent," having been largely rounded up in 1966: "We saw that as students and youth we should do something." Indeed, strike action at industrial centers in the South was preceded by marches at secondary schools in northern Namibia, in particular Ongwediva, following the June 1971 ICJ ruling.[86] But, Nehova says, the student activists felt that their protests in the North were not enough and thus set their sights much higher—to pull off a national strike that would paralyze the economy and would "hit the apartheid authorities where it hurts most."

Indeed, the marches at Ongwediva had resulted in the mass expulsion by the authorities of several hundred students who then went south to the towns and industrial centers of central Namibia. Nehova and others such as Ndali Kamati, Helao Nafidi, Ndaxu Namolo, and David Shikomba eventually found themselves organizing a national strike. They based themselves in Walvis Bay, where many were able to procure jobs in the fish and canning factories to be among the contract workers, and from where they were also able to rely on the support of SWAPO stalwarts such as Nathaniel Maxuilili. In their organizing efforts among the workers, according to Nehova, they did not say that the strike was for the purpose of obtaining independence or hastening the process of liberation; rather, "we simply said we must strike in order to improve the working conditions and salaries and other remunerations for ourselves." As one contemporary observer recalls, "The OPO/SWAPO call was clearly in the air: 'Odalate Naiteke' [Let's break the 'wire' or contract, in other words, let's go on strike]."[87]

When the strike broke on Monday, 13 December 1971, in Windhoek it was not, and should not have been, a surprise.[88] Commissioner General De Wet says that from early 1971 he had indications that people were very dissatisfied, that "the disturbance was there," and he repeatedly informed his superiors in South Africa that trouble was imminent.[89] Especially in Walvis Bay, meetings had been held among the workers in the weeks preceding the date set for the strike.[90] De Wet's comment that men went to the contract system voluntarily was used to mobilize workers.[91] According to Nehova, support for a strike was overwhelming, and the decision was taken to send letters and envoys to other work centers throughout the land to inform workers of the strike plans.[92] Just a few days before the strike, Nehova, Kamati, and Namolo sent a letter to De Wet, the administrator, and the South African prime minister, again referring to De Wet's comment and saying that "they would soon witness our true feelings about the contract labor system."[93] On 13 December, the day the strike began in Windhoek, a final meeting was held with workers in Walvis Bay attended by the chief Bantu affairs commissioner for SWA Gert White, a group of Ovambo headmen (from the Ovambo Executive Council), the workers, and Bishop Leonard Auala. The workers demanded higher wages and an end to the contract labor system or they would hand in their contracts; the authorities tried to dissuade the workers from their strike plans. At the meeting fourteen workers (and students) spoke out against the request to call off the strike and were promptly arrested. In the event, the strikers' demands were not met, nor could they be persuaded to call off the strike. By the end of that week most of the thirty-six hundred workers in Walvis Bay had joined the strike.[94]

On Friday, 10 December 1971, the *Windhoek Advertiser*'s headline from Walvis Bay read: "Massive Strike Is Planned by Hundreds of Ovambo." On 12 December, the day before the strike began in Windhoek, special police contingents were flown into Namibia from South Africa and in Windhoek a "mass meeting lasting two and a half hours" was held at the Ovambo Compound. Once the strike started, it spread rapidly throughout the territory. For the rest of December and into January almost daily newspaper accounts reported on the new work sites hit by the strike and tallied the growing number of workers who had downed their tools and joined the strike. By 28 December it was revealed that "a labour crisis looms"; not only were existing workers on strike, but no new recruits were reporting to the SWANLA offices. SWANLA Manager J. H. Louw in Grootfontein reported that whereas in the past, five hundred workers per week had applied to the association's offices, by the end of December there were none. By 4 January 1972, ten mines were shut down and more than 12,000 workers were on strike.[95] Eventually the total number would reach 13,500 workers on strike, shutting down eleven mines and affecting twenty-three work centers.[96]

As soon as the labor action began, striking workers were deported to the North, to Ovamboland. Special trains were arranged by South African Railways after 16 December from Walvis Bay and Windhoek to Grootfontein, from where other transport was provided. The trains were "protected" by the

South African police, although the striking workers were peaceful; in fact, one newspaper reporter wrote that the "mass exodus gave the impression of a holiday tour rather than people who went on strike" and that "the Ovambo occupants" sang hymns as they boarded the trains and buses. Until all of the workers actually boarded the trains, the authorities were convinced that most of them would not, certain that a core group was intimidating the rest. These fears were, of course, proved wrong.[97] Up in Ovamboland, meanwhile, a torrent of violence was about to be unleashed.

Once the workers were back in the North, "there was real fighting, real fighting," according to Nehova. Not only the returned workers but others as well decided "that the time has come for the colonial authorities to be told that enough is enough." Armed with "primitive weapons" (bows and arrows, pangas, assegais), but also with guns, many fought and were killed. Commissioner General De Wet reported on 12 January (when the strikers' demands were made known in a widely circulated leaflet) that the "the intimidation in Ovambo is at an end," the same day the first planeload of police from South Africa touched down in Ondangua "to reinforce the existing task force"—with promises of more police to come from Pretoria and elsewhere in South West Africa. On 18 January police helicopters began patrolling the Namibia/Angola border after reports that the fence was being cut in several places. By 26 January South African minister of Bantu administration and development M. C. Botha revealed in Cape Town that units of the South African Defence Force would be sent in to assist the police in "the protection of international borders."[98] Not only was the fence cut, but the animal kraals and property of headmen, chiefs, and others who collaborated with the South African authorities (for example, by participating in the homeland governments or informing on others) were burned, and many were killed.[99] By the beginning of February a total prohibition on travel through Ovamboland was implemented and no more permits for transit to Angola were issued.[100]

Once in Ovamboland, the striking workers held meetings and elected a Contract Committee, chaired by Johannes Nangutuuala, leader of the Democratic Cooperative Development Party, to make known their demands to the authorities. A first meeting was held on 3 January and another a week later on 10 January 1972 at Oluno in Ondangua. A pamphlet drawn up by the Contract Committee formed the basis for a series of resolutions passed at the 10 January meeting. Minutes from the meeting listed the "evils of the contract system" (no choice of job, meager wages, absence of family, mandatory anal examinations, no respect for Ovambos among other blacks, no protection in the law) and outlined how the "contract system is a form of slavery" (jail-like compounds, only one way to exit or enter the Police Zone, ill-treatment throughout the employment period). Finally, the minutes called for a more "favourable system for looking for labour" (by doing away completely with the contract system; allowing the freedom to choose one's job, to leave an unsatisfactory job, and to have one's family nearby; being paid according to the work and not the race; opening labor offices in every town and advertising vacancies; and creating jobs in government and giving first preference to blacks, especially in the homelands).[101]

Meanwhile, attempts by the authorities to resolve the crisis culminated in meetings on 19 and 20 January in Grootfontein (planned in any case for February of that year). On 19 January the South African minister of Bantu administration, M. C. Botha, and his deputy, met with representatives of SWANLA, the South West Africa Agricultural Union, the South African Railways, the Department of Posts and Telegraphs, the South West Africa Administration, the Department of Labour, the South West Africa Municipal Association, the Fish Factories Executive, Consolidated Diamond Mines, the Tsumeb Corporation, the South West Africa Company, and others; this meeting was a follow-on to an earlier meeting (29 December) between representatives of SWANLA, employers, and the South African government in Pretoria at which it had been decided that in future the homeland governments (Legislative Councils) would run the labor recruitment system. On 20 January a meeting was held between Minister Botha, his deputy, and representatives of the Ovambo and Kavango Legislative Councils at which the agreement of the previous day was accepted.[102] Despite the demand at the 10 January meeting that a delegation of the Contract Committee attend these meetings, no representatives of the striking workers were present. According to South African newspaper reports, however, Johannes Nangutuuala, "the workers' designated spokesperson," accepted the new agreement and announced over Radio Ovambo that it met most of the strikers' demands. Other sources dispute the newspapers' reports of agreement.[103] Nangutuuala's intervention once the striking workers returned to the North is seen as largely opportunistic and as evidence of the lack of sustained leadership in the organization and implementation of the strike.

AFTERMATH OF THE STRIKE

Thus a "historic document" was signed on 20 January 1972 between the South African government and the homeland governments of Ovambo and Kavango, in the hopes of bringing to an end the labor crisis that had "plagued South West Africa" since 13 December 1971. The agreement between the South African government and the two homeland governments listed sixteen points, which made provision for the major changes to emanate from the discussions, namely, that SWANLA would be abolished to be replaced by labor bureaus (employment offices) established in the homelands by the homeland governments and that a new contract of service would replace the old one. The new contract indicated most of the remaining changes: each worker was contracted on a separate form (four to a form in the past) and the contracts were in English, Afrikaans, and Oshivambo, rather then English, Afrikaans, and German; the terms "employer" and "employee" replaced "master" and "servant"; although both contracts stipulated basic minimum wages, the new one made provision for overtime and for specified working hours; both contracts required the employer to provide free food, free accommodation, and free medical treatment, although in the past the SWA administration was responsible for the cost of hospitalization, which under the new contract became the province of the employer; under the new contract the employer was no longer obliged to provide the employee with a shirt, shorts, and blanket when a contract was signed; under the old contract the employer was responsible for travel costs to and from the workplace, while under the new one the employer could recover the costs of travel through deductions from wages and was responsible for the return journey only if the contract was completed.[104]

In addition, under the new contract the employee was allowed unpaid home leave during his period of service and paid leave when the contract expired. Also, the worker could enter into a new contract with the same employer or another before his first contract expired instead of being compulsorily repatriated to his home, as in the past. The new contract could be terminated by either party, and breach of contract was no longer a criminal offense as in the past. The system of medical classification of potential employees into different categories would cease.

The new system cost the employer even less than in the past. Although for the workers there were one or two favorable changes, the basic parameters of the contract labor system remained intact—just what the striking workers did not want—"a new name for [the] 'wire.'" And, as John Kane-Berman noted, several factors served to "render nugatory the theoretical improvements in the contract system"; for example, the pass laws, which continued to regulate all movement of blacks outside the homelands, required the carrying of (unchanged) identification passes and hampered the ability to find a new job before the old one expired.[105] Workers were still to be housed in compounds, food was still produced on a mass basis, transport was still provided rather than giving sufficient wages to pay one's own, families were still unable to accompany workers to the work site. De Wet readily conceded that the workers' demands were only partially met. Freer movement, which he saw as the overriding goal, was still not achieved for the workers or for their families.[106]

The official regulations governing the new labor bureaus and the new labor recruitment system generally came in the form of the Employment Bureaux Regulations, gazetted on 30 March as Proclamation 83 of 1972. The regulations covered those black workers living outside the homelands, while the regulations for the Ovambo homeland came in the form of Ovambo Legislative Council Labour Enactment 6 of 1972 gazetted as Government Notice R1417 of 18 August 1972.[107] What were essentially emergency regulations were also put into effect in Ovamboland from February 1972 (Proclamation R17 of 4 February and Proclamation R26 of 14 February); these prohibited the holding of most meetings (except church services or sports gatherings) unless they were authorized in writing by the native commissioner. Individuals might be prevented from attending meetings, and it became an offense to say or do anything that might undermine the authority of the state, the Ovambo government, officials of these bodies, chiefs, or headmen. Prohibitions could be imposed on persons leaving or entering Ovamboland. Persons could be arrested without warrant and detained for questioning until the authorities were satisfied that their questions had been fully answered. By 11 April 1972, 213 persons had been detained under the emergency regulations in Ovamboland; 130 had been released after periods ranging from one to fifty-three days; 83 were still in detention. By 26 May a further 54 persons had been detained. In mid-January 1973 the Ovambo Legislative Council decided to ban political meetings "to protect innocent Ovambos."[108]

Employers' reaction to the new labor recruitment system was swift and predictable. To them the new system represented "free bidding for a job, bilateral agreements between employees and employer [as opposed to between SWANLA and employers], free choice to resign and take on any other job, better payment, holiday bonuses and leave pay and many other benefits."[109] They responded by forming committees to ensure uniformity of wages and to eliminate competition for labor among employers. During late January and early February representatives of the Chamber of Commerce, Windhoek Municipality, the Afrikaanse Sakekamer (Afrikaans Business Chamber), the Railways, Post, and Telegraphs, civil engineering firms, the hotel industry, and the Master Builders' Association came together to address the problem. Members of the South West Africa Agricultural Union met on their own, feeling particularly vulnerable in a system that allowed some freedom of choice to potential employees; farmers asked for a "fixed wage for Ovambo workers or chaos would ensue."[110]

By the end of January 1972 some workers from the North began returning to the South to resume employment, with the apparent expectation of substantial change under the new contract system. Indeed, by 18 February seven employment offices had been opened in Ovambo and five in Kavango, and 6,148 workers returned to work in the South.[111] The *Windhoek Advertiser* reported from several quarters "unreasonable attitudes on the part of Ovambo workers," including their refusal to be transported by trucks (demanding buses or taxis instead), dissatisfaction with food given them, refusal of medical examinations, and demanding excessive wages. Employers told the newspaper simply that "we told them that we were not interested in their demands." Workers returning to the Ovambo Compound in Katutura in early February destroyed more than four thousand beds with hammers in protest over the squalor of that compound and the compound system in general.

In July 1972 Johannes Nangutuuala stated in a newspaper interview that "the Ovambo worker was still not satisfied" and that if nothing happened unrest would continue (and warned that the Oshivelo crossing point could be the next site of destruction); he also said that the provisions of the new contract system were not being adhered to. Moreover, in a letter to the Ovambo Legislative Council in 1972, Nangutuuala requested the establishment of a workers' society (trade union) and a joint meeting of the Legislative Council and earlier Contract or Workers' Committee so that members of the Workers' Committee could visit various workplaces in Namibia.[112] Also in July 1972, some branches of the South West Africa National Party called for the reintroduction of the Masters and Servants Act, in particular the provision making it a criminal offense to breach contract and leave one's place of employment. In September, members of the South West Africa Agricultural Union complained at their annual congress that their workers were blackmailing them through a "go-slow strike," while others cautioned that the world was watching SWA's labor situation and that farmers might better pay their workers more. By January 1973, amendments to the labor regulations of the previous year were being made. In August 1973 farmers were still complaining that their workers were deserting them and the police force would take no action.[113]

It seems that the strike did have an effect on wages in the territory. Most observers suggest some, if not considerable, increase in wages for black workers in the wake of the strike. Gottschalk writes that actual cash wages for migrant workers rose between 10 and 20 percent while minimum wages rose more (although employers were no longer obliged to provide their workers with clothes or the fare for the return journey home).[114] *A Survey of Race Relations, 1972* cites a newspaper in which the divisional inspector of labor in Windhoek said in August that since the strike, "African wage rates had increased by 66 to

100 percent."[115] According to the *South West Africa Survey, 1974,* at CDM all jobs were reevaluated and renumerated in 1972 on the basis of "the rate for the job."[116] From then on, the lowest grade workers received from R49.14 to R62.34 per month, to which could be added R25.09 per month in in-kind payment for clothing, food, medical care, and recreation. From 1974, provision was made for a noncontributory retirement allowance for migrant workers. At Tsumeb Corporation average cash earnings for black workers were R36.63 at the end of 1973 and noncash benefits totaled R34.78. Laborers working for the South African Railways received a starting wage of R45 per month, rising to R57 per month after four years of service. In the fishing industry, "an ordinary worker from the northern territories" received a basic cash wage of R27.30 per month, to which was added another R36.09 in overtime, bonus, and leave pay; noncash payment for clothing, housing, and medical services totaled R18.85 for such a worker. Operators in processing plants at Luderitz received a basic weekly wage rate of R45 to R60 plus overtime, while an artisan, "irrespective of race," could earn about R350 per month.

Data on salaries and wages for Namibia, especially before 1980, are scant. The mining industry, which provided the best paid job opportunities for black laborers, was always an exception. Paul Hartmann gives salaries and wages and average earnings in the mining industry from 1950 to 1980.[117] His data indicate a considerable narrowing in the gap between average annual earnings of white and black workers in the industry. While the white:black wage ratio in 1950 was 19:1 (R1,430 to R75), in 1960 it was 15:1 (R2,432 to R163), in the year of the strike it was 11:1 (R4,667 to R429), by 1975 it was 6:1 (R7,170 to R1,113), and by 1980 (when apparently such figures by race were no longer kept) it was down to 4:1 (R13,682 to R3,265).[118]

While wages were increasing slowly during the 1970s, education and skill levels among the black population were also increasing, indeed at a faster rate. Between 1970 and 1979 the number of "black and Bushmen" secondary school students increased more than fivefold (from 1,943 to 11,609) and the number of "brown" secondary students more than doubled, from 1,195 to 4,659, while the number of "white" secondary school students dropped from 6,651 to 6,618.[119] The number of black and Bushman primary school pupils increased from 90,282 to 160,786 and the number of brown primary school pupils from 17,785 to 24,408 while the number of white primary school pupils fell from 15,043 in 1970 to 12,883 in 1979. Still, the figures for tertiary education reveal how far was yet to go: the number of black students at universities in South Africa (including "black" universities) rose from 47 in 1971 to 98 in 1978; the number of coloured students at South African universities in those years rose from 44 to 157, while for whites the number rose from 1,564 to 2,268. There was no tertiary education in Namibia at the time.[120]

The strike also prompted the first public acknowledgment of the need for trade unions for black workers in Namibia. Many companies, hoping to fend off worker discontent, attempted their own internal adjustments. In the mid-1970s, Metal Box and Walvis Bay Containers, both in the Walvis Bay fishing industry, appointed their first personnel officers, and other companies attempted to use liaison committees to consult with their workers.[121] At the trial of those charged in the early days of the strike in Windhoek with intimidating other workers, the magistrate, in the course of his judgment, reportedly said that as a result of the strike most employers realized that they had been underpaying their workers.[122] Pleading in mitigation at the same trial, in the sentencing of eight of those found guilty, Advocate Brian O'Linn said that the workers had exercised their only option, namely, to strike, because they had no trade unions through which to express their grievances. By their action, he said, they had brought about the realization that the two groups, white and black, could not do without each other.[123]

That same month, in June 1972, Enno Harms, the president of the Windhoek Chamber of Commerce, reportedly made a plea at the Chamber's annual general meeting (AGM) for the organization of "Ovambo" workers into trade unions. Because workers were not organized into representative trade unions, he said, there was no body with which an employers' organization could negotiate. In Harms's view, the government of Ovambo could not be regarded as a suitable body to represent workers' interests.[124] At the same AGM one year later Harms continued on the reformist note: he claimed that much of the labor unrest and dissatisfaction in SWA could be attributed to the lack of facilities for "the non-white worker," in addition to poor wages. In the interest of increased productivity, he urged greater efforts to train black workers and increased liaison between employers and employees.[125] A few years later, in 1976, the president of the Association of Mining Companies of South West Africa, J. L. P. McKenzie, would go so far as to call for scrapping migrant labor in the territory in favor of a "non-migratory labour force, one that was well housed, well paid and well trained." He outlined a scenario in which all "shared in the profits of industry": revenue and infrastructure for the state and jobs, good wages, and training and development for the workers.[126]

Meanwhile, a certain influence from capital in South Africa was being felt inside Namibia as well. Officials from the Afrikaanse Sakekamer in South Africa would come to address the AGMs of the Windhoek Afrikaanse Sakekamer and say, for example, that labor legislation and the relationship between management and employees or management and trade unions were important. Recognizing that "without the Bantu we will never be able to achieve our economical aims," such officials made a plea for better understanding "Bantu ambitions and aspirations," for more training, for the establishment of liaison committees in the workplace, and so on.[127] Developments in industry in South Africa received wide coverage in Namibia, such as when the Federated Chamber of Industries in late 1976 called for the scrapping of residential, business, and job apartheid because, inter alia, of the way it forced employers to pay "unrealistic and artificial premium wages"—or when the Anglo American Corporation declared in late 1977, in elaborating its labor policy, "that there are no grounds on which racial discrimination can be justified."[128]

O'Linn and Harms were not the only ones during the 1970s to observe the need for trade unions for black workers in Namibia. A 1976 paper on the labor regime, the Namibian worker, and human rights asserted that it was "a major failure of the 1971 strike that it did not lead to any concession in the direction of collective bargaining."[129] "This is not surprising," it continued, "as the authorities are well aware that recognition of the right of African workers to form trade unions will enhance their bargaining power." The International Labour Organisation (ILO), in particular, had an ongoing concern with the lack of trade union rights in Namibia. A report of the Ad Hoc Working Group of Experts of the Commission on Human Rights in February 1973 found that "the main feature of the recruitment system of Namibian workers is the absence of a trade union system." The group found that despite the changes introduced after the strike, the denial of freedom of movement and freedom of association to black workers meant that the new system maintained the contours of the old. The group recommended that ways and means be found by which trade union rights could be "factually and legally" applied in Namibia.[130]

But at that time in Namibia trade unions were not an option for black workers.[131] The 1952 Wage and Industrial Conciliation Ordinance provided for the organization of trade unions but excluded black workers from the definition "employee" and therefore precluded their effective participation in trade unions.[132] Indeed, the climate even toward white trade unions was very hostile at the time. According to Francois Adonis, onetime president of the Local Authorities Union of Namibia (LAUN): "When SWAMSA [South West Africa Municipal Staff Association, predecessor to LAUN] started in 1969, trade unions were not very acceptable in society. Municipalities thought of us as communists, really. Some of our previous leaders had to disguise themselves when they wanted to go into certain communities—and they were white guys."[133] The legal environment for black trade unions would change only in 1978, and attitudes would take much longer than that.

In exile, however, where there were no workers, a trade union was being organized—at least in name. By 1970 SWAPO in exile, then based in Dar es Salaam, had created the posts of secretary for labor and assistant secretary for labor and founded—again, on paper—the National Union of Namibian Workers. At the Consultative Congress in Tanga, Tanzania (26 December 1969 to 2 January 1970), Solomon Mifima had been made the first secretary for labor and Luther Zaire the assistant secretary for labor, although Andreas Shipanga contends that Mifima had been acting in that capacity for some time.[134] At the congress itself, despite a report in at least one SWAPO publication that "the idea of a national strike to abolish the system of contract labour altogether had been discussed in general terms in SWAPO's ranks at least as far back as the Tanga Congress,"[135] there was no discussion of an NUNW or further labor matters, except that, according to John Ya Otto, Mifima "informed the SWAPO leadership that it was essential that the workers of Namibia not only be defended by the Department of Labour but that the workers should realize a movement of their own, a trade union movement," and the idea was accepted.[136]

The date for the official launching in exile of the National Union of Namibian Workers is always given as 24 April 1970. The earliest written reference to the NUNW seems to be an article by Mifima himself, which appeared in a SWAPO publication printed in the German Democratic Republic in 1972. Describing the labor situation generally in Namibia at the time, Mifima concludes: "The National Union of Namibian Workers calls upon all . . . the world to condemn the brutal action of Vorster's illegal government in Namibia, and offers full moral and material support to the Namibian workers in their legitimate struggle against exploitation for freedom, justice and independence."[137] Later, in 1974, an article in the *Windhoek Advertiser* reported that "in the latest move in what appeared to place South West Africa's black workers on an organised footing," circulars had made their way into the country informing of the formation of a National Union of Namibia [*sic*] Workers as "the sole representative of the struggling workers of Namibia." According to the report, the circular claimed that the union was affiliated to SWAPO and called upon black workers to contact an address given in the circular (though not in the article). Offices of the union in Lusaka were said to be staffed by full-time trade unionists.[138]

Indeed, Solomon Mifima, as "secretary of the NUNW" is reported to have represented his organization at the International Trade Union Conference against Apartheid in June 1973 (sponsored by the ILO).[139] In June 1975 Mifima, as secretary for labor of SWAPO, represented the United Nations Council for Namibia at the annual ILO meetings in Geneva.[140] But Mifima did not last long in either of his two roles. By the early 1970s SWAPO in exile had largely shifted its base in Tanzania to Lusaka and environs in Zambia. It was here that the "SWAPO crisis of 1974–76" occurred,[141] resulting in the arrest by SWAPO of Mifima and others in the SWAPO leadership, including Andreas Shipanga and Immanuel Engombe, on 21 April 1976, and the subsequent detention of these three and eight others in prison in Tanzania for two years. The SWAPO crisis of 1974–76 is important because of the way the SWAPO leadership dealt with some of its "organized wings" (in this case the youth and military) and because of the precedent it set.[142]

Upon their release from prison, Mifima and Shipanga returned to Namibia; Mifima, in the meantime was replaced as secretary for labor by John Ya Otto. Among other things, SWAPO's own internal investigation into the crisis, the "Ya Otto Commission" report, recommended that dormant and inactive departments such as Foreign Relations, Information and Publicity, and Labour, be revitalized.[143] Ya Otto calls Mifima "the father of the establishment of the National Union of Namibian Workers" although he says that when he (Ya Otto) arrived in exile in 1974 Mifima was "preoccupied primarily with this underground organization to overthrow the SWAPO leadership." Therefore, when Ya Otto took over, he says, he essentially attempted to build a Department of Labour anew.[144] An initial focus was admission to the ILO for Namibia as well as building support for trade union activities among international trade union movements and solidarity organizations.

Parallel to the developments in the labor field were changes in the internal political situation in Namibia that, especially later, would affect the situation facing black workers in Namibia. In the early 1970s the South African government was moving ahead with its plan for self-government for the homelands; in 1968, 1970, and 1972 nominated Legislative and Executive Councils were instituted in Ovambo, Kavango, and Caprivi, respectively. In 1973, according to the Self-government for Native Nations in SWA Act 20 of 1973, Ovambo and Kavango became "fully self-governing" territories with partially elected Legislative Councils. Also during 1973 the South African prime minister appointed an Advisory Council, consisting of representatives of eight of the eleven "population groups" in Namibia—but no political parties or groups—to begin discussions about Namibia's "constitutional future."[145] This Advisory Council met until September 1974, when the decision was made to convene a constitutional conference under the auspices of the National Party of SWA.[146]

One year later, in September 1975, Dirk Mudge and Eben Van Zyl, senior members of the all-white Legislative Assembly's Executive Committee, convened the Constitutional Conference, which took place in Windhoek's

Turnhalle building. More than 150 delegates from the eleven different population groups participated in the conference and within two weeks issued a Declaration of Intent to formulate an "independence constitution." By August 1976 the conference made proposals for an interim government for the territory and independence by 31 December 1978. A draft constitution, including a Bill of Rights, was completed by March 1977 and a three-tier system of ethnic government for the country was proposed. In mid-May 1977, 95 percent of white Namibians voted in a referendum in favor of the Turnhalle proposals for independence by the end of 1978 and for the proposed constitution.

In anticipation of independence for the territory, the position of administrator, in place since 1915, was abolished by the South African government and the first administrator general (AG) was appointed on 1 September to act on behalf of the South African government as a one-person interim government to prepare the territory for the elections. With the appointment of the first administrator general, direct representation for Namibia in the South African Parliament, first introduced in 1950, came to an end. In addition, most of the functions that had been transferred to the South African government in 1969 were transferred back to a South West Africa administration.[147] The Turnhalle Constitutional Conference was dissolved on 7 November 1977 just days after all of the delegates to the conference, with the exception of the National Party of SWA, joined a new political organization, the Democratic Turnhalle Alliance (DTA) with Clemens Kapuuo as president and Dirk Mudge as chairperson.

From mid-1975 the first steps had been taken toward doing away with various "petty apartheid" laws.[148] In June, Dirk Mudge announced that such legislation would be repealed, with the result that the right of admission to hotels, restaurants, and cafes would be left to the discretion of owners and managers, and all signs segregating races at the entrance to public buildings would be removed.[149] In the course of the Turnhalle Conference in March 1976 a decision was made to remove discrimination in wages and salaries based on race or color and to adopt a policy of equal pay for equal work. Just one month after his appointment, the administrator general repealed by special proclamation the Immorality Proclamation of 1934, the Prohibition of Mixed Marriages Ordinance of 1953, and the Immorality Amendment Ordinances of 1953 and 1954 and further repealed or amended a series of influx control laws that abolished the identification passes required of black Namibians, did away with the requirement of a permit for blacks to remain in an urban area for more than seventy-two hours, and eliminated the powers of authorities to remove unemployed blacks from urban areas. But black people still had to obtain permission to seek work and be employed in urban areas.

Spurred on largely by the SWAPO Youth League, resistance to the notion of self-governing ethnic homelands was immediate and widespread; indeed, it had followed nearly uninterrupted from the strike and its aftermath.[150] Mass meetings were held in Katutura throughout 1973 to oppose the prime minister's Advisory Council and the implementation of "self-government" in the homelands. Disturbances continued to occur in the Ovambo Compound in Katutura, especially in protest over the August 1973 elections in Ovamboland for members of the Legislative Council (a strong campaign to boycott the elections was successful as only 2.5 percent of those eligible to vote in the election voted). In the wake of the election, resistance in the North continued unabated and those arrested or detained began to be handed over to "tribal courts," which meted out brutal punishments of flogging with the "epokolo"—the central rib of a makalani palm branch—resulting in severe wounds or even death to the flogged individual.[151]

In the North and in other parts of Namibia the SWAPO Youth League continued to hold illegal meetings and even rallies to protest the restrictions on political activity and freedom of speech, the policy of separate development under way (the homelands), and the emergency regulations. Student unrest in the form of school boycotts took place at Martin Luther High School and the Augustineum. Hundreds of SWAPO and SWAPO Youth League members were routinely arrested, detained, and tortured. The arrests and detentions in 1973 and 1974 and eventually a series of "SWAPO Youth League trials" from 1973 to 1975 even led to a momentary international outcry against South Africa's policies inside Namibia.[152]

The detentions and trials also contributed to an exodus of thousands of Namibian youth, from mid-1974, into Angola and Zambia. Of course, the fall of the Portuguese in Angola served to facilitate the youths' flight from racial discrimination and political repression at home, from beatings and floggings in the North, in search of education and training abroad, or to join the SWAPO military effort against the South Africans. Those who left included most of the militant SWAPO Youth Leaguers as well as older SWAPO leaders such as John Ya Otto.

Still the protest continued, especially after the authorities announced a second election in Ovamboland in January 1975. Only seven months later, on 17 August, Ovambo Chief (and recently "reelected" Legislative Council chief minister) Filemon Elifas was assassinated, prompting a further spiral of violence and arrests. By late 1975 the situation in the North had not eased; the war had been stepped up, another consequence of the fall of the Portuguese in Angola; and in October civilians were ordered to withdraw from the border areas of Ovambo, which then became security zones. From November, South African

Defence Force troops were airlifted into the area. In 1976 schoolchildren intensified their boycotts against their inferior "Bantu" education.

State authorities responded, in part, with additional security legislation and with the additional use of force. In early 1974 it was announced that the SWA Riotous Assemblies Act (Ordinance 9 of 1930) would be amended to give the authorities still greater control over black political meetings in the urban locations. SWAPO publications such as *Kalahari Sands* and *Namibia News* were banned. In May 1976 new legislation widened the provisions of the 1950 Suppression of Communism Act in the territory and martial law was declared in the North; in addition, the emergency regulations first imposed in Ovambo in 1972 were extended to the Kavango and to the Caprivi by Proclamation R89 of 1976. By July a shoot-to-kill order was in place in "no-go" areas of Ovambo (along the border), and in mid-1977 the South African Defence Force began military training for volunteers for ethnic military units. Such was the situation on the eve of the "independence elections" that were to take place in Namibia in 1978.

The analysis of the origins and aftermath of the 1971–72 strike in Namibia in this chapter has revealed the conflicting versions of this important event in Namibian history. Some have described it as a largely spontaneous outbreak, others as the organizational effort of the SWAPO Youth League and SWAPO students. Still others have claimed a role for the NUNW. I have presented the strike as a politically inspired event, loosely organized by SWAPO secondary school students, for which long-standing worker grievances were successfully galvanized. Although it may not have appeared so at the time, the strike clearly had a significant result—setting in motion a contradictory process of labor and political reform, on the one hand, and an intensification of war and repression, on the other—as the colonial authorities and capital grappled with the need for a new strategy in Namibia.

On the labor front, the first steps toward dismantling the decades-old contract labor system, symbolized most vividly in the "recruiting" agency SWANLA, were taken. As some employers began to confront the need for labor reform in the aftermath of the strike, wages were raised in some industries and working conditions improved in others. For the first time, faint reference was made to the possibility of allowing workers to organize themselves into trade unions. In the 1970s the state embarked on some political reforms—for example, abolishing many of the existing "petty apartheid" laws—but it imposed even more draconian security legislation and intensified its war effort in the North.

This chapter has also explored the earliest relations between the liberation movement SWAPO (and its predecessor organization the OPO/OPC) and workers in Namibia. Although most SWAPO accounts attribute the movement's origins to a group of contract workers gathered in Cape Town, the leadership, at least, was largely composed of students, teachers, and journalists. Like other liberation movements in Africa at the time, SWAPO was very much a nationalist movement whose early goals were and remained freedom and national independence. Unlike other nationalist movements in Africa, however, SWAPO did not emerge from an organized labor movement. SWAPO made its early appeals to the contract migrant workers in Namibia in an effort to win widespread political support through an issue of vital concern to thousands of ordinary Namibians.

In 1979 Richard Hyman observed that "Third World" strikes rarely occur "against an established background of 'free collective bargaining' between recognized unions and employers. . . . Commonly they are a form of pressure or protest directed against the government rather than individual private employers; accordingly, they are likely to possess an overt political dimension."[153] Certainly in Namibia political and labor issues have always been inextricably linked. For Namibian workers there was no distinguishing the economic exploitation they encountered at the workplace from the oppression they endured as black Namibians—with no political rights—in the wider apartheid society. Thus for SWAPO and Namibian workers, the coincidence of political and labor issues was natural. Not surprisingly, then, according to Kandy Nehova, one of the main accomplishments of the strike was that it raised the consciousness of workers; for thousands of Namibian workers the strike and its aftermath made clear the connection between the economic and the political.[154]

Still, with a few exceptions, in the aftermath of the general strike life continued much as before for the workers of Namibia. The strike did not lead to an effort to achieve greater economic gain through organization; rather, the plight of ordinary workers continued to be subordinated to specific aims of the broader political struggle. But this struggle had not extended to economic emancipation. This trend continued during the late 1970s and early 1980s, as is demonstrated in the next chapter.

Three

NATIONALISM CONFRONTS TRADE UNIONISM, 1978–1984

In many respects, a new era in political developments inside Namibia began in 1978. Although there would be no independence in that year, as many had anticipated, politicians and political groups initiated the first of two attempts at an "internal settlement" in the form of an interim government established in 1980. A process of lifting many of the petty apartheid laws continued, although this was one of the most repressive periods in recent Namibian history. In the labor arena, an amendment to one labor law for the first time allowed black workers to form and join trade unions, although new security legislation restricted freedom of movement and, in the process, freedom of association. And restrictions on trade unions' political affiliations further dampened the effect of the new amendment.

On the side of capital, reform initiatives gained greater impetus during this period. Organizations such as the Private Sector Foundation, the Institute for Management and Leadership Training, and the Namibia Institute for Economic Affairs were formed, introducing into the public discourse the notion of "labor relations" and holding seminars on the subject. The larger mining companies in particular, facing a more capital-intensive production, mindful of an impending independence, and subject to considerable international pressure, led the reform initiative. Their employer organization, the Chamber of Mines, put forward the first suggestions for broad changes to existing labor laws although, especially with hard economic times in the early 1980s, these suggestions were not eagerly embraced by other factions of capital, especially commercial agriculture.

In other respects, however, developments during this period were crucial in setting the stage for the later emergence of trade unions in Namibia. Following the above-mentioned change in the labor law, for the first time, a few black trade union bodies such as the Namibian Trade Union Council and the Namibian Federation of Trade Unions were established, although they never gained a significant following. More important, an effort linked to the South West Africa People's Organisation to organize a black trade union was attempted, only to be crushed as part of a wider repression of political activity after the union was moved from its worker base at the Rossing uranium mine to a headquarters in Windhoek. Examination of this effort reveals the marked differences at the time in the conceptions of trade unionism of those organizing among workers inside Namibia and those based in exile with SWAPO in neighboring Angola.

In exile, the activities of the SWAPO Department of Labour and the nascent National Union of Namibian Workers continued with ever-increasing support from international trade union movements and anti-apartheid organizations. Training of future trade unionists and labor administrators began in earnest, and a school for trade unionism was established in Kwanza Sul. By the early 1980s, however, SWAPO's labor and trade union activities in exile were under attack by the nationalist organization itself. Along with hundreds of other SWAPO cadres, trade unionists in exile were arrested and imprisoned by SWAPO's security apparatus, accused of being South African spies. Moreover, those involved in trade unionism in exile were leveled with the special charge of attempting "to form a party within a party."[1]

INSIDE NAMIBIA: THE NAWU AND THE NUNW

Although various SWAPO histories claim that during the 1970s the NUNW was active inside Namibia (though "of necessity operating underground")—with "branches firmly established in most of the big mines"[1]—there is little confirming evidence. Namibian workers interviewed in Walvis Bay, Windhoek, and at the Rossing uranium mine in Arandis in January 1977 spoke passionately about the absence of trade unions in Namibia, the conditions under which they could be formed, and the improvements they could bring to workers' living and working conditions.[2] Indeed, the evidence that does exist suggests a story quite different from one of the linear and parallel development of a NUNW inside and outside Namibia. Rather, it seems that although the NUNW was established in 1970 in exile (even if it existed mostly only on paper), inside Namibia the first stirrings of a general workers' union were under the guise of the Namibian Workers' Union (NAWU), which later became known as the National Union of Namibian Workers—neither of which was particularly successful in this early incarnation.

From 29–31 May 1976 a SWAPO party congress was held in Walvis

Bay; among other things, this congress elected a new internal leadership.[3] Jason Angula, a young activist who had been involved in the school marches and strikes in the North in the early 1970s and eventually came back south to Martin Luther High School, was given the portfolio of Economics, Labour, and Natural Resources, a new position.[4] In 1977, according to Angula, the position was split; he stayed on as secretary for labor and Alexander Gaomab was given the portfolio of Economics and Natural Resources.[5] Angula describes his terms of reference as "enormous": "It was, inter alia, my duty as the Labour Secretary to keep a close working relationship with especially the workers because at that time we had no trade unions . . . and also it was part of my terms of reference to look into the question of forming a visible trade union. It was also my work to serve as the link between the grassroots and the top leadership of the Executive Committee [of SWAPO] and also with our colleagues outside."[6] Angula describes himself at the time as a mobilizer, a fieldworker, and an officeholder, "preparing speeches, conference addresses, information and also standing before the press in defense of the party and also putting forth the party's aims and objectives." Indeed, Angula says, each portfolio holder "was virtually a one man show."[7]

According to Angula, SWAPO initiated efforts to form a black trade union in Namibia in about 1977. He recalls that he and others were in close contact with SWAPO comrades outside and requested that a constitution for a trade union be drawn up; when the constitution was sent back, it bore the name Namibian Workers' Union.[8] Indeed, a draft constitution of a Namibian Workers' Union apparently did exist; it was published in a special issue (on Namibia) of the *South African Labour Bulletin* in 1978, and the introduction to the draft states that it was an "important landmark in the efforts of Namibian workers to organise in their own interests."[9] SWAPO's own *Historical Profile* of 1978, published in Lusaka, cites the "newly-formed Namibian Workers' Union" as further evidence of the growing resistance inside Namibia.[10] Gerson Max, a Lutheran pastor who worked throughout the 1970s and early 1980s with migrant workers all over Namibia ("preaching" in the worker compounds on Sundays), also claims he had close contact with John Ya Otto in exile and recounts his own extensive involvement in the formation of the Namibian Workers' Union around 1977.[11]

That SWAPO in exile should have sent back to Namibia a draft constitution of an NAWU when the NUNW so clearly already existed in exile seems unlikely, although the 1978 SWAPO document as cited above does indeed refer to a newly formed NAWU. Peltola ascribes this discrepancy to the fact that the contacts between those SWAPO cadres inside and outside Namibia were so few that those inside did not even know of the existence of the

NUNW outside.[12] Others tend to gloss the discrepancy: Gillian Cronje and Suzanne Cronje write of the NUNW as "also referred to as the Namibian Workers' Union (NAWU)." An NUNW/COSATU history argues that workers, together with Jason Angula, Pastor Max, and Arthur Pickering, "spoke of building a trade union which they first called the Namibian Workers Union (NAWU). But as their union grew stronger, they gave it the name of SWAPO's union—which had been organising underground since 1970—the National Union of Namibian Workers (NUNW)."[13]

While it seems that initial efforts to organize a general workers union were being made around 1977, in the name of NAWU, and meetings held in towns such as Walvis Bay, Windhoek, Swakopmund, Tsumeb, and Grootfontein (according to Angula), a more specific effort to organize industrial workers began at the Rossing uranium mine in 1978. During that year a "coloured" advocate named Arthur Pickering went to Rossing as a personnel officer;[14] Pickering went to Rossing from Windhoek although he had previously been active with Manuel de Castro trying to organize Luderitz fishermen into a trade union. At Rossing, Pickering found that the workers had many grievances stemming in particular from rampant racial discrimination at the mine: for example, employees were divided into day rate workers and staff, with all of the staff—except for thirty blacks, including Pickering—being white, regardless of their qualifications. In certain jobs, where the lack of competence on the part of the white workers was particularly evident, there was considerable animosity and tension over the privileges they enjoyed merely by virtue of being white. The mine at that time had instituted liaison committees for communication with workers, but these were organized along ethnic lines—one for the Ovambos, one for the Damaras—and therefore particularly disliked.[15]

Pickering began organizing meetings in and around Arandis to explore the idea of starting a trade union. At first workers were not particularly receptive: "There was still a great deal of ignorance; at the time there was so much politics going on as the DTA had just been formed and there were many of the exiles who were coming back and so people were very suspicious of anything new." Soon Pickering's efforts came together with those of others to organize black workers in Namibia; at Camp A at Rossing Pickering found a worker in possession of membership cards for the Namibian Workers' Union and became aware of the efforts of Pastor Max and Jason Angula to organize workers. Then he was approached by a Swede by the name of Palle Carlsson who had been sent into Namibia, via SWAPO and the NUNW in exile, to assist in the organization of trade unions.[16] Carlsson, together with Max, organized a large meeting in Windhoek mostly with mine workers from

Consolidated Diamond Mines, although, according to Pickering, nothing much came of this initial effort.

At Rossing, meanwhile, events took another turn when in December 1978 workers simply downed their tools and went on strike.[17] Pickering and Henry Boonzaaier, another Rossing worker active in the effort to organize a union, set about drawing up a list of demands and indicated their desire to meet with management. In the aftermath of the meeting, during which the striking workers and their representatives were preparing for further negotiations with management, a bomb exploded in a bakery in nearby Swakopmund and Pickering and Boonzaaier were picked up by the police.

They were eventually released, but, according to Pickering, "by this time we did not have a union as such, no structures, it really depended on one or two people to do all of the work and it really became too much." By that time management at Rossing was "gunning for" Pickering, and in March 1979 he left the mine.[18] Pickering returned to Windhoek, where he was again picked up by the police (Boonzaaier, still at the mine, had already been taken in), part of a more general roundup of SWAPO activists; he and Boonzaaier and about one hundred others spent six months in four prison cells of twenty-five each in Gobabis, east of Windhoek. Upon their release, Pickering was once again approached by Carlsson, still intent on fostering trade unionism in Namibia; together Pickering and Boonzaaier then established a union office in Windhoek with money from the Swedes; for some months Boonzaaier and Pickering went out to organize workers, especially at the mines, gaining access to the workers' compounds as lay preachers on Sundays.

In December 1979 Boonzaaier and Pickering left Namibia for a meeting in Botswana and were picked up once again by the police, with Pastor Max as well, upon their return. And while the three and others were in jail, the police went to the newly established union office, confiscated equipment, documents, and vehicles, and closed the office. After they were released in early 1980 Pickering was placed under house arrest; Boonzaaier decided to leave Namibia for exile in Angola and Pickering left in October 1980 for further studies in Britain. Efforts to organize mass-based trade unions in Namibia had ended temporarily.

These activities were the basis for the myriad reports of extensive organization by the NUNW in Namibia in the years 1978–80.[19] More accurately, the relationship with the NUNW seems to have been as follows: early efforts by Pastor Max and Jason Angula had revolved around a Namibian Workers' Union, but in the course of 1978 and 1979, through Palle Carlsson and Jason Angula, more information began to reach Namibia and Pickering and others about the NUNW in exile.[20] Efforts to organize an NAWU became efforts to organize an NUNW. Finally, a meeting of NUNW inside and outside Namibia had been arranged. In December 1979 Boonzaaier and Pickering and two of Max's people had met with John Ya Otto in Francistown in Botswana.

At this meeting the ideas and experiences of those trade unionists who were actually organizing workers inside Namibia confronted those waging a political struggle on behalf of Namibian workers from exile. Although Pickering and Boonzaaier were SWAPO activists, Pickering, at least, was not happy with the SWAPO/NUNW concept of trade unionism he encountered during the week-long meeting in Botswana: "It was quite obvious to me that Ya Otto . . . was basically a politician and saw the union as a wing of SWAPO and was more concerned about us having T-shirts and NUNW having SWAPO colors and so on. And he had ideas of trade unions that were East European . . . very bureaucratic, with various departments—information and publicity etc.—a political organization." Still, Pickering concedes that "the only people who had any interest at the time in promoting unions were SWAPO or Ya Otto or any people connected with them."[21] Moreover, Ya Otto also reportedly felt that trade unionists in Namibia should have nothing to do with South Africa, while Pickering and Carlsson had already made a very useful trip to Durban to meet with organizers from the Federation of South African Trade Unions (FOSATU), and this was another source of tension.[22] More broadly, Pickering felt at the time that while a SWAPO-based union might work at a place like CDM, which had a relatively homogeneous migrant workforce and always a very strong SWAPO branch, at a mine such as Rossing, "which was multi-ethnic—where there were DTA people and SWANU people and NIP [National Independence Party] people—you just could not have a party base." In the event, these first efforts to organize a general trade union in Namibia did not survive long beyond the Botswana trip; they fell victim to the repression of the wider political struggle. But the idea of an NUNW and of a SWAPO-based trade union had been introduced and the groundwork for later efforts was laid.

SWAPO IN EXILE: FEAR OF SOLIDARNOSC

In the wake of the "SWAPO crisis" in 1976, SWAPO held an Enlarged Central Committee meeting 28 July to 1 August in Nampundwe outside Lusaka,[23] at which John Ya Otto replaced Solomon Mifima as secretary for labor. Two documents resulted from this meeting: the Political Programme of the SWAPO of Namibia and the Constitution of the SWAPO of Namibia. As Saul and Leys note, while some considered the Political Programme, in particular, with its "left-leaning" language, to be a concession to the rebellious youth who had just been put down, it could also be seen as an attempt for greater appeal among the movement's increasingly important military supporters in Eastern Europe, the Soviet Union, and Angola.[24] The constitution, meanwhile, set out in some detail the tasks of the various party officials, including the secretary for labor: he or she was responsible for encouraging and supporting efforts of the working people to organize themselves into trade unions; for encouraging bona fide trade unions in Namibia to seek affiliate membership with SWAPO; and for maintaining contacts with national and international labor movements and representing SWAPO in conferences of such movements.[25]

Initially at least, it seems that the secretary for labor spent much of his time in the last activity. Already in 1973 the International Labour Organisation had stated its commitment to providing, in cooperation with the United Nations commissioner for Namibia, assistance "towards ensuring trade union rights for Namibian workers."[26] By 1974, in conjunction with the proposed creation of an Institute for Namibia, the ILO stated its further willingness to provide lecture courses on trade unionism and other labor questions as well as scholarships for students of labor administration. In that same year the decision was taken to invite the United Nations Council for Namibia to all sessions of the International Labour Conference and all other ILO meetings of relevance to Namibia, and by 1975 discussions were taking place within the ILO on how to formalize such participation.[27] By December 1976 SWAPO had been accorded observer status within the United Nations system as a whole and thereafter the particulars of Namibia's participation at the ILO were worked out.[28] According to Neville Rubin, who was then working on the southern Africa program at the ILO, Namibia was admitted as a member state to the ILO by special resolution in 1978, the government in this case being represented by the UN Council for Namibia. As always at the ILO, the "government" designated the worker and employer representatives, who, in this case, were always exiled SWAPO members; throughout the entire period John Ya Otto represented workers and for much of the period Ngarikutuke Tjiriange represented employers.[29]

The activities of the SWAPO Department of Labour/NUNW in exile were many, but they revolved primarily around education and training—the only option, perhaps, in the absence of workers and employers. Because facilities in the SWAPO camps were insufficient, students were at first sent abroad for training; according to Ya Otto, in the late 1970s, trade unions in the Soviet Union and Eastern Europe provided short courses and resources to the growing number of Namibian students of trade unionism in exile. From 1977 the Soviet Union invited two Namibian students annually to study at the Moscow

High School of Trade Unions, and East European trade unions offered more training abroad and equipment to the future Namibian trade unionists.[30] When some of these students returned to SWAPO in exile, they set about teaching their colleagues what they had learned about trade unionism in schools literally under a tree. The first of these was in Nyango in Zambia and known as NYASOTU (Nyango School of Trade Unionism) and a later one was in Kwanza Sul and known as KWASOTU (Kwanza School of Trade Unionism).[31] Very soon northern European and Scandinavian trade unions and solidarity organizations became more intensively involved, sending instructors to Angola for trade unionism courses and eventually deciding to fund and help to build a trade union school for SWAPO in exile; the Nduuvu Nangolo Trade Union Centre (NNTUC) was opened at the Kwanza Sul Resettlement Centre in 1983.[32] Also in 1983 publication of the *Namibian Worker* began from Luanda, another initiative with much support and input from the Central Organisation of Finnish Trade Unions (SAK).[33] During these same years the ILO sent SWAPO cadres to its training institute in Turino, Italy, for courses in labor administration, industrial relations, and employment services; one of the ILO's main contributions during this period was to build a Vocational Training Centre for SWAPO cadres in Zumbe, Angola.[34]

Meanwhile, John Ya Otto, in his dual role as SWAPO secretary for labor and NUNW general secretary, was immediately active in strengthening links with international trade union and solidarity organizations above and beyond the ILO. Among other things, this included the decision to affiliate the NUNW in exile to the World Federation of Trade Unions (WFTU), arch rival at the time to the International Confederation of Free Trade Unions (ICFTU).[35] It is not clear exactly who made this decision or when, although it is clear that those active inside Namibia at the time with a fledgling NUNW were not consulted.[36]

Outside, in exile, there can be little doubt that the SWAPO Department of Labour and the National Union of Namibian Workers were one—indicated first and foremost by the fact that the same individual headed both. The NUNW's origins in exile were as a simple creation of the party at the suggestion of the one who headed the nascent Labour Section (Mifima) in 1970, and later constitutions of SWAPO outlined the responsibility of the secretary for labor to organize trade unions. Those who were in exile at the time recall the congruence: "NUNW was part of [the] SWAPO Department of Labour and the trade unionism or trade union activities there were mainly around May Day, and when a trade union organization visited SWAPO or [the] SWAPO Department of Labour they actually visited [the] NUNW"; "when we were in exile working for NUNW . . . NUNW and [the Department of] Labour were one. We couldn't make a distinction because at that time the situation also did not allow it"; "the Labour Department and the trade unions, there was a very thin line [so] that one could at times not see that the two were separate things—because it was run by the Labour Secretary who was the head of the trade union activities as well and it was also the responsibility of the SWAPO Labour Department to organize trade unions."[37] In the view of others, NUNW in its early days in exile was nothing more than a "name on paper," a "letterhead."

Given the complete overlap of party and trade union (and indeed the models learned during short courses abroad), there can be little surprise that the difference between the two was neither drawn nor well understood by the students of trade unionism or those working within the two organizations at the time (as was true of their political leaders in a previous era). As an instructor, Peltola found that when he tried to lecture on the difference between the government and a trade union, students "couldn't see the difference at all."[38] Indeed, a thesis written in the mid-1980s by one SWAPO student in exile reveals a predominant attitude among SWAPO cadres toward this issue: in an independent Namibia a "strong state" in unity with the trade union movement was envisaged; in addition, "the labour movement will be expected to change from its pre-independence confrontational role to one of active cooperation. To this effect, this dissertation suggests that the State/Party–Union relations should be defined along lines approximating those in Tanzania where there is special representation of unions in [the] party apparatus. There should be interlocking leadership, or control over [the] appointment/elections of union functionaries particularly the top executive posts of the national trade union centre."[39] More important, the thesis noted, "The purpose of trade unions in post-independent Namibia will be determined by the objectives of the state."

But the issue of trade union/party/state relations was, for the moment, minor compared with the new crisis that would befall SWAPO in exile in the early 1980s. In the February 1982 issue of the Luanda-based publication the *Combatant*, SWAPO reaffirmed its support for the government of Poland, which had just declared a state of emergency and therefore saved the country and socialism from "the chaos, civil war and terror the counterrevolutionaries could have brought about."[40] The "counterrevolutionaries" were the "400 reactionary organizations" united in Solidarnosc and "masquerading as a trade union." Indeed, the Polish example was not one the SWAPO leadership wished to see replicated any time soon, and it took the requisite precautions. By the early 1980s another "SWAPO crisis"—with a trajectory that was to be far worse even than the worst aspects of the crisis of 1974–76—was unfolding. Saul and Leys have described in some detail this episode in SWAPO's history in which "the revolution was consuming its own children"—in which "a system of organised terror . . . enveloped the entire organisation."[41] Accused of being South African spies, more than one thousand SWAPO members in exile were arrested from the early 1980s, beaten, and tortured until they signed "confessions" and then sent to "the holes"—literal dungeons in the ground in Lubango, Angola, sometimes holding up to one hundred people at a time— where they languished for years with the barest minimum of food, water, and clothing, deprived of exercise, reading material, and other amenities. In the end, several hundred died—from physical abuse, poor food, lack of medical attention, or natural causes—or were killed.[42]

Saul and Leys identify, in brief, the following ingredients contributing to the dungeons of Lubango: "military reverses, declining morale, misgivings about the competence of the army command, insecurities, extending even to rivalries between successive generations of exiles and between different ethnic groups, the arrival of a new wave of exiles from the south, and a pervasive tradition of authoritarianism, reinforced in the aftermath of the 1976 crisis."[43] Indeed, it seems that the trade union movement in exile also came in for special attention from the SWAPO leadership and security apparatus. Peltola reports that by late 1981 SWAPO leaders were voicing publicly their concern about trade unions: "that a trade union in an independent Namibia would perhaps upset the economy and politics through strikes."[44] Peltola reports that some in the SWAPO leadership were highly suspicious of the trade union education that was taking place in the camps, in particular that provided by the foreign instructors. A general attempt was made to maintain control over the trade union movement by, for example, preventing it from selecting its own leaders.

Those active in trade unionism in exile were increasingly thrown into the dungeons. Trade unionist Henry Boonzaaier, after fleeing persecution and torture in Namibia and South Africa, found himself in Lubango for eight years after 1982. According to Africa Watch, at least one former detainee reported being told to implicate the SWAPO labor secretary as "an enemy agent," along with certain other SWAPO officials in Luanda.[45] Several of the successive directors of the Nduuvu Nangolo Trade Union Centre were arrested during this period and spent up to five years in the dungeons.[46] The accusation was simple, according to one former director of Nduuvu Nangolo: that the trade unionists were "counterrevolutionaries," that they were trying "to form a party within a party." Another former NNTUC director cites the "crisis of Solidarity in Poland" and confirms that the trade unions were "becoming a threat." Both attribute the situation, to some degree, to a leadership that did not understand what trade unions were all about:

> Basically there were many others in the leadership and some ordinary people who did not understand, who felt that the [Labour] Department should be done away with, especially the trade union section, should be done away with, because you are training people who are going to take from you tomorrow. Because if today you give them that opportunity to organize freely, to go and attend seminars . . . they can build influence there and they can organize themselves until they are strong and take over the leadership. Or thus it happens maybe like Poland that the trade union eventually caused such big havoc in the country until they had to take over. So there was this fear.[47]

One labor activist from exile reports that those active in trade unionism were made to feel "like outcast people" and that "it was only later that people came to like trade unions, understand trade unions, and trade unions were regarded as part and parcel."[48]

In 1986, Peltola was sent by the Ministry of Labour in Finland and taught his last course with SWAPO in exile—this one in labor administration. It should have been held in Kwanza Sul at the Trade Union Centre but was held instead in the transit camp of Viana just outside Luanda; people were not being let through to the SWAPO camps inside Angola because of the "detainee paranoia . . . because people were just talking." Indeed, the first word of the detentions in Lubango began to filter back to Namibia around 1984 especially after the 10–13 May "peace summit" convened jointly in Lusaka by Zambian president Kenneth Kaunda and Administrator General Willie Van Niekerk and attended by SWAPO and other delegations from Namibia. SWAPO students abroad began to hear of the detentions after 1984 as well.[49]

Ironically, perhaps, SWAPO's own proclaimed ideology served to protect the trade union activities in exile to a certain extent. Although individual members could be arrested and sent to "the holes," the trade union movement that had been formed in exile, including the trade union school, could not be completely eliminated. The main reason, according to one labor activist, seems to have been the international support that had contributed so much to the establishment of the Department of Labour and the NUNW in the first place and SWAPO's own professed ideology:

> Well, it was so that the leadership could at that point in time not do away with activities because they were already so well known by the international community . . . it could have been a type of a lie—that SWAPO is a bourgeois party—because they were very close to the socialist countries and because they were the people who used to give us more support than anybody else. So it could have been a conflict between the socialist block and the movement itself. Because they would

have needed a very clear explanation . . . they would just feel that SWAPO is a bourgeois party and it is against the working class.[50]

Only from the mid- to late 1980s with the real development of trade unions inside Namibia did the attitude change somewhat, especially as the mobilizational value of the unions in the final days of the liberation struggle became clear to the nationalist movement.

CAPITAL CONTEMPLATES REFORM OF LABOR RELATIONS

The first concerns about labor relations in Namibia expressed openly by employers followed on the strike of 1971–72 and have been discussed in the previous chapter. The concern continued in the late 1970s and early 1980s and began to take more tangible form with concrete proposals for changes to labor legislation and the establishment of organizations aimed at influencing employers and employer organizations. Although these efforts in large part reflected evolving conditions in Namibia, developments in South Africa in the business and labor communities certainly had an enormous influence. For a variety of reasons, by the late 1970s in South Africa big business, with the exception of agriculture, "was agreed on the need for significant reforms in economic and political policy."[51] During these years a significant dismantling of many apartheid controls and a gradual reform of the labor relations dispensation commenced. For example, in the labor arena, following the recommendations of the Riekert and Wiehahn Commissions, constraints on the movement of African workers were loosened, job reservation was scrapped, and African workers, for the first time, were allowed to form and join trade unions.

In Namibia, the multinational mining companies were at the forefront of this initial reform effort, reflecting their increasingly sophisticated methods of production, a fear of the postindependence dispensation, and a response to a concerted international campaign against them.[52] As Alastair MacFarlane notes, in the late 1970s "the contract labour system did not actually suit the planned operational needs" of a mine such as Rossing Uranium : "Whilst every other mine in Namibia was operated using large quantities of cheap black unskilled labour, the Rossing mine was building a highly sophisticated, capital intensive process which did not lend itself to operation by an unskilled, semi-proletarianised and transient workforce. Rather, what was required was a fully proletarianised, settled and trained workforce committed to industrial values who would be committed to employment at Rossing."[53] In addition, there were other more political considerations for a company like Rossing. Again, according to MacFarlane, with independence seemingly imminent in 1978, "Rossing was concerned to make itself acceptable to a future black government which was likely to be dominated by the South West African People's Organisation." Though independence did not transpire in 1978, it was clear to Rossing management "that any internationally acceptable settlement would involve UN supervised elections and a SWAPO dominated government. . . . Rossing was concerned to endear itself to the Namibian population and the international community in order to help guarantee its post-election presence."[54]

In September 1980 the Chamber of Mines in Namibia produced "A Working Paper on Labour Law and Labour Practice in South West Africa/ Namibia."[55] The introduction stated that "as a major industry and a large employer of labour the Chamber of Mines believes it should take the lead in examining the existing industrial relations system in SWA/Namibia and in recommending the changes it perceives necessary to promote industrial peace and prosperity." The paper expressed a desire to minimize conflict between management and labor and to maximize the growth of the country; improving labor relations, it was felt, could be achieved by changing the legal framework and by changing attitudes. The study found that both managers and workers had limited experience, skills, and knowledge of industrial relations and that a strong, independent trade union movement could be an asset to management as well as to workers.

The paper's "fundamental recommendations consist[ed] of compulsory recognition of trade unions under certain circumstances and the facilitation of industrial councils composed of employers and trade unions." In the absence of trade unions, or where trade unions might represent job classes that were "temporarily racially exclusive," works councils were recommended, although it was acknowledged that because of their history (especially in South Africa) "the works council suffers from a lack of credibility with the workforce." While the paper recognized the "merit in working towards one union per industry," it felt that "the ideal of one, non-racial union per industry or company is not achievable in the near future." It recommended that "the act of [union] registration be made as objective as possible without the grey issue of representativeness clouding matters." Industrial councils were recommended to institutionalize bargaining between employers and employees or their trade unions. A legislated minimum wage was considered undesirable, but there was recognition that in some instances, especially in the absence of collective agreements between management and employees, a wage determination, encompassing "only those conditions of employment that are absolutely basic to the individual's well being," might be necessary.

The 1980 *Annual Report* of the Chamber of Mines reiterated the need to minimize conflict and maximize economic growth in the territory mentioned in the "Working Paper" and proposed amendments to the Mines, Works, and Minerals Regulations, in particular the removal of racially discriminatory provisions. In 1981 the *Annual Report* noted that the Chamber's efforts to have the Wage and Industrial Conciliation Ordinance amended had "met with no success," in part prompting the formation of a Labour Committee to pursue the matter. By 1982 the *Annual Report* revealed that meetings had been held with the Chamber of Commerce and the South West Africa Agricultural Union (SWAAU) to discuss the Chamber's proposed amendments and that the two bodies had requested more time to study the documents; the *Report* also noted that Chamber officials were meeting with representatives of government. In 1983, according to the *Annual Report,* the original "Working Paper" was resubmitted to the government, this time to the new administrator general, Willie Van Niekerk, who also agreed to meet with the Chamber's Executive Committee on a regular basis. The *Report* stated that relations between management and employees continued "to be cordial and of a high standard with no serious industrial unrest during the year." By 1984 labor relations were reported to be "extremely good"—"a tribute to the strong and continuing efforts which the mines have directed towards good communications between management and employees, as well as to the ever-improving conditions under which employees work and live"; regular meetings with the administrator general were continuing as well.[56]

The Chamber of Mines was not the only organization on the side of capital to begin to explore labor relations in the territory. In late 1980 the Private Sector Foundation (PSF) was established in Windhoek, modeled, according to its past and present directors, on the Urban Foundation in South Africa.[57] The PSF was meant to be "a voluntary, non-ethnic, non-political association of businesses and individuals in SWA/Namibia concerned about the welfare of the community and committed to improving the quality of life of all people of this country according to their needs."[58] Initially, the PSF worked in four program areas: labor relations, housing and community services, education and training services, and small business development.[59] In May 1981 the PSF presented employers with a *Statement of Employment Principles* which called for selection and promotion in employment solely on the basis of ability, an active commitment to employee training and development, acceptance of the principle of equal pay for equal work, and concern for employee benefits and quality of life and for employers to acknowledge workers' rights to join trade unions and not be victimized for joining them.[60]

Activities of the Private Sector Foundation with respect to labor relations included conducting seminars with lecturers, mostly from South Africa, on topics such as "Negotiations Between Labour and Management," "Labour Relations," "The Formation and Operation of Industrial Councils," and "Industrial Relations Within an Organization"; lobbying the government "to accept defensible principles of labour management"; conducting a survey of labor relations in Namibia; and doing more general research on employment issues in the country.[61] The PSF also had two fieldworkers in labor relations.

And yet, despite the PSF's efforts, according to Miriam Truebody, PSF general manager in 1992, during 1982 and 1983 the foundation had to curtail its labor relations activities because of opposition by member organizations, mostly to the idea of trade unions, which the foundation was seen as promoting.[62] While organizations such as the Private Sector Foundation recognized the advantage of co-opting trade unions by promoting them, not all employers could fathom the strategy. According to Charles Truebody, first executive director of the PSF, "Trade unions were the bogeymen . . . trade unions to them [employers] meant less profit . . . the legal situation in this country was a Master and Servant situation and one doesn't give up that sort of position very easily . . . people were hoping that the thing would go past, that you live in a Third World country and there is so much labor in the place anyway, what's the point of having a trade union around . . . there was probably more than anything else a fear of what trade unions might do." Truebody continues: "People, I think, were very, very concerned about making sure that politics would go the way of the white man and because trade unions were used as a political tool they were part of the enemy and therefore had to be eliminated or prevented from establishing themselves."[63]

Another organization, the Namibia Institute for Economic Affairs (NIEA), was founded in 1982. Following the trend in southern Africa the NIEA was meant to be a centralized employers' organization in Namibia, although it never succeeded as such.[64] Instead, in its early years the NIEA became involved in drawing up development plans with government—only later to be joined by various professional organizations. From 1984, according to founder Henk Schoeman, the institute became involved in labor matters, eventually hosting seminars on labor relations as part of a larger Labour Relations Project and making the first recommendations that a commission of inquiry into labor matters in Namibia be established.[65] More important perhaps, the NIEA continued its attempts to organize employers in Namibia, eventually working with the ILO in this endeavor.

As might be expected, an employers' organization such as the South West Africa Agricultural Union did not have an agenda similar to that of the Chamber of Mines during these years, though even SWAAU apparently recognized that the labor relations situation must change. Indeed, during these years the section of SWAAU's *Annual Reports* devoted to their Employers' Association showed a growing preoccupation with workers' conditions of employment.[66] While in the late 1970s the association was still concerned with simply securing sufficient labor (working out a suitable labor recruitment system in the absence of the old), by 1979–80 the organization had begun to offer courses for both its members (for example, in personnel management) and their employees. The health, education, and housing needs of farmworkers began to be mentioned, if not exactly addressed. In 1982 representatives of the Employers' Association met, through the auspices of the NIEA, with members of the International Employers' Organisation of the ILO.

By 1984–85 the SWAAU Employers' Association listed better relations between workers and employers and improvements in the overall living standard of farmworkers as two of the goals of its ongoing education and training program. By 1986 the association had instituted a work competition (not unlike health and safety competitions in the mining industry) which considered a farmer's record on education and training—for himself and his employees—employee wages, housing, and general environment such as health, alcohol abuse, literacy, and church services. So though in general the living and working conditions for employees on the commercial farms remained the worst in the country, it appears at least that the farmers' organizations recognized that circumstances were changing.

And yet these initial forays did not constitute a linear process. In late 1984 the administrator general attempted to tighten control over the Namibian labor force through the implementation of manpower bureaus. While the legislation was officially intended "to bring work-seekers and employers together in an orderly manner" through the establishment of a central and local manpower bureaus (employment offices), the information, registration, and certification that would be essential components of the new system led many to consider it an attempt "to try to smuggle through the back door the old, hated pass laws."[67] In no time both employers' and employees' organizations voiced their opposition to the proposed legislation, with the most vocal and effective resistance coming from community-based organizations.[68] Ultimately, largely through the efforts of the Aksie-Mannekragburo (Action Manpower Bureaus), formed from residents' associations and other groups in Khomasdal and Katutura, the proposed legislation was defeated and in June 1985 quietly withdrawn by the administrator general.[69]

None of these reform efforts came to fruition in the early 1980s when they were first initiated; certainly Namibian workers did not feel the difference. Indeed, most of the stated goals of this period have been realized only in very recent years. Still, the movement that was afoot among employers and their colleagues in government at the time was important. In fact, some of the political reforms of the late 1970s and early 1980s had greater implications for the workers of Namibia and their prospects for organization inside the territory.

FIRST ATTEMPT AT AN INTERNAL SETTLEMENT

The changing political dispensation during these years provided the backdrop against which capital and labor were exploring new roles. Independence, slated for December 1978, and which in the minds of many, though illegitimate, had been so imminent, did not come to pass. An election was indeed held from 4 to 8 December 1978—a contest between only the DTA and the National Party—in which the DTA gained forty-one out of fifty seats in a "Constituent Assembly."[70] In May 1979 the Constituent Assembly was transformed into the National Assembly, and the South African–appointed administrator general remained the sole figure in the executive. In June 1980 a twelve-member Council of Ministers to assist the AG was established with DTA leader Dirk Mudge as chairman; as such, Mudge also appointed the ministers.[71] This "interim arrangement" constituted the first attempt at an internal settlement in Namibia, but it collapsed in January 1983, when the DTA government, under the leadership of Mudge, resigned, leaving the Administrator General Willie Van Niekerk to rule the country by decree. Van Niekerk was instrumental during 1983 in the formation of the Multi-Party Conference (MPC), a coalition involving eight political parties and alliances (not including SWAPO; two of the eight later withdrew). By April 1984 the MPC had agreed on the basic principles for a coalition government and the Transitional Government of National Unity was established by the South African government in June 1985. This second attempt at an internal settlement remained in place until 1989 when the United Nations–sponsored transition to independence commenced.

The period of the first interim government in Namibia was noted for its repressiveness. Following the intensification of the war effort by combatants of SWAPO's People's Liberation Army of Namibia (and the relocation of bases to Angola) the South Africans enhanced their own security efforts. All public meetings in the North were banned in 1979 and in southern Namibia in 1981. A counterinsurgency unit, called Koevoet, which would inflict terror on the people of Ovambo especially, was established in 1979 and a general military buildup in the North took place. In 1980 the South West Africa Territorial Force (SWATF) was created, and all men outside of the northern homelands were subject to military conscription (contributing to a new exodus of youth into exile).[72] A campaign to Win the Hearts and Minds (WHAM) of the people was also undertaken with the creation of cultural organizations for the Ovambo, Kavango, and Caprivi regions.

SWAPO activists were constantly being harassed, arrested, detained, and tortured. The beginning of 1978 saw the organization of rallies in Katutura followed by violence and killing, in particular the assassination of Clemens Kapuuo, president of the DTA, on 28 March. On 19 April 1978 the administrator general, M. T. Steyn, announced the promulgation of emergency regulations contained in new security and detention legislation (AG 26).[73] In early June 1979 Danny Tjongarero, SWAPO deputy national chairman, closed the SWAPO office in Windhoek, which had been bombed, and dissolved the National Executive, saying that the party could "no longer guarantee the lives of people and the protection of property." The bureaucracy would be scrapped, and the movement become "a pure people's movement."[74] Not until February 1984 would SWAPO again attempt to hold a rally inside Namibia.[75]

At the same time one change to existing labor legislation occurred that can be seen as in keeping with the initial steps toward labor reform suggested above. In July 1978 the Wage and Industrial Conciliation Ordinance 35 of 1952, the primary law governing labor relations in Namibia at the time, was amended to include black workers, for the first time, in its definition of an "employee."[76] The most significant aspect of this change (and so it was reported in Windhoek newspapers) was that "members of all races in the Territory will now be entitled to belong to trade unions."[77] For a trade union associated with a political party, however, the lifting of one restriction was offset by the levying of others. Discretionary powers on the part of the state administration in the registration of trade unions continued, concerning a trade union's constitution and its "representative" character and in particular whether it contained any provisions "contrary to any law or [which] are calculated to hinder the attainment of the objects of any law" or whether the union had "been formed for the purpose of evading the provisions of any law." New provisions brought the Namibian law in line with new South African law, which prohibited the affiliation of trade unions and employers' organizations to political parties and unions and employers' organizations granting funds to or receiving funds from political parties.[78]

Still the change in legislation does seem to have prompted a few tentative forays into black or at least multiracial trade unionism. In August and September 1979 the first disparate signs of attempts to organize black workers (apart from those of NAWU and the NUNW already discussed) appeared in the *Windhoek Observer*: a Working Committee linked to the SWAPO-D announced its plans to form a trade union in the mining industry.[79] At the same time, according to the same newspaper, black mine workers at the Tsumeb Corporation Limited's (TCL) Tsumeb mine began to join the South West Africa Mineworkers Union (SWAMU), which had previously been a white union but then declared itself multiracial.[80] By 1981 the Namibian Trade Union Council (NTUC) was established by Solomon Mifima, then SWAPO-D vice-president and person responsible for labor affairs.[81] In 1983 Mifima, by then a member of the Christian Democratic Action Party, ran a "labour complaints service" in Windhoek and received "a steady trickle of complaints."[82] Also in 1983 Jackson Kambode, another early SWAPO supporter who had left SWAPO and returned to Namibia, established the Namibian Federation of Trade Unions (NFTU), based in Oshakati; by 1986, however, neither the NTUC nor the NFTU still existed.

Otherwise, in the early to mid-1980s, the unions that existed were primarily "white" unions or staff associations that were attempting to become multiracial. The South West Africa Municipal Association (SWAMSA) had been founded in 1969, and in 1981 the Government Service Staff Association (GSSA) was founded, according to the stipulations of the Public Service Act 2 of 1980. SWAMSA became multiracial in 1978, in part reflecting the increasing numbers of "nonwhite" staff in the municipalities (anyone working for the municipalities had to join SWAMSA), and from its inception the GSSA also accepted "nonwhite" members.[83] The South West African Confederation of Labour (SWACOL), founded in 1983, was an organization to which "mostly white-dominated staff associations" were affiliated, although some, such as SWAMSA, refused to join.[84] One of the aims of SWACOL was to gain international recognition for the "labor federation" and the unions and staff associations it represented from, for example, the ILO and the ICFTU, thereby conferring some measure of legitimacy on the reform process under way in Namibia.[85]

In 1983 only five trade unions were registered with the Department of Civic Affairs and Manpower: the Typographical Workers' Union, the Building Workers' Union, the Fisherman Workers' Union, the SWAMU, and the SWAMSA; the latter two were described as the only "functioning unions."[86] In any case, the authorities at the time were willing to deal only with registered trade unions. At a SWACOL conference, AG Willie Van Niekerk said that unregistered unions could not be recognized as legitimate bargaining partners and that "no enforceable agreement can emerge between an unregistered trade union and any employers' group."[87] With a few notable exceptions, however, none of these trade unions survived the 1980s, and the real beginning of a trade union movement, as it is known in Namibia today, can be dated from the mid-1980s.

In conclusion, the nationalist movement's emerging attitude and practice toward its labor wing (and to the whole notion of organized labor) became evident by the early 1980s in the course of the attempt, first, by workers at the Rossing uranium mine to organize a National Union of Namibian Workers in Namibia in the late 1970s. In covert meetings of trade unionists from inside Namibia and those from SWAPO in exile, two different conceptions of trade unionism confronted each other. Some of those organizing workers at Rossing turned to FOSATU in South Africa—an emerging black trade union federation that was explicitly "workerist" in philosophy, wary of the national liberation movement, and careful to avoid any political alliances (refusing, for example, to join the United Democratic Front in 1983)—much to the dismay of the SWAPO labor activists from exile. While those from exile envisioned a trade union built along party lines, a political party–based union in Namibia was viewed by some organizers inside the country as potentially divisive of diverse workforces. In the event, the attempt to organize a black trade union in Namibia around 1980 was unsuccessful, eventually crushed as part of a wider repression of political activity.

Meanwhile, education and training for trade unionism and labor administration formed the bulk of the activities of the SWAPO Department of Labour and NUNW in exile. The model of labor relations conveyed in the course of these activities suggested the complete subordination of trade unions to political party and state. At about the same time, the nationalist movement's fear of the threat posed by potentially autonomous organizations, such as trade unions, was revealed when future trade unionists and labor administrators were arrested along with other SWAPO cadres in exile and accused of spying for South Africa. Those arrested were charged, in particular, with attempting to form a party outside of SWAPO. This period, then, is critical for understanding the later evolution of trade union/party/state relations in Namibia, especially in the postindependence period.

This period is also crucial for understanding the later position of capital in Namibia. For it was during these years that some few employers in Namibia, taking their cue from their counterparts in South Africa, came to the conclusion that "apartheid policies were anachronistic, atavistic remnants of nineteenth-century attitudes that had no place in the modern world."[88] The formation of organizations such as the Private Sector Foundation and the Namibia Institute for Economic Affairs encouraged employers to consider adopting "employment codes" and perhaps even to countenance the organization of their workers. The Chamber of Mines, representing the most important and most advanced industry in Namibia, led the reform effort.

So, by the mid-1980s, although trade unions had been organized for decades elsewhere in Africa, there were still none to speak of in Namibia. A slight easing of the restrictions on the formation of black trade unions in 1978 had been countered with enhanced security legislation and a prohibition on political affiliations for unions. While Namibian workers continued to strike in large numbers during this period,[89] such collective action had not been translated into concrete gains for workers, either in the organization of trade unions or in significant changes to the existing labor relations dispensation. In part this static condition can be attributed to a highly repressive colonial rule and an archaic labor relations framework. More important, however, it can be ascribed to the continued blurring of the distinction between nationalist movement or political party and trade union (and the consequent reluctance to organize from the shop floor rather than the party cell) and to the growing notion that only following independence could the grievances of workers be addressed. In a 1983 interview, onetime SWAPO labor secretary Solomon Mifima (then of the NFTU) reported that workers did not know what a trade union was or how it operated. And he found that the high degree of politicization among workers tended to hinder their participation in trade unions: "People feel they have work problems or are exploited because there is no independence. *After* independence, they say, we'll sort it out."[90] Even into the late 1980s, "after independence" remained the refrain of the Namibian trade unions that were finally organized on a mass basis, a development to which we now turn.

Four

VIVA NAFAU: THE EMERGENCE OF THE NUNW, 1985–1989

Since the National Union of Namibian Workers finally emerged in Namibia in the mid-1980s, its original organization has been seen largely as the work of the "Islanders"—those SWAPO activists and combatants imprisoned on Robben Island off Cape Town in South Africa and finally released in 1984 and 1985, in particular Ben Ulenga. Although there is no doubt of the crucial inspirational and organizational role played by Ulenga and others, I argue that an equally important impetus came from two other sources: from workers and community activists in Windhoek's Katutura township and from mine workers at Namibia's two largest mining enterprises. In the end, however, SWAPO activists ultimately spearheaded the effort to organize workers, especially as the mobilizational value of trade unions in the final years of the liberation struggle became clear to the nationalist movement.

In the process, growing tensions and contradictions within the broader nationalist struggle were revealed—for example, over whether community-based organizing, or indeed any organizational activity outside of the formal structures of the nationalist movement, could be tolerated, and over whether there could be any "development" activity inside Namibia before independence or only after the nationalist victory. But by the time the effort to organize the majority of Namibian workers became clearly a SWAPO endeavor, these tensions and contradictions had essentially been resolved in favor of the nationalist movement. Indeed, the final "birth" of the major trade unions in Namibia firmly within the nationalist camp and the simultaneous stifling of autonomous social movements and community-based organizations inside Namibia has served, I believe, to weaken both in independent Namibia.

The emerging trade unions were a target of much attention, as well, from the Transitional Government of National Unity installed in Namibia in June 1985. Together with some employers, this "interim government" continued the effort to reform labor relations in Namibia started in the late 1970s and 1980s. "Nonpolitical" trade unions were actively encouraged by the government with the result that Namibia today has a highly fractured organized labor movement. In addition, legislative initiatives were undertaken, May Day was made a nationally observed holiday, and a Commission of Inquiry into Labour Matters was appointed. Employer organizations such as the Namibia Institute for Economic Affairs continued to sponsor seminars on labor relations and to encourage employers themselves to organize, albeit unsuccessfully. An impending independence lent urgency to all of these efforts as employers and government alike sought, ultimately in vain, to reconfigure labor relations before a SWAPO government came to power.

In some respects this entire period may be seen as a transition to independence, even to the "democracy" of an independent Namibia. Indeed, with independence imminent, under the aegis of United Nations Security Council Resolution 435, the mid- to late 1980s was a period of political liberalization during which, for the first time, the political space for activities such as those described in this chapter was appropriated. Indeed, the period was marked by a heightened mobilization of workers and of labor unrest, typical features of periods of transition from authoritarianism.[1]

THE NUNW AS "THE FIGHTING ARM OF SWAPO":

Social Workers and CBOs in Katutura

Many accounts of the revival of the NUNW in the mid-1980s tell of the triumphal return of the Robben Island prisoners to Namibia and their pivotal role in organizing the unions.[2] While the role of Ben Ulenga and others was indeed key, community activists had been handling workers' grievances and considering organizing workers before the "Islanders" were released from prison. Thus an early impetus for the organization of workers in Namibia came from those working through the churches and other community-based organizations (CBOs).

The late 1970s and early 1980s had been a period of particularly severe repression in Namibia.[3] The war effort on the part of the South Africans had been greatly enhanced so that by the mid-1980s more than one hundred thousand South African–controlled troops (including Namibian conscripts since 1980) were inside the territory—for a soldier to civilian ratio of about 1:12—the majority of them in only a small area in the North. Eighty percent of the population lived under emergency regulations with 50 percent under virtual direct South African Defence Force rule. Thousands of people had been forcibly removed from their homes along the Angola border, their lives further disrupted by the wanton destruction of agriculture and daily violence and brutality on the part of the security and military forces. By 1985 the South African government was spending R3 million ($1 million) per day on its military effort in Namibia.[4] Upon his release from Robben Island in 1984, after sixteen years in prison, Helao Shityuwete found Windhoek to be a "military bastion": "Everywhere you looked there were army camps, army personnel, army vehicles."[5]

The repression was successful for a time in stifling political activity, but by the early to mid-1980s new movement "on the ground" began to build. Community activist and founder of the nongovernmental organization (NGO) Bricks Andre Strauss wrote in 1987 that following a "relative impasse locally" in the early 1980s, during which "state repression increased to the level of almost constituting a ban on all political activities," two processes unfolded: while some Namibians became increasingly cynical and despondent about the prospects for independence, others reconsidered the situation, "and a new phenomenon was born, namely, to organize at grassroots level."[6]

Strauss saw the struggle of the Namibian people against apartheid and colonialism taking place at three levels, not necessarily mutually exclusive (or inclusive): at the level of the national liberation movement, of community-based organizations, or spontaneously, in response to specific short-term crises.[7] Community organizing, which centered around the Windhoek townships of Katutura and Khomasdal, was a response to longer-term crises—in housing, employment, health, education, social welfare—"the chronic conditions caused by these factors and the inability of the colonial power to redress these issues." According to Strauss, the formation of community organizations "surged" in 1984 (some of this organized activity was prompted by a severe and prolonged drought in the early 1980s); by 1986 he was able to list eighteen CBOs in Katutura, including trade unions, a community newspaper, a primary school, women's organizations, a social research unit, and health and residents' committees. By 1987 the list of "some of the major community organisations in Namibia" had expanded to twenty-eight, including unions and workers' organizations.[8]

In addition to being a response to the crisis of daily living in the townships in Namibia, the turn to community-based organizing reflected an influence from South Africa. By the late 1970s and early 1980s more and more (though still very few) black Namibians were making it to university[9]—and being allowed to pursue subjects other than nursing, teaching, or theology— which generally meant going to South Africa, where they were quickly incorporated into, and learned from, the struggles on the ground there. According to Namibian community activist Lindy Kazombaue, "South Africa played a big role because of what happened from '73 in South Africa . . . a revolution took the streets and you were drawn in. Even if you thought 'I am from another country,' you became part of it. So we were all involved in politics." And when students returned to Namibia they applied their new experiences back home: "So when those people came back, they actually took part in development issues or in trade union problems. So to me it was actually the South African influence, politics in South Africa just blew over to Namibia."[10]

It is in this context that the beginnings of the trade union movement, as it exists in Namibia today, must be put. In the absence of many other accessible institutions, the churches—and especially some church employees—were an integral part of this initial groundswell of organizing activity. In the early 1980s ordinary workers began to turn to the churches with their numerous problems. At the time, Rosalinde Namises was a development education officer and Lindy Kazombaue a social worker at the Roman Catholic Church in Windhoek; during 1984 and 1985 they found themselves increasingly besieged by workers complaining about their problems from the workplace—unfair dismissals, low wages, no leave, inadequate housing and transport.[11] The same was happening at the Council of Churches of Namibia, with which Vezera "Bob" Kandetu was working.[12] Feeling insufficiently equipped to take on the problems of workers on their own, however, these church workers turned initially to church and trade union activists they knew in South Africa for guidance.

Community organizers Namises, Kazombaue, Kandetu, and others decided to call together a group of workers—from the airport, the nearby Otjihase mine, domestic workers, and farmworkers—for a workshop in Katutura with a South African activist experienced in trade unionism, who could talk to them about how best to address the workers' plight. According to Rosalinde Namises:

> As people who were traveling to South Africa we met activists and church people whose contextual theology was based on working with trade unions and organizing workers and so on. So what we did was we called one of the priests to come and run a workshop for us on workers and their issues, because they were having problems and there was nobody who was really concentrating on the workers at that time. So we invited the workers and we had this workshop and it was in Soweto [in Katutura], I remember, at the Catholic Church. Out of that we said there needs to be a steering committee so that we can really continue to work with the workers and meet them regularly, let them discuss their problems and see what they can do.[13]

From this meeting of almost one hundred people in early 1985, a Workers' Action Committee (WAC) was formed. The WAC met several more times until eventually other events overtook it.[14]

Down on the Mines

Meanwhile, also during 1984 and 1985, another strand of organizing had been taking place that would weave together with that of the WAC and the work of others in 1986 for the eventual establishment of the National Union of Namibian Workers and its affiliated unions. Somewhat independently of each other, mine workers had begun to organize at the Consolidated Diamond Mines in Oranjemund on Namibia's southern border and, especially, at the Rossing uranium mine in Arandis near the coast.

At CDM, in late 1984, organizers from the National Union of Mineworkers (NUM) in South Africa had begun to recruit workers. As a wholly owned subsidiary of De Beers Consolidated Mines, which is in turn a subsidiary of Anglo American Corporation, CDM was an NUM target as part of a wider union project for the organization of all diamond mines in southern Africa.[15] According to Howard Gabriels, who was organizing diamond mines in Namaqualand just south of the Namibia border, NUM organizers approached and were approached by CDM mine workers. In Oranjemund itself NUM organizers found a highly organized SWAPO branch—to which most of the migrant workers in this company town belonged—but no workplace organization except a management-created consultative committee.[16]

According to one longtime CDM employee and senior shop steward at the mine, the Work Affairs Committees, as management-created consultative structures, left no scope for negotiation. Workers' problems, such as unfair dismissals, were usually referred to the SWAPO branch, officials of which would then attempt to resolve them with management. With no other venues available to workers, efforts to improve working conditions were through political struggle and not "worker oriented," according to this source. Although the early NUM effort at CDM was significant, it mainly reached those South African workers employed at the mine.[17]

From the start, NUM organizers were concerned not to build simply a Namibian branch of the NUM at CDM but to foster the growth of a Namibian union. Indeed, this was apparently also a concern of external SWAPO leadership; according to Gabriels, Anton Lubowski and Nico Bessinger consulted with SWAPO leaders in exile who wanted assurances that a Namibian and not South African trade union would result.[18] In an initial trip to Windhoek, Gabriels and others made contact with members of the Workers' Action

Committee in Katutura. It was also through the WAC, according to Gabriels, that a connection was made with the Rossing Mineworkers Union (RMU) with which the NUM organizers then began to work, although on a much more limited scale.

At the Rossing mine organizing efforts were also under way. For black workers at the mine the discrimination that had prompted strikes and other collective action in the late 1970s and the initial attempt inside Namibia to organize an NUNW in 1978–79 still persisted.[19] While Rossing management, like CDM management, had set up consultative committees for worker representation, according to MacFarlane, "Employee views on the committee structure ranged from apathetic to hostile. . . . A typical comment from both the black electorate [of the committees] and the representatives was that 'the system is bullshit.'"[20]

Trade unions were seen as a much more effective way of representing and defending workers' interests, and meetings were held among workers at church halls and clubs around the mine. A decision was taken to form a union,[21] links were made with members of the Workers' Action Committee in Windhoek, and the Rossing Mineworkers Union was founded. Indeed, on 25 April 1986 the *Namibian* reported that the Rossing Mineworkers Union had been established at the mine; this announcement followed "in the wake of abortive attempts on behalf of workers to establish a union last year, and enter into negotiations with the South African National Union of Mineworkers (NUM)."[22] Organization of the RMU continued in earnest until eighteen months later newspapers reported the signing of a recognition agreement between the Rossing Mineworkers Union and Rossing management.[23]

The "Robben Islanders" Return

These two developments were brought together, and to a certain extent subsumed, by a third development that would finally lead to the launching of the industrial unions of the NUNW and later the federation itself. In early 1984 the release of all Namibian prisoners on Robben Island began; the first to be let go, on 1 March, was Andimba Toivo ya Toivo, who had served sixteen years of a twenty-year sentence.[24] Toivo ya Toivo's release came on the eve of the "peace summit" in Lusaka in May 1984. In general, the release of the Namibian prisoners was seen as an attempt by the South Africans to relieve some of the international pressure on them at the time and to lend credibility to the "transitional government" in whose name the releases were said to take place. Another of the released—in November 1985—was Ben Ulenga, a SWAPO combatant who had been wounded and captured during an incursion into northern Namibia in mid-1976 and sent to Robben Island about one year later. Upon their arrival in Namibia, Ulenga and others released with him went first to the SWAPO and SWAPO Youth League structures in Windhoek to see where and how they could best reintegrate themselves.[25]

One of their early activities with the SWAPO Youth League was to hold a rally in Katutura in late January 1986. The rally was broken up by the police, however, and about fifty to sixty people—mine workers from nearby Otjihase, SWAPO Youth Leaguers, and others—were arrested and taken away to jail where they spent the night together in a cell talking about what to do next. According to Ulenga: "We were together there that whole evening, including Anton Lubowski and other people, almost everybody who was actually active. We just spent the evening talking about the things that we could do and we don't do and so on, and one of the things we really emphasized was having a strong militant workers' movement."[26]

Although there was not necessarily unanimity of opinion during this discussion, at a follow-up meeting in April a committee was formed to "reactivate" the NUNW inside the country; this committee consisted of four fieldworkers, Ben Ulenga, Jappie Nangolo, Gabriel Ithete, and Ruben Itengula, who were to start traveling around the country organizing workers.[27] Some months later, members of this committee formed in April met with members of the Workers' Action Committee. According to one written account, at this later 1986 meeting it was decided to merge the two existing committees into one, a Steering Committee, later known as the Workers' Steering Committee (WOSC),[28] with the following officeholders: Barnabus Tjizu, chairperson; Bob Kandetu (from WAC), vice-chairperson; Ben Ulenga, organizer; Rosalinde Namises (from WAC), secretary; Elia Kajamo, deputy secretary; Anton Lubowski, treasurer; Lindy Kazombaue (from WAC), deputy treasurer, and Gabriel Ithete, transport secretary. In addition, four fieldworkers were appointed: Ruben Itengula, Jappie Nangolo, Loide Kasingo, and Gabriel Ithete.[29]

The Workers' Steering Committee continued with its task. According to a December 1986 Progress Report by treasurer Anton Lubowski, the response by workers to the organizing efforts of the fieldworkers was "overwhelming" and by August 1986, thirty-five workers' committees were "fully operative"—from Oshakati in the North to Luderitz in the South, the bulk of them in the food and allied industries. The constraints, however, were many: funds were scarce, and only one vehicle was available to traverse an enormous country. Most important, according to Lubowski, the task "was made extremely difficult, firstly, by the fact that there was absolutely no worker organisation whatsoever on the ground."[30]

By August 1986, thirty-five to forty workers' committees had been established, most in the food industry, and in late September the first union to result from this effort was launched—the Namibian Food and Allied Union (NAFAU)—led by former Robben Islander John Pandeni as general secretary.[31] Just two months later, at the end of November 1986, the various efforts to organize mine workers were brought together when a congress of one hundred delegates founded the Mineworkers Union of Namibia; the first general secretary of the MUN was Ben Ulenga.[32] In 1987 two more unions were launched—the Metal and Allied Namibian Workers Union (MANWU) in May and the Namibia Public Workers Union (NAPWU) in December.[33] Also during 1987, pressure surfaced to create proper structures for the emerging NUNW and an initial step in that direction was taken with the establishment in late 1987 of the Joint Union Committee (JUC) to replace the Steering Committee.[34] Over the next few years three more industrial unions were created out of this nascent NUNW/JUC effort: the Namibia Transport and Allied Union (NATAU) was established in July 1988, the Namibia National Teachers Union (NANTU) in March 1989, and the Namibia Domestic and Allied Workers Union (NDAWU) in April 1990. The NUNW itself was not formally constituted until a Consolidation Congress was held in Windhoek in June 1989.[35]

Tensions and Contradictions

Of course, the origins of the NUNW and affiliated unions did not follow the simple trajectory suggested by this narrative. First, tensions emerged over whether community-based organizing, or indeed any organizational activity outside of the formal structures of the nationalist movement, could be tolerated. Second, dissension emerged over whether there could be any "development" activity inside Namibia before independence or, indeed, only after the nationalist victory and independence. In essence, these tensions and contradictions were resolved in favor of the externally based nationalist movement. Community-based organizing was discouraged, if not thwarted, or, as in the case of the trade unions, incorporated. In a similar vein, development efforts were to be postponed until after independence. This turn of events in Namibia in the late 1980s contributed enormously to the postindependence situation of weak social movements.

The fate of the Workers' Action Committee and the attempt to establish other community-based organizations provide an illustration of the first of these issues. On 22 November 1985 the *Windhoek Advertiser* reported that seven SWAPO Youth League members, including Rosalinde Namises, had been suspended from the party for six months unless they dropped their community activities.[36] In this particular case the issue was the formation of a women's organization—Namibian Women's Voice—outside of and separate from the SWAPO Women's Council. Lindy Kazombaue, also active in the formation of Voice, recounts: "SWAPO was pressurizing us also to bring our women's organization, which was started on a church base, under the SWAPO Women's Council, which was also not fair because we couldn't organize, mobilize people on a church basis and tell them tomorrow 'you are all SWAPO members.'"[37] While the suspension order came from external SWAPO, a skepticism of community-based organizing activities existed among SWAPO cadres inside Namibia as well, according to Namises: "I think in our branch, the Windhoek branch itself, people felt that we must not be involved in community activity and they wanted us to make a choice between whether you will stay a member of SWAPO or you will join a community group. And they created lots of rumors around us, that we were supported by South Africa, we were spies and so on."[38]

This conflict extended to the attempt to organize workers, with considerable suspicion directed toward those church workers who first founded the Workers' Action Committee. According to Kazombaue, people thought "'why should things be done outside SWAPO, in the church?' We were all SWAPO members but they were saying we should do it under the banner of SWAPO, so there was a lot of tension about it. They felt 'why should we have this Workers' Action Group?'" According to Bob Kandetu, there was opposition to what was seen as the church organizing workers, and members of the WAC were accused of "selling out."[39]

Indeed, the suspicion of community organizing was so great that, according to Ben Ulenga, even at the prison meeting in late January 1986, at which forming trade unions was mooted and seriously discussed, not all agreed: "There was at that time a very negative attitude towards new formations, and some people felt that 'no, this was an attempt to hijack attention away from SWAPO' . . . people were very sensitive."[40] Months later, merging the Workers' Action Committee with the committee of Ulenga and others to form the Steering Committee could be achieved only by "overpowering our mutual suspicions." As Ulenga notes, "they [the suspicions] didn't really die," and soon some of the founding members of the WAC found themselves off of the Workers' Steering Committee.[41]

This conflict quickly became framed in another way, namely, "development now or after independence?" Although it is not clear how widely, if at all, this question was debated, Andre Strauss argued in a 1987 article for "development now." Strauss elaborated the following reasons: independence would not be delivered on a silver platter by those who sympathized, rather it must be fought for at all levels; progressive community development work would not retard, rather it would advance the struggle; progressive community development work embodied important features such as critical analyses of daily survival issues, empowerment in the face of utter desperation and apathy, and pride in the acquisition of nation-building skills; finally, community organizations would not replace the national liberation movement, rather they reflected a worldwide trend toward enhanced community-based organizing.[42] Rosalinde Namises recalls the attitude of some SWAPO cadres at the time: "I think they felt threatened. Because they felt it must only be SWAPO that needs to do things. And if you are maybe a SWAPO member you must only stick to that program and maybe you don't go beyond that. Because they felt you don't need development, they said development will be done after independence."[43]

For the nationalist movement independence took obvious precedence over development; indeed, there could be no development without independence.[44] SWAPO secretary for publicity and information Hidipo Hamutenya, in a 1988 interview published in the *Namibian,* responding to a question about "independent yet affiliated" trade unions, made clear the nationalist position:

> We consider it unrealistic, even dishonest, to argue that workers should be organised only to fight for higher wages and better conditions of work because in Namibia today the economic exploitation of the workers is in itself an aspect of the principal political contradiction. Although contradictions in Namibia abound, the contradiction between labour and capital is for the moment secondary to the main contradiction between the overwhelming majority of the Namibian population which is denied the right to self-determination and subjected to the sovereignty of the South African state, on the one hand, and the privileged minority group built around the state on the other hand.
>
> The workers' struggle for economic betterment and that of the nation to achieve independence, are essentially inter-woven. It is, for instance, inconceivable that the Namibian workers would be able to achieve significant improvement in their lot without the achievement of independence.[45]

The struggle for independence was paramount and, as had happened with the general strike of 1971–72, ongoing worker grievances were used by the newly formed trade unions (and by extension by the nationalist movement) to mobilize the Namibian populace in the final days of the independence struggle.[46] Certainly in the case of the early NUNW committees and NAFAU, the organizers were SWAPO cadres, many rooted originally in the SWAPO Youth

League branch in Windhoek, organizing mostly SWAPO workers around the SWAPO goals of freedom and national independence.

Various sources report on the influence of the external SWAPO leadership on these unfolding events in Namibia in the late 1980s. Leys and Saul have documented that "some significant instrumentalization and demobilization of internal SWAPO by the external leadership did occur."[47] According to one trade union activist in Namibia at the time, the SWAPO leadership "didn't really care about the unions, they were useful to them." For the party "the trade union was simply a way to regain the SWAPO support from the migrant workers and workers . . . they used the union . . . they got excited about this pretty quickly, but not in any way thinking even about economic issues, thinking about the future." As the mobilizational value of the trade unions became clear, "Viva NAFAU" became the rallying cry of the masses: "NAFAU, the word NAFAU, you know in the townships . . . it worked like 'SWAPO is back in town.' NAFAU meant SWAPO. That word NAFAU . . . people didn't know what it means. But it was a new medium for expressing a whole host of grievances."[48] John Ya Otto, years later, noted of this period that "of course the trade unions inside the country were very vocal and they came out, they became even stronger than the political organization SWAPO at one stage."[49]

Of course, the significance of what was happening inside the country was not lost on the nationalist movement outside. Peltola reports from an interview with SWAPO secretary for labor in exile (and NUNW general secretary) John Ya Otto that "in Luanda the SWAPO leadership was happy of the developments. Perhaps for the first time it looked positively at the activities of the trade unionists among its ranks."[50] SWAPO publications from Luanda, such as the SWAPO Information Bulletin, brought out monthly articles with such titles as "Racists Reel Under Workers' Power" in which workers were exhorted to continue with strikes and other acts of industrial unrest.[51] In the New Year's messages in 1986 from Luanda workers were urged to "turn the factories, mines, colonial farms, construction sites, railway stations and colonial offices into battlegrounds against the occupationist regime and its treacherous puppets." On 1 May 1987, the Namibian printed a story on the call by the National Union of Namibian Workers in Luanda for all Namibian workers to "cripple the colonial economy in order to speed up the liberation of Namibia." If all else failed, workers were reminded in the New Year's message of 1988 that "it is right and proper for the dismissed and retrenched workers to join the People's Liberation Army of Namibia in order to speed up the process of liberation."[52]

Although the externally based nationalist movement ultimately embraced the nascent trade union movement, as in earlier years there were clear differences of attitude and approach between those involved with trade union-ism inside and outside the country. When asked about the influence of external SWAPO on the trade union movement inside Namibia, one trade unionist noted with respect to the NUNW general secretary in exile: "I had not known him before, apart from reading his book, and if the way he performed here [in Namibia after the exiles returned] while general secretary of the NUNW is anything to go by, then I don't think there could be any significant influence from his side, as the secretary for labor, on what we were doing here [inside Namibia]. Because I think we were much more dynamic and much more active and much more militant than he could ever think." Another trade unionist related his impression of a draft constitution presented to Namibian unionists when SWAPO/NUNW cadres from inside and outside Namibia met in Harare in 1989: "I thought that the examples they were using were the advanced ones that they picked up in Europe or wherever they were going to. . . . They were not aware of the real level of trade unionism inside the country, so some of the things that they were referring to were sometimes not even heard of here, while some of the things that we were talking of here were strange to them."[53] These differences would emerge in still greater force after independence.

THE EARLY DIVIDE AMONG ORGANIZED WORKERS

Even before the revival of the NUNW unions, other trade unions were being organized inside Namibia in the mid-1980s. Some observers have suggested that this development may have prompted the SWAPO and NUNW activists in their own efforts. An article in the *Namibian* in early January 1985 reported on the call of Jackson Kambode, of the Namibia Federation of Trade Unions (NFTU), "for unity among Namibia's unions to form a democratic and non-violent trade union movement." According to the article, four trade union federations existed at the time in Namibia: the NFTU, the Namibian Trade Union Council under the leadership of Solomon Mifima and allied to Peter Kalangula's National Democratic Party for Social Action, a Namibia Confederation of Trade Unions attached to NUDO, and an "independent" National Namibia Workers Union led by Hidipo Shikondombolo. The four bodies together were said to have a membership of fifty-two hundred workers.[54]

Although there is no indication of any sustained activity on the part of any of these trade union "federations," other bodies formed during the mid-1980s spawned unions that have, in some cases, and after various permutations, survived into, and even found a considerable following in, independent Namibia. In December 1985 the Namibia Trade Union (NTU), "open to all Namibians," was founded, according to a report in the *Namibian*.[55] The acting president of the NTU was Alpha Kangueehi, who had left Namibia for exile in Botswana in 1975 and returned in the mid-1980s. At the announcement of the new union, according to the *Namibian*, Kangueehi disavowed links with any political party: "We are trying to build a totally independent trade union and have no connection with any political party at all." Kangueehi said the union's aims would be "organising and protecting workers from exploitation in all job categories, to create unity and solidarity, to strive for better and equal working conditions and, 'insofar as this is compatible with the workers' desire, to do everything in our power to bring change to the present economic, social and political order.'"

According to Kangueehi, the NTU was the first union to operate from the Katutura Community Centre, the first "to initiate the notion of trade unionism" in Namibia—before the Robben Islanders returned and "reactivated" the NUNW. Kangueehi found that "trade unions were a new idea to the workers . . . because for many years workers were not organized into a trade union. They were only organized into a political mass, SWAPO or SWANU and so on and so on. There were no trade union movements . . . it was a new idea."[56] According to Kangueehi, the NTU began as a general union and then grew to have member unions, first a Domestic Workers Union and then an Automobile and Metalworkers Union. While newspaper accounts do record further interventions by the NTU during the late 1980s and early 1990s[57] and the NTU continues to have an office in Windhoek and to claim affiliated unions and a membership, on the whole, this union has had a negligible impact.[58]

At about the same time, between August and November 1985, the Namibia National Trade Union (NNTU) was established under the leadership of Theo Ngaujake, who had also spent some years outside of Namibia in exile before returning in the mid-1980s. The NNTU was meant as an umbrella body that would "conscientize and educate the Namibian workers as to their rights so that they could realize the importance of their contribution to the liberation struggle in Namibia and NNTU cause of restoring social justice to Namibian society."[59] In late February 1986 the NNTU called on the interim government to commit itself to civil rights and workers' rights or face the prospect of a "protest campaign in the form of shop boycotts."[60]

By September 1986 the NNTU claimed three affiliates: the Epukiro Agricultural Organization, representing more than 70 percent of farmers in Epukiro in eastern Namibia, the Namibia Wholesale and Retail Workers Union (NWRWU), registered with the Department of Manpower and Civic Affairs, and the Drivers, Transport and Allied Workers Union (DRTAWU)— for a total membership of seventy-six hundred.[61] By June 1987, however, allegations that Ngaujake and the NNTU had taken funds from the interim government, via the police, began to surface.[62] At the time Ngaujake attributed the accusations to a smear campaign by Kangueehi and the NTU, but he now admits to taking the funds.[63]

This incident seems to have resulted in Ngaujake's expulsion and the dissolution in June 1987 of the NNTU, to be replaced in July 1987 by the Namibia National Allied Unions (NANAU).[64] The NANAU was led, however, by some of the same people who had led the NNTU, and it incorporated some of the same unions that had belonged to the NNTU.[65] According to Henoch Handura, one of the founding members of the NNTU (with Veripi Kandenge, who revealed the transfer of funds from the interim government), NANAU was formed when Aloysius Yon, of the Namibia Building Workers Union, asked the NNTU to join forces with the member unions but wanted the federation (name) to be changed.[66] The NANAU seems to have existed for about another year before it was transformed into the Namibian Christian Social Trade Unions (NCSTU), a federation headed by Aloysius Yon;[67] after a rocky start with some member unions that existed only on paper, the NCSTU by the late 1980s had a core membership including the Namibia Building Workers Union, the Namibia Wholesale and Retail Workers Union, and the Government Service Staff Association, which became the Public Service Union of Namibia (PSUN) in November 1990.[68] Only in mid-1992 did the South West Africa Mineworkers Union and the Namibia Municipal Staff Association (NAMSA) join the NCSTU; in the early 1990s these five unions constituted the affiliated member unions, under the continued leadership of Aloysius Yon.[69]

All of those involved in organizing these particular unions and union federations—Kangueehi, Ngaujake, Yon—stated at the time an intention to remain unaffiliated to any political party or tendency.[70] At the same time they were variously accused of being "puppets" and "stooges" acting in collaboration with the interim government.[71] The issue of collaborating with the interim government carried over to the issue of registering trade unions and participating in recently created "government" structures such as the National Labour Council. Handura recalls that the NNTU initially registered the Wholesale and Retail Workers Union and purposely did not register the Drivers, Transport and Allied Workers Union because they did not know the implications of registration and because of the charge of "collaboration" that inevitably followed from registering.[72] But without registering, Handura and others quickly found that they could not make use of even the few dispute resolution mechanisms or strike provisions that existed at the time. Indeed, unions of the nascent NUNW, such as the MUN, also registered with the interim government of the day.[73]

Transitional Government and Employer Initiatives

Encouraging the creation of "nonpolitical" trade unions was a clear goal of the Transitional Government of National Unity, installed on 17 June 1985. Indeed, an enduring legacy of this policy has been the marked divide in Namibia's already very small organized labor force, manifest most clearly in the existence of two trade union federations. But promoting nonpolitical trade unionism was just one aspect of the transitional or interim government's effort to reform labor relations, preferably before independence. Indeed, the transitional government undertook a variety of initiatives on the labor front, according to Moses Katjiuongua, minister of labor in the transitional government: "We thought that doing things like this, like improving labor relations and so on, improving health services and things like that, was a way of building up political goodwill in the process of also improving the quality of life of the people of this country. We don't have to wait until we are independent. So, on the one hand, it was an attempt to improve conditions, an opportunity to help. On the other hand, it was self interest to try to create a local political base, to compete with SWAPO when 435 came along."[74]

Almost as soon as the new regime came into place, changes to existing labor legislation were proposed. In October 1985 a draft bill aimed at "modernizing and rationalizing" labor laws and improving conditions of employment for workers was announced by Minister Katjiuongua. He believed that the bill would "lay down the beginnings of civilised, modern and humane and much more business-like labour relations in this country."[75] Two pieces of labor legislation were passed in 1986: the Conditions of Employment Act No. 12 of 1986 and the National Labour Council Act No. 9 of 1986. The Conditions of Employment Act covered a wide range of conditions of employment and provided for the appointment of inspectors to deal with alleged transgressions of the act, although apparently not in sufficient numbers or with sufficient commitment to carry out their task effectively.[76] The act did not cover all workers in Namibia, however; for example, farm and domestic workers and casual workers and civil servants were excluded. The National Labour Council Act set up a tripartite Labour Council, with members to be appointed by the government. The purpose of the council was to advise the minister of manpower on labor policy matters.

At the time the conditions of employment legislation was passed, it was criticized mainly for failing to provide for a minimum wage. Moreover, there was little indication of any serious effort to enforce the provisions of the act.[77] According to Koerner-Damman, in many cases the new conditions went no further "than what had already been general practice in some companies," and important regulations concerning, for example, unfair labor practices, were not included.[78] But the fundamental shortcoming of the act was that it addressed only individual conditions of employment and made no provision for a broader collective labor relations framework. According to attorney David Smuts, the act "only had an effect on individual worker rights and not on the collective labor rights . . . they weren't the rights that could be collectively asserted."[79]

The National Labour Council was even less effective, according to Charles Truebody, who chaired the council: "There was clearly an attitude in the Department of Labour at that stage that they wanted to keep this very short reined and under the control of the Department, which was part of the philosophy of the apartheid system, I mean it was control. . . . The Labour Council was completely stymied by the Department; it wasn't allowed to do anything except where the Department said yes. . . . The net result was that it didn't achieve anything." Truebody eventually resigned from his position as chair, and the National Labour Council was "disbanded" after independence.[80]

In November 1985, the interim government announced promulgation of another bill, which many interpreted as a clear reaction to organizing efforts of the National Union of Mineworkers at mines in Namibia. The bill, the Wage and Industrial Conciliation Amendment Act, removed the right of a branch of any trade union or employers' organization in South Africa to acquire registration in Namibia or for anyone "not normally resident in Namibia" to become a member or official of a trade union or employers' organization in Namibia or to help to establish such a body. The right to establish unions in Namibia was "reserved for the inhabitants of Namibia," according to Moses Katjioungua.[81] The bill was "rushed through" the National Assembly on 18 November without opposition or discussion. By the end of December the cabinet of the interim government was seeking legal advice on whether, as many, such as the Workers' Action Committee, charged, the amendment contravened the government's Bill of Fundamental Rights.[82] By April 1986 no decision had yet been taken on the Amendment Act, although by early May 1986 the *Namibian* reported that the bill, which had been referred back to the cabinet, "appears to have died a natural and appropriate death."[83] In the event, the legislation did not succeed in hindering those organizing the mines in Namibia.[84]

The interim government also made May Day a public holiday in Namibia, effective for the first time in 1987. On that day ten thousand people turned out for a rally in Katutura, and thousands of others gathered at rallies around the country. In 1988 and 1989, similar turnouts were recorded at May Day rallies in townships around Namibia. Trade unionists proclaimed the May

Day public holiday a victory—one not handed down to them but won through their own battles and sacrifices.[85]

Finally, in October 1987 and amid much protest, the Ovambo Compound in Katutura, an enduring symbol of the old contract labor system and continued home to hundreds of migrant workers in Windhoek, was destroyed. Opposition to the implosion of the compound, which took place on 9 October, came from the unions and from the Committee for the Preservation and Renovation of the Katutura Hostel who felt, on the one hand, that the workers' hostel could be used to provide facilities for schools, libraries, sports clubs, and other organizations and, on the other hand, that insufficient alternative housing was being provided for those formerly resident in the hostel. Some residents found accommodations on their own elsewhere in Katutura while others were moved to a new location, Hakahana. Eventually offices for the Katutura Community Centre were created on the premises.[86]

Not surprisingly, the rapid mobilization and organization of workers into trade unions in the mid-1980s led to increased labor unrest in Namibia and the harassment and arrest of union leaders. One source notes that from 1980 to 1985 there were three reported strikes in Namibia, and the number increased to six in 1986 and twenty-four in 1987.[87] Indeed, 1987 saw a spate of often protracted strikes and other activity. For example, in May 1987, seven hundred workers at SWAVLEIS went on strike after twelve fellow workers were dismissed, following which police raided the workers' compound in Katutura. In June 1987 the offices of the NUNW Steering Committee, MUN, NAFAU, MANWU, and advocate Anton Lubowski were raided, and in August several SWAPO and union activists were arrested and detained under the Terrorism Act. In July workers at Taurus Chemical plants in Luderitz went on strike after the dismissal of one of their colleagues, followed again by police raids on the workers' hostel in Luderitz. In July most of Tsumeb Corporation's workforce at its Tsumeb mine went on strike (following a consumer boycott in Tsumeb in June), only to be fired en masse in August when they refused to return to work. Also in August, three hundred workers at LTA Construction Company in Windhoek went on strike for higher wages. In early September workers at MKU Enterprises in Okahandja struck, also demanding higher wages.[88]

The strikes and generally deteriorating labor relations situation are generally credited with the appointment on 15 September 1987 of the Commission of Inquiry into Labour Matters in Namibia, chaired by South African professor Nic Wiehahn. Wiehahn had headed a very similar commission in South Africa, appointed in 1977. That commission presented its first report on 1 May 1979, suggesting, among other things, that the right of African workers to form and join trade unions be recognized. Because unions were growing, leaving them outside the system would leave them beyond control.[89] In Namibia the Wiehahn Commission's brief was "to report and make recommendations on all aspects concerning labour matters in South West Africa/Namibia." In the process, special attention was to be given to certain of the existing labor laws in the country and to the "methods and means by which a foundation for the creation and expansion of sound labour relations may be laid for the future."[90] According to Moses Katjiuongua, as unions began to make demands in the mid-1980s, "employers became conscious of workers' power. . . . They had to begin to be sort of responsive." This situation "opened a new chapter in labor relations in our country" of which the Commission of Inquiry and new labor legislation were only a beginning.[91]

Commission members offer a variety of reasons for the appointment of the Commission of Inquiry. Johann Van Rooyen (then director of manpower in the interim government) identifies "the general deterioration of the labor relations situation in Namibia"; Aloysius Yon feels that Moses Katjiuongua "had a problem"—made clear by unions such as the Building Workers Union—"to a great extent it came because of our insistence that the laws are not just . . . Katjiuongua and Dirk Mudge and all those guys, they had to do something in order to show that they are not just for the employers." In so doing, Yon adds, the government hoped to gain votes. Charles Kauraisa (then labor relations manager at Rossing) also saw "labor" as one of the problems that was emerging for the interim government; there was a desire for "harmony in work relations" but no proper framework for achieving it: "We continued to rely on the archaic sort of labor legislation then which was applicable here in Namibia." According to Dave Smuts, labor reform was also a way to achieve credibility: "The interim government was desperately looking for some sort of credibility and one of the issues that could very easily get some credibility would be to have some labor reform. It was an area that was crying out for reform." In addition, such a move on the part of the interim government might serve to preempt the growing labor movement: "The union movement was starting to make gains and it would also take quite a lot of the wind out of their sails if they [the government] could themselves bring it about."[92]

Initially, the NUNW unions were reluctant to participate in a commission operating "from an illegal mandate" that would likely attempt merely to reform or "adjust" the existing labor relations system. The unions did, however, decide ultimately to make representations before the commission, for which they enlisted the help of South African labor lawyers Halton Cheadle and Clive Thompson.[93] The first part of the Wiehahn Commission Report was handed over to the interim government in March 1989; the second part was submitted in December 1989.[94] Because the recommendations of the commission were largely incorporated into the postindependence labor legislation, they and the unions' submissions will be treated in the following chapter.

The attempt to incorporate and depoliticize the emerging trade union movement was also evident in the ongoing activities of some Namibian employers and employer institutions. In April 1986, the Institute for Management and Leadership Training (IMLT) held a seminar on labor relations at which Minister Katjioungua pledged the government's commitment to healthy labor relations based on collective bargaining. Trade union leader Tom Chalmers told the assembled employers at the seminar that not all trade unions were "leftwing or socialistic" and that the objects of a union and of "good management" were the same: a contented workforce.[95] The Namibia Institute for Economic Affairs held a major seminar on the Wiehahn Commission Report in June 1989. The government's Department of Manpower was actively involved with the NIEA and other organizations in such endeavors, according to then director of manpower Johann Van Rooyen: "The whole idea was to sensitize the social partners. The unions were invited, the employers were invited, but primarily it was the employers . . . we wanted to improve matters with employers . . . the Inspectorate of the Directorate of Manpower was very weak and very small. It was very easy for employers just to ignore us. So we really tried to influence their attitudes . . . and tell [them] that it was also to their own benefit to increase productivity and things like that. It was mainly a sensitizing campaign."[96]

The knowledge of impending independence added urgency to the efforts to reform labor relations. In October 1985 the chairman of the Labour Promotion Fund Control Board in the interim government had requested a study on the feasibility of introducing courses on industrial relations at the Academy in Windhoek. In the end this study, concluded by Theo Mey in July 1986, contained mostly an assessment of labor relations in Namibia at the time.[97] The study identified in Namibia only six employees' organizations (SWAMU, SWAMSA, NWRWU, NUM of South Africa, RMU, and GSSA) and one federation of organized labor (SWACOL) with five affiliates. No extensive survey of employers' organizations was carried out although discussions were held with representatives of the South West Africa Agricultural Union, the Chamber of Mines, and the NIEA.

The study found that "the absence of a union 'tradition' makes it impossible to make predictions on the future. . . . The history of unions does not bear witness to dynamic growth and expansion." It saw the most potential for union activity in the mining industry and "asked if workers will not be more enthusiastic if unions were front organizations for political parties" as had been the case in Ghana and Kenya. As for employers, the study found that "it is regarded as essential for management and the labour force to establish a 'partnership' before independence and determine the rules of the game according to which conflict can be settled. The opinion is that the government's involvement in management-labor relations should be minimal and concern has been expressed about the political susceptibility of trade unions."

In a January 1988 speech to the Private Sector Foundation titled "Industrial Relations in an Impoverished, Politicized and Polarized Society," Bob Meiring, Tsumeb Corporation manager, noted that Namibia was far from the "ideal situation where industrial conflict is resolved through collective bargaining, industrial democracy and political conflict through the vote and parliamentary government." In such a situation there was "an overflow of political issues into the industrial relations sphere. Indeed, we can state that militant trade unions will become the Trojan horse of frustrated politicians." Meiring advised that "business" could best "depoliticize the situation it faces by actively addressing every component of the issues that make up the Industrial Relations field." Most important, however, he noted, "there is little prospect for sound Industrial Relations and prosperity under the present state of conflict and form of government."[98]

In July 1988, in the wake of the previous month's two-day stayaway led by students and workers, the Chamber of Commerce reportedly issued a statement welcoming "all developments that lead to a successful industrial relations system." The Chamber sought a reduction in conflict between labor and management and for developments to proceed in an evolutionary manner, avoiding provocation. The statement acknowledged the necessary role of trade unions: "Genuine grievances and genuine causes for conflict should not be suppressed but rather brought out into the open, discussed, actioned, and resolved. The constructive role of organised labour in this regard is greatly appreciated."[99] A series of articles in the *SWA/N Ekonoom* on the new labor legislation, "good human relations in the workplace," and government labor relations policy show the effort to ease employers toward what was presented as an inevitable new industrial relations dispensation. In 1987 the newspaper urged employers to see the granting of May Day as a public holiday as an indication that "we have thus progressed one step further on the road to establish an own identity, and have again proven our willingness and ability to take our rightful place in the international community." Reports of a Labour Working Group established by the NIEA encouraged the formation of employers' organizations, while management in general was "urged to act now" to "address labour relations matters as a priority."[100]

THE TRANSITION TO INDEPENDENCE

On 1 April 1989 the official transition to independence began in Namibia following a series of lengthy external negotiations culminating in the Brazzaville Accord of December 1988.[101] During this year, Namibia was inundated with members of the roving international press corps, numerous delegations of foreign election monitors and observers, and the "Blue Helmets" of the United Nations Transition Assistance Group (UNTAG). More important, the tens of thousands of Namibians who had been in exile, most for at least a decade, if not two or three, and the SWAPO leadership returned home to Namibia. The year started grimly with the killing of about three hundred SWAPO combatants in search of United Nations bases in northern Namibia by the South African Defence Force but ended relatively peacefully with "free and fair" elections for the Constituent Assembly in November. Members of the Constituent Assembly then drafted a constitution for the Republic of Namibia and transformed themselves into the first National Assembly. A few minutes after midnight on 21 March 1990, in drizzling rain and a balmy warm wind, the South African flag was lowered at the Independence Stadium in Windhoek's Olympia suburb, the Namibian flag was hoisted high, and a new era—national independence—was ushered in.

In many ways, 1989 was a crucial year for the nascent labor movement in Namibia. A Consolidation Congress of the NUNW was held in Katutura from 23 to 25 June 1989. The congress was meant to launch the NUNW officially as a federation. The agenda included a keynote address by Hidipo Hamutenya for SWAPO of Namibia, a review of the workers' movement and discussion with Ben Ulenga, and a report from the NUNW Joint Union Committee by Barnabus Tjizu.[102] Resolutions from the congress called for an end to the plunder of Namibian resources by multinational corporations, the starvation wages paid to workers, the migrant labor system, the continued occupation of Walvis Bay, and the preindependence privatization campaign. In addition, resolutions called for a strengthening of unity with the Congress of South African Trade Unions (COSATU), Cassinga Day as a national holiday, looking forward to socialism, education programs for workers and training for union officials, greater health and safety measures, supporting the government during the transition to socialism and developing an economic policy, concluding recognition agreements with employers, and working with government to compile a nondiscriminatory Labour Code.[103] The NUNW's general secretary from exile, John Ya Otto, then SWAPO campaign manager for the Windhoek district and SWAPO Politburo and Central Committee member, was elected, in absentia, general secretary of the newly launched federation.

John Shaetonhodi was elected NUNW president and Bernhard Esau treasurer. A National Executive Committee (NEC), made up of mine workers, was selected to oversee the daily activities of the federation. Provision was also made for a Central Executive Committee (CEC) composed of NEC members plus member affiliates.[104]

Resolutions from the congress suggested that a unification congress would take place in June 1990, which, however, did not happen. Such a congress would have tackled the issues of integrating the internal and external wings of the NUNW and of the NUNW's various affiliations, both to international trade union bodies and to SWAPO;[105] in fact, the next congress was the Extraordinary Congress from 28 March to 1 April 1991, at which these issues were addressed. Indeed, the issue of NUNW's relationship to SWAPO was already divisive; newspapers reported that delegates to the 1989 congress faced a crucial issue—"potential conflict of interest between itself as a movement representing workers, and SWAPO as a political movement and potential government." According to the newspaper report, "The congress appointed an ad hoc committee to look into the question and to seek resolutions." The following day, however, John Ya Otto stated that there was no "conflict of interests" between SWAPO and the NUNW because workers had always supported the national liberation movement SWAPO. Bernhard Esau was quoted as saying that the only committee formed had been one to ratify resolutions adopted at the congress. The NUNW, according to Ya Otto, was an autonomous body with its own constitution and though it was affiliated to SWAPO this did not mean that the federation would be controlled by SWAPO if a SWAPO government were elected.[106]

The arrival back in Namibia of the exiled SWAPO movement had an important impact on the NUNW that will be explored more fully in the following chapter. For example, the *Namibian Worker,* published inside Namibia since early 1988 in a magazine format by the then existing unions, changed dramatically with a special issue on 1 April 1989. Originally, the *Namibian Worker* was published almost monthly in two editions, one in Afrikaans and one in Oshivambo, languages that literate workers would be able to read and illiterate workers to understand when read to them. From April 1989, in newspaper format, the *Namibian Worker* was primarily an English-language publication with translation into other languages, a practice common among some of the daily newspapers in Namibia. In addition, the publication had an altered masthead—the SWAPO flag was added. In late February 1990 the SWAPO flag was replaced by the NUNW logo, which is superimposed over the SWAPO green, red, and blue. And in a pattern familiar throughout Africa and foreshadowing events to come, three longtime SWAPO veterans and top trade unionists went to the Constituent Assembly when it was formed following the November 1989 elections: recently elected NUNW general secretary John Ya Otto, Namibia National Teachers Union president Marco Hausiku, and the union movement's most forceful and articulate leader, MUN general secretary Ben Ulenga.[107]

Jon Kraus has argued that in assessing trade union strength and organizational autonomy it is necessary to know "whether the union developed autonomously or emerged in tandem with nationalist or other party organisations and [to know] the early character of trade union-political ties."[108] I have argued in this chapter that the final formation of the NUNW unions grew out of separate efforts by mine workers at Rossing and CDM and by social workers in Katutura township—efforts that were quickly submerged within an initiative led by some SWAPO cadres to organize trade unions in Namibia. Thus, in strong contrast to the pattern in many African countries where organized trade unions spawned nationalist movements, in Namibia, SWAPO was ultimately responsible for the formation of the unions of the NUNW during the five years before independence. Among other things, this has meant continued confusion in the minds of many over the difference, if any, between a trade union and nationalist movement or political party, a reluctance on the part of some of the unions to operate independently of the party, and, more important, an apparent unwillingness on the part of the ruling political party to sanction a strong and autonomous trade union movement.

In the process of organizing the unions, two sources of tension with implications for the postindependence period emerged. The first concerned the question of whether community-based organizing outside of the nationalist movement could be tolerated, and the second centered around the question of whether development could take place before independence or only after the nationalist victory. Although nationalist support for the union effort was ambivalent at first, once the mobilizational value of the unions in the final years of the liberation struggle became clear, they were embraced by the exiled movement. At the same time, in forming the unions, little or no attention was given to building strong organizations at the shop-floor level and to addressing workers' economic grievances or to contemplating the unions' own role after independence and their relationship to the nationalist movement turned ruling political party. In many respects, then, the Namibian case stands in marked contrast to the South African case, where, according to Robert Fine, the black trade unions that emerged in the late 1970s represented an attempt to "construct a new political culture 'from the bottom up.' In this sense, they represented the practical rebirth of civil society before its explicit conceptualisation." Again in strong contrast to the Namibian case, in South Africa, "the unspoken premise was that there could be no revolution without reformation:

without prior reformation, liberation from apartheid could not lead to the constitution of freedom."[109]

Finally, the five-year period before independence was characteristic of a transition to independence and to democracy. During this period, for the first time in Namibia, the political space became available for organizational activity. The Transitional Government of National Unity undertook labor reform initiatives. This "reform strategy," which had been building slowly since the general strike of 1971-72, was a classic one encountered by labor movements throughout the world. As Collier and Collier note in their study of the emergence of worker protest and an organized labor movement in several Latin American countries, "An earlier pattern—in which repression was generally a far more central feature of the state response to worker organization and protest—gave way to state policies that launched the initial incorporation of the labor movement. State control of the working class ceased to be principally the responsibility of the police or the army but rather was achieved at least in part through the legalization and institutionalization of a labor movement sanctioned and regulated by the state."[110] In the Namibian case, government—together with employers and a handful of employers' organizations—continued efforts to incorporate and depoliticize the nascent trade union movement with the result that a highly fractured organized labor movement emerged. All of these developments contributed to a weakened and largely co-opted trade union movement after independence, as described in the next chapter.

Five

THE EARLY YEARS OF INDEPENDENCE, 1990–1996

After twenty-three years of armed struggle and even longer effort in the corridors of the United Nations and International Court of Justice, Namibia finally attained its independence on 21 March 1990. In elections for the Constituent Assembly in November 1989, contested by ten political parties, SWAPO won 57 percent of the vote, just short of the two-thirds majority it had hoped for to be able to write its own constitution. Instead, members of the Constituent Assembly, through a highly consensual process, drafted one of the most liberal and democratic constitutions in Africa. In early 1990 the Constituent Assembly was transformed into the National Assembly, one of two houses in the national Parliament, and elected SWAPO president Sam Nujoma as president of the Republic of Namibia.

In the first few years of independence the government and ruling party SWAPO emphasized the peace and stability that prevailed after decades of war and unrest. The guiding principle of postindependence policy has been one of national reconciliation—promoting harmony among previously hostile parties but also, in the minds of many, maintaining the status quo. On the economic front, in strong contrast to its previous doctrine, the SWAPO government has embraced a "mixed economy" that accords the leading role to the private sector and leaves to government the primary task of creating "an enabling environment" for growth in the private sector. Indeed, a new foreign investment code and generous tax concessions and other incentives have led to increases in foreign direct investment. At the same time, the unemployment rate is estimated to be at least 30 percent, and the previous apartheid dichotomy of white employers and professionals and black, mostly unskilled, workers remains largely unchanged.

The new government has been more successful in altering the political and legal framework of an independent Namibia. The new constitution is noted, inter alia, for its guarantee of fundamental human rights and freedoms, which have been carefully monitored since independence. New legislation, in particular a new Labour Code, represents a dramatic improvement over the old for Namibian workers. Embodying the International Labour Organization's notion of tripartism, the new labor law, for the first time, covers nearly all workers in Namibia and encourages and facilitates collective labor relations between employers and trade unions. At the same time, however, the new legislation applies mainly to the formal sector workforce, thereby excluding the majority from its provisions. And because of the trade unions' considerable lack of capacity, even the organized wage workforce is having difficulty taking advantage of the new law.

For trade unions in Namibia the transition to independence and a new dispensation has only just begun. Despite the favorable legal and political environment, the trade unions have been hard-pressed to make their voices heard. As part of the transition from their political role in the nationalist struggle before independence, the unions are having to confront their relationship to the ruling political party SWAPO as well as their considerable lack of capacity in such crucial arenas as organization and administration, finances, leadership, research, and policy. Many unions are struggling to service their members as trade unions and to reverse many apartheid practices from the past. Most important, perhaps, the unions have yet to articulate a clear socioeconomic and political vision to enhance their position and to guide their interactions in the new tripartite dispensation.

All of this has made for turmoil in labor relations in independent Namibia. In the early years of independence, several tense confrontations between employers and workers occurred, marked grimly by the beating death of one factory owner by disgruntled employees in November 1992. Throughout much of 1996 striking workers at the Tsumeb Corporation Limited copper mine battled bitterly with their bosses. A real test of the unions' power came in the confrontation with government over the labor regulations to prevail in newly established export processing zones.

THE INDEPENDENCE COMPROMISE: A MIXED ECONOMY AND NATIONAL RECONCILIATION

Just a few years after independence the structural limitations of Namibia's economy are abundantly clear. During the transition and in the immediate postindependence period, external studies portrayed an economy in dire straits.[1] The World Bank, in a 1991 report, described the "dual economy" inherited by the independence government: one marked by two societies and economies—north and south of the "Red Line." One was "wealthy, educated, healthy and European—the other poor, illiterate, malnourished and African," with gross inequalities in income and access to public services between the two. The same dualism marked the productive sectors of the economy as well, according to the report, for example, in the contrast between mining and commercial agriculture, on the one hand, and subsistence agriculture, on the other.

Despite the dualism, according to a macroeconomic and sectoral overview of the Namibian economy by the United Nations Development Programme, the outstanding characteristics of the economy at independence were the overwhelming but declining importance of the primary sectors and the economy's export orientation. During the 1980s mining and commercial agriculture were contributing less to gross domestic product (GDP) than in the past because of depletion of resources and falling demand (diamonds and uranium, respectively), and drought. Some of the fall in the primary sector had been made up for by growth in the secondary sector (although manufacturing still accounted for only 5 percent of GDP), resulting from growth in the construction industry in the 1980s, and in the tertiary sector since 1980 with the establishment of the ethnically based "second tier" administrations and increased military and police expenditures.

According to the World Bank report, the trade-off for the government as it sought to dismantle the inherited apartheid system would be between immediate redistribution of assets and income and long-term sustainable growth. The bank's recommendation for the medium and long term was for a focus on economic growth and the creation of greater employment and a more skilled and productive workforce. Reactivating the economy called for stimulating investment, increasing public investment, and maintaining an enabling environment for private sector activity. In other words, the specific tasks of the government would include addressing the equity problem without jeopardizing growth, creating enough employment opportunities to absorb the currently unemployed and new entrants into the workforce, and changing the composition of expenditures, increasing their efficiency and containing their growth.[2]

For all practical purposes, the new government has followed the prescriptions of these outside agencies. Following the early advice of the auditor general Fanuel Tjingaete, the government has sought to "set the market free."[3] One of the government's first acts, following a donors' conference in June 1990 to raise foreign aid, was to host a Private Sector Investment Conference in Windhoek in February 1991 in an attempt to attract increased foreign and domestic investment. At the opening of the conference, then minister of trade and industry Ben Amathila stressed the access to markets provided by Namibian membership in the Southern African Customs Union (SACU), Namibia's strategic location and excellent relations with its neighbors, its access to international trade routes, healthy infrastructure, managerial capacity, low operating costs, and high standard of living. Amathila cited Article 98 of the constitution, which reads, in part, "The economic order of Namibia shall be based on the principle of a mixed economy with the objective of securing economic growth, prosperity and a life of dignity for all Namibians." Amathila translated that statement to mean that the Namibian government was "committed to a mixed market economy based on social responsibility and [that] the private sector is the pivot of our recovery and growth."[4]

The SWAPO government's commitment to a private sector–led economy remains steadfast. At the Economics Conference of the National Union of Namibian Workers in October 1992, then permanent secretary in the Ministry of Trade and Industry Tsudao Gurirab reiterated the government's views on industrial development: "We see the government's role in this sphere mainly as the creation of an enabling environment for a prosperous private sector." President Sam Nujoma, in his address to the assembled worker delegates, outlined the "pragmatic liberal approach" adopted by his government in which the private sector was seen as the prime generator of economic growth, foreign investment was strongly encouraged, and nationalization was explicitly not envisaged.[5]

That the new SWAPO government would favor a "mixed economy," with primacy given to the private sector, was clear already by the late 1980s. In 1988 SWAPO revealed its thinking on economic policy in a document entitled "Namibia's Economic Prospects Brighten Up" issued from Luanda. While noting that the "SWAPO leadership does not hide its belief in the moral superiority of social ownership and control of the economy," the document conceded that "the movement is realistic enough to know that for the immediate future, independent Namibia will not have sufficient finance or technical and managerial expertise to maintain reasonable rates of economic outputs." It stated that "SWAPO's economic policy at independence is that there will be state, cooperative, joint venture and private participation of a significant part of the country's resources [sic] than is the case now." Wholesale nationalization of the mines, land, or productive sectors was not envisaged "for the foreseeable future." The "central plank" of SWAPO's economic policy was to be "to achieve a necessary measure of national control over the country's resources and to bring about a balance between just economic returns to the Namibian people, on one hand, and reasonable profits for foreign and local private investors, on the other."[6] SWAPO's 1989 Election Manifesto repeated verbatim the text of the 1988 document.[7]

To some, the SWAPO government's apparent retreat on previously articulated socialist economic policies may have come as a surprise.[8] Lauren Dobell attributes the apparent switch to the nature of the liberation struggle waged by SWAPO; she argues persuasively that the way "this erstwhile guerrilla movement shed the 'scientific socialist' philosophy which had ostensibly guided its struggle for liberation, to adopt, with little apparent regret, the capitalist orthodoxies of the post–Cold War global economy" (and the ease with which SWAPO was able "to market neocolonial solutions to its constituents") must be seen as "predictable consequences of the externally-oriented diplomatic strategy pursued by SWAPO's leadership" throughout the liberation struggle.[9] Others attribute the apparent switch in SWAPO's approach to the dramatically changed international context, in particular to the collapse of the Soviet Union and former Eastern European allies.[10]

More likely, however, the bulk of SWAPO's leaders and members never particularly embraced socialism and its tenets.[11] Throughout the years of the liberation struggle, SWAPO leader Sam Nujoma identified its goals in strictly nationalist terms: "freedom and national independence." In 1975 Nujoma told an interviewer that SWAPO's aims and objectives "were, and are still, to liberate Namibia from South African colonial oppression and to achieve independence as a unitary state."[12] In an interview ten years later, Nujoma said, in response to a question about SWAPO's commitment to Marxist-Leninist principles: "SWAPO is first and foremost a Namibian liberation movement. I recall when we formed SWAPO we had never met a single communist."[13] On the question of a future economic or social system, Nujoma deferred to the future independence government: "You can only plan your economy when you have the country and the land where the resources are. Therefore our main concern is now to achieve freedom and independence and then we plan our economy, depending on what Namibia possesses."[14]

Careful reading of these and other interviews would have rendered obvious the independence government's choice of a mixed economy and "national reconciliation" as leading policies. For Sam Nujoma, among others, a policy of national reconciliation was paramount from the start. Immediately upon his return to Namibia, Nujoma made clear the need for a such a policy: "The first thing we have to do is pursue a policy of national reconciliation and open a new page of history, founded on a respect for human life, human rights and equality, and build a new life for the whole of society. Everybody has suffered; this war has affected everybody. Even whites."[15] In a conference on reconstruction and reconciliation in southern Africa shortly after independence, then minister of information and broadcasting Hidipo Hamutenya explained the policy's origins: "Namibia has achieved its independence barely seven months ago as a country whose multi-racial, multi-ethnic and multi-cultural population has been torn asunder by a protracted political and military struggle. To bring these previously and mutually antagonistic social groups in this country to some kind of accommodative peaceful co-existence, is the driving force behind the government policy of National Reconciliation." The main objective of the policy, according to Hamutenya, was to foster national unity and consensus: "to mould a cohesive nation state out of the divergent and formerly hostile racial and ethnic groups in this country."[16]

In addition to the obvious social and political aspects, national reconciliation since independence has had an economic dimension as well, most clearly evident in the government's efforts not to antagonize the largely white private sector, whether local or foreign. One of the National Assembly's early acts was to pass the Foreign Investment Act in December 1990 which sets out the conditions for foreign investment and provides various guarantees on the security of those investments.[17] Indeed, SWAPO's overtures to the white business and professional community inside Namibia began in the decade before independence when groups of white professionals and businesspeople from Namibia met with SWAPO leaders abroad. These meetings were arranged by various organizations and individuals within Namibia, including Anton Lubowski, members of the Interessengemeinschaft Deutschsprachiger Suedwester, or IG (Organisation of German-Speaking Namibians), and, later, the Namibia Peace Plan Study and Contact Group.[18]

Meetings took place between white Namibians and the exiled SWAPO leadership, for example, at a United Nations–sponsored conference in Paris in January 1981 and again in 1982 and 1984 in Paris. Several white Namibians attended the Lusaka "peace summit" in May 1984 as well as the ten-year anniversary of the United Nations Institute for Namibia, also in Lusaka, in August 1986. Further meetings took place in Harare and Lusaka in 1986 and in March 1987 and May 1987. In June 1988 a large meeting took place in Stockholm, and in October 1988 another large meeting was held in Kabwe in Zambia.[19] At the Stockholm meeting in June 1988, participants discussed a range of topics, including national reconciliation, democratization of society, economic reconstruction and development, and land, judicial, and public service reform. SWAPO gave assurances that private property would not be expropriated without just compensation, no mention was made of nationalization of industry, and the trade-off between distributive justice and economic productivity was raised.[20] Consistently, those white Namibians who met with SWAPO abroad were startled by the unexpected moderation and pragmatism they encountered. For example, one founding member of the IG says that the more he spoke to SWAPO, the more positively impressed he was; "they were moderates"—something people inside Namibia could not see. This IG member spoke mostly with the top leaders—about everything—and found them to be pragmatic and willing to compromise.[21]

Not surprisingly perhaps, given SWAPO's policies, many of those in the white business community have viewed the new government charitably, thankful that the transition to independence has been as uneventful as it has been and reluctant to blame the SWAPO government for the economic malaise during the early independence period. In early 1993, then (Windhoek) Chamber of Commerce and Industry general manager Harald Schmidt noted: "I think the business community will tell you that it [independence] went better than everybody expected. They are very grateful. The dire economic recession is not the doing of the government. It is more external factors which we have become victim of. It doesn't matter which government was the first government, we would not have been better off."[22] A foreign journalist observed: "A certain trust has progressively won over the white community, the private sector and businessmen. All have observed that they had sufficient opportunity to express themselves. The government had promised that there would be no expropriations, nationalizations, or expulsions. Up to now, it has kept its word."[23] Up to now, there is little reason to believe that the government will not continue to keep its word.

Tripartism: The New Labor Relations Framework

One of the first priorities for the SWAPO government after independence was a new labor dispensation. Shortly after independence, a report commissioned by the International Labour Organisation attempted an investigation of labor relations in Namibia, including an analysis of the old labor legislation—much of which remained in effect until the enactment of a new labor law in November 1992. The report reiterated the sentiments of an August 1988 news release from the preindependence Department of Civic Affairs and Manpower that "in the past . . . labour matters in this country have been neglected to a minor level and have not been accorded sufficient leverage and status in both the public and private sectors."[24] The ILO report concluded that "the development of a labour law based on democratic principles is vital for a newly independent country not only as a reaction to the apartheid rooted labour law of the past but also in order to ensure that rights are guaranteed in statutory form, not only through agreement."[25]

In July 1990 the government announced the adoption by the cabinet of a document entitled "National Policy on Labour and Manpower Development" which indicated the government's intention to proceed as the ILO report had suggested.[26] The document highlighted the "urgent need to restructure labour and manpower development programmes and procedures so that all vestiges of apartheid, racism and the colonial past may be replaced by a system of equality, justice and full potential development and participation by all able-bodied Namibian citizens." In particular, the document expressed the government's concern about the "present inherited high rate of unemployment of over 30 percent," which the government hoped to alleviate through the introduction of affirmative action programs and labor-intensive projects. The document indicated that the ILO notion of tripartism would form the core of a new labor relations framework in Namibia, one that would encourage collective bargaining between employers and trade unions. The policy called for the establishment of a labor court, a national labor exchange (employment office), and a national labor council to serve the Ministry of Labour in an advisory capacity. The document advanced tentative support for notions such as "flexible and voluntary" industrial councils, worker "co-determination" in management issues, "industrial self-government" by employers and employees in respect of some conditions of employment, and a minimum wage "in sectors in which it is most needed." Finally, the policy touched on broader conditions of service, occupational health and safety, and international cooperation.

But this document was merely an initial statement of policy intent, not all of which would later be adopted. The actual new labor legislation would not be implemented until November 1992. Indeed, the drafting and enactment of the new labor legislation was a much more lengthy and involved process than initially anticipated even though much of what was ultimately included in the new legislation had been recommended in the Wiehahn Report handed over to the administrator general in two installments in March and December 1989.[27]

The Wiehahn Report was the culmination of two years of work on the part of the nine-member Commission of Inquiry into Labour Matters in Namibia, appointed in 1987. In a late 1989 article, the commission chair, Professor Nic Wiehahn, called Namibia's existing system of industrial relations "underdeveloped and unsophisticated," lagging behind that of South Africa on whose legislation most, if not all, Namibian labor legislation was based. The most important reason for this situation, according to Wiehahn, was "the uncertainty which has surrounded the country's political and constitutional position ever since the Second World War."[28] The introduction to the report notes that three basic principles were decided upon at the outset of the commission's work: that the existing system should be "de-South Africanised and the new one be indigenised as far as possible," that the new system should "in the greatest degree" conform to international labor standards, and that the new system should be flexible and allow for maximum future growth and development.[29]

Accordingly, the commission recommended that Namibia become a member of the International Labour Organisation, ratify and adopt the relevant ILO conventions and recommendations, and, as a rule, conform to international labor standards. The commission report recognized the need for protective conditions of employment legislation and recommended improvements to the existing 1986 legislation; it also recommended the establishment of a wages commission to set minimum wages in certain sectors. Most important, the report proposed the further development of a system of collective bargaining as the cornerstone of labor relations in Namibia and called for adherence to the principle of freedom of association for all categories of employees, the right to strike, and the adoption of the notion of an unfair labor practice. The report further recommended the establishment of industry councils, a labor court, and an office of the labor commissioner. The report recommended that all labor-related legislation be consolidated into a single Namibian labor code and that the prohibition on trade union affiliation to political parties be repealed. A second volume of the report dealt with employment, training of human resources, social security and protection of labor, and labor administration.[30]

In a symposium organized by the Namibia Institute for Economic Affairs in June 1989, members of the commission presented and elaborated upon initial findings to a group of employers and a few trade unionists.[31] In "Critical Analyses" delivered by employer representatives, Paul Smit of the South West Africa Agricultural Union and Paul van der Bijl of Olthaver and List expressed their objection to legislated minimum wages. On the whole, however, employers' comments were favorable. Bob Meiring of the First National Development Corporation welcomed the commission's support for freedom of association and collective bargaining, though he warned against possible "unpredictable outcomes." Alan Hattle of the Government Service Staff Association endorsed the recommendation that public sector trade unions be able to engage fully in collective bargaining procedures. Trevor Solomon of Afrox Ltd. also praised the recommended improvements and expressed concern about potential challenges and paternalistic approaches. Barry Tapson from Consolidated Diamond Mines worried about the potential ambiguity in terms such as "unfair labor practice" and questioned some of the details of the proposed labor court before calling for the formal recognition of the recommendations of the report.[32]

The four unions at that time grouped loosely around the National Union of Namibian Workers, namely the Namibia Food and Allied Workers Union, the Mineworkers Union of Namibia, the Metal and Allied Namibian Workers Union, and the Namibia Public Workers Union, "despite deep reservations," made two submissions to the Commission of Inquiry, in December 1987 and May 1988. In their first written representation before the commission, the unions stressed the differences between Namibia and South Africa and urged that new legislation not be based on that from South Africa. They, too, recommended codification of the new legislation into one law and suggested that it be based on several fundamental principles: the right to work, to freedom of association, to bargain collectively, to strike, to a living wage and healthy and safe working conditions, and to social security benefits.[33] They insisted that the new legislation should embrace all workers, including the public service, farmworkers, and domestic workers. In addition, the unions called for the establishment of a national labor court and proposed several examples of unfair labor practices. They called for reform of workers' compensation procedures, comprehensive unemployment insurance, and greater manpower training and development. In a supplementary written representation, the four unions indicated how the basic principles outlined in the previous representation could be translated into legislation. In essence, this written representation constituted a draft Namibian labor code.[34]

Of course, none of the recommendations of the Wiehahn Commission Report could be implemented in the months before independence so when the new government took over in March 1990 the old labor legislation was still in effect. At independence there began anew a lengthy process of drafting comprehensive new labor legislation for an independent Namibia. From the start, the International Labour Organisation was intimately involved in the drafting of the new legislation.[35] According to one ILO document—a technical memorandum to the government of Namibia—new labor legislation was the "first priority imposed on the MLMD [Ministry of Labour and Manpower Development] by the Government of Namibia after independence."[36] In July 1990 the ILO provided an expert consultant on labor law—Professor Bob Hepple of the University College of London—to write an initial draft. An early "consultative document" from the MLMD—a proposed labor code—resulted, outlining the government's proposals for a labor code and inviting comments in writing from employers and their organizations, workers and trade unions, and the general public.[37] According to the "Technical Memorandum," this process continued until April 1991, when a two-day tripartite seminar was held to explain and discuss provisions of the draft legislation. Then, according to the "Technical

Memorandum," the draft was revised and presented anew to the Namibian government in May 1991, after which representations continued to be made to the MLMD before the draft was submitted to the cabinet for approval on 17 July 1991. The cabinet deferred approval of the draft "pending more detailed consideration of its implications for conditions of employment in the public sector and in certain other technical respects." The bill was finally approved by the cabinet on 17 September 1991, after which it was sent to the Ministry of Justice, which significantly altered the form of the draft legislation.

By January 1992 the minister of labor was able to submit a new version of the legislation to the cabinet for approval, and in mid-February a second national tripartite forum was held in Windhoek to explain provisions of the bill to interested parties. The Labour Act was passed by the National Assembly in mid-March 1992, signed by the president on 26 March, and promulgated as the Labour Act No. 6 1992 on 8 April 1992. But the new Labour Act was not enacted until 1 November 1992.

Trade unions have remained dissatisfied with several aspects of the new labor legislation. In the area of basic conditions of employment, for example, they favor a forty-hour rather than a forty-five-hour work week, they would like to see the implementation of a minimum wage, and they would like a clear definition of what constitute "essential services."[38] At the same time, many employers fear the provisions of the new legislation will be far too expensive to implement; they charge that while workers' rights are explicitly stated, workers' duties and obligations are not and that the legislation is too sophisticated for a developing economy such as Namibia's.[39] The failure to enact the new legislation until more than six months after it was passed was a concern for many. The problem, according to some reports, was that the structures and new positions created by the Labour Act had to be set up before the legislation could become law.

As Hyman has noted, when there are no "strongly entrenched liberal-democratic traditions . . . there is no reason to expect much latitude for trade unions to build up membership loyalty and commitment in the workplace." Similarly, when workers have little industrial muscle, "employers have no urgent incentive to seek collaborative bargaining relationships."[40] Labor legislation that facilitates, even mandates, collective bargaining can foster employers' participation. Indeed, the new legislation in Namibia is by most standards progressive and offers significant opportunities to workers and their trade unions. Among other things, the Labour Act introduces fairness into the labor relations context, for example, with the notion of an unfair labor practice. Employees may be dismissed only for a "valid and fair" reason and in a "procedurally fair" way. Guidelines for disciplinary action are clearly laid out, and the onus lies with employers to show that disciplinary actions and dismissals have indeed been fair. Labor relations are now decriminalized in that complaints are processed in district labor courts. Provision is made for the introduction of a minimum wage in certain sectors following the directives of the Wages Commission. Concerning collective labor relations, unions must no longer demonstrate "representativeness" in registering with the labor commissioner, and they may seek recourse in the Labour Court if an employer will not accept a proposed bargaining unit or reach agreement with the union. Union members are allowed access to employers' premises for the purposes of organizing workers. And the act provides for an extensive, though qualified, right to strike.[41] In general, according to Andrew Corbett, "the act has the capacity to substantially alter traditional employment relationships and to challenge managerial prerogative in a numbers of areas . . . [and] the law has the potential to regulate employment relations in such a way that there is more job security and more equity in the workplace."[42]

A fundamental principle on which the new labor dispensation in Namibia is based is tripartism. In presenting the Labour Bill to the National Assembly, then minister of labor and manpower development Hendrick Witbooi noted on 4 March 1992 that "one of the major objectives of this legislation is to promote the principle of tripartism—that is, to encourage the discussion of major issues affecting employment, including industrial relations, working conditions, enactment of new legislation, ratification of international labour conventions—by unions, employers and Government."[43] Indeed, several of the structures provided for in the Labour Act promote tripartism in labor relations or are tripartite bodies themselves. For example, a Labour Advisory Council—composed of four representatives each from government, registered employers' organizations, and registered trade unions—has been established to advise the minister on "any labour related matters." The Wages Commissions that may be called to set minimum wages in a given sector would also consist of a chairperson appointed by the minister and one representative each from registered trade unions and registered employers' organizations. In addition, the act provides for the establishment of a labor court and district labor courts whose assessors may be appointed in equal numbers from among representatives of trade unions and employers' organizations. Finally, the Office of the Labour Commissioner has been established to facilitate healthy labor relations between the "social partners."[44]

But in the early years of independence, one of the partners in the tripartite relationship—organized labor—had a difficult time asserting its position. Indeed, one of the first acts of the postindependence Ministry of Labour was to orchestrate a "tripartite" May Day celebration. The rally, usually a show of strength for organized labor, was reported as a "fiasco" in the Namibian press.[45] Instead of the usual twelve thousand workers at May Day rallies in years past, only three thousand attended this government-sponsored celebration—the first in an independent Namibia. Indeed, participation in subsequent rallies has been even more dismal. A rally held in November 1990 in Katutura—billed as the unions' first postindependence mass rally apart from May Day—drew only three hundred people. In 1991 three thousand workers again attended the May Day rally in Katutura, but in both 1992 and 1993 the turnout was only a paltry three hundred. Asked one reporter in the days after the 1992 May Day: "Does last Friday's dismal turnout at the Katutura May Day rally, combined with other low turnouts around the country, indicate that something is seriously wrong with Namibia's union movement?"[46]

Trade Unions: The Transition Continues

Indeed, times have been tough for the nascent trade union movement since independence. Most fundamentally, as the unions acknowledged in a 1992 editorial in the *Namibian Worker*, the unions are experiencing a period of transition: "We do not blame the present passivity on the workers, but view the two years after independence—and perhaps some to come—as a transition to disentangle political activities from trade union activities. It is a period of organising and educating workers in trade unionism."[47]

Disentangling political activities from trade union activities has meant for the NUNW unions, among other things, addressing the question of the federation's affiliation to the political party SWAPO. In the early days of independence the issue of the trade unions and their role vis-à-vis government and the ruling political party frequently came to the fore. In 1989, during the transition to independence, there had been no question where trade union sympathies lay as all energy was channeled toward a SWAPO victory in the November election.[48] But shortly after the election one reporter would note that "a matter for some debate at the moment is whether or not the NUNW, and its six affiliated unions, should retain its SWAPO-affiliated status under a SWAPO government. Some observers have expressed the belief that this could lead to a conflict of interests between the unions and the government, particularly when union demands are made by workers at government institutions."[49] By 1991 the relationship between trade union and party had to be addressed at the level of a national congress.

The March 1991 issue of the *Namibian Worker* noted the decision of the National Executive Committee of the NUNW to call an Extraordinary

Congress from 28 to 31 March 1991 in Windhoek. According to President John Shaetonhodi, the congress was necessary to discuss the NUNW's direction after independence, labor issues in the country, the NUNW's relationship to other movements in Namibia, including political parties, the NUNW's role in the international labor movement, and financial policy.[50] Resolutions adopted at the congress addressed expanding worker education, building constitutional structures, encouraging trade union unity, preventing dual leadership, remaining nonaligned in the international labor movement, and supporting land reform in Namibia and a nonracial South Africa. On the subject of political policy, that is, affiliation to SWAPO, the congress resolved that "NUNW to reaffirm [*sic*] its affiliation to SWAPO as a historically tested organisation committed to the total liberation of the working people and the realisation of their interest." In adopting the resolution the congress noted that "the political nature of trade union movement cannot be denied" and "the aims to affiliate to any organisation or body are to enable the affiliates to fully take part in decision making; to seek greater unity for the common cause; dictated by the similarities in aims and objectives; to obtain greater support."

A headline in the *Namibian Worker* in May 1991 reported, "NUNW Stays with SWAPO." Union leaders explained the congress's decision: "We are aware that SWAPO is about to transform into a political party, but today SWAPO is not a political party. What we did at the congress was to reaffirm our affiliation to the liberation movement as it is." The article continued: "The congress decided, that once SWAPO changes into a political party, there must be open consultations between NUNW and SWAPO."[51] At its first congress in an independent Namibia, 6–11 December 1991 in Windhoek, SWAPO did indeed transform itself from a liberation movement into a political party.[52] And at the NUNW's First Ordinary Congress, 22–25 September 1993 in Windhoek, the issue of affiliation was revisited.

Newspaper headlines before the 1993 congress revealed that assembled delegates would "debate SWAPO ties."[53] Indeed, at the opening day of the congress, outgoing NUNW president Tjekero Tweya made the "bold statement," according to the *Namibian*, that "the affiliation of the NUNW to SWAPO was not in the interest of workers, and the federation should reexamine its relationship with the ruling party." Tweya added that disaffiliation would not mean an antigovernment stance on the part of the unions and suggested that uniting all unions in Namibia would be difficult given party political affiliations.[54] Three unions—NANTU, NAFAU, and MUN—introduced a resolution calling for the disaffiliation of the NUNW from SWAPO that was quickly defeated. The issue did not even go to a vote, according to newspaper accounts, but was rejected during debate in the house. A South

African journalist who attended the congress wrote that "journalists and observers accused the congress of undemocratic procedures in this regard [the resolution not to disaffiliate]. The motions for disaffiliation were scantily debated and not voted on."[55] After the congress, the newly elected leadership told the press that the congress had "resolved to continue with the historical ties to SWAPO, as it was felt that affiliation to the ruling party has caused no concrete damage."[56]

The affiliation of the NUNW to SWAPO has both supporters and detractors. Within the trade union movement itself, the issue has been controversial. While everyone acknowledges the historic relationship between Namibian workers and SWAPO, those opposed to actual affiliation to the party feel that it prevents the unions (and the party) from developing their own programs and identity and keeps the unions from most effectively serving the workers' interests: "The struggle from SWAPO was started as a workers' party, so you can't really separate those two, but in one way you have to [separate the two] in order to strengthen the party. You cannot align the workers with the party because they would never develop the union."[57]

Others express concern that affiliation places the unions in a position subordinate to the party, despite the unions' latent potential strength: "Affiliation to me is not a problem, it has never been a problem, but the interpretation of this affiliation is a problem . . . somehow one gets the feeling that people are awaiting instructions and orders in a field where they are supposed to be independent and ruled by the decisions of their members."[58] One trade union activist who worked in the NUNW Media Unit around independence suggests an alliance rather than affiliation: "But to affiliate, actually that is, you lose your identity, you lose your initiative, even your power base. If you affiliate to a political party that means that the political party becomes the main deciding body and you yourself, you become an appendage and you are subservient to the party."[59]

One union general secretary considers himself warned by the experience of trade unions elsewhere in Africa: "To my point of view it is a clear, clear principle that any trade union in the world should, it is one of the tasks of the union—you should unite the workers, you should be independent and should be very democratic. These are the principles of any trade union in the world and if you don't fulfill this then you are not a proper trade union . . . if you turn to Zimbabwe, the colleagues will tell you 'my brother, this is the second, third year, don't worry, just wait, you will detect the problem. You will come to loggerheads with the government.'"[60]

Still others worry that affiliation to one political party discourages members of other parties from joining the trade unions. In 1992 then NANTU general secretary Markus Kampungu denied a definition of NANTU according to political persuasion: "Because if we are representing 10,000 members out of 14,000 [potential] members, those 10,000 members, they are not [only] members of SWAPO. They are members of different parties. They support us based on the aims and objectives as reflected in the NANTU constitution."[61] Indeed, by late 1992 NANTU announced publicly that it was an independent teachers' union neither affiliated nor allied to any political party. A press release stressed that the union was open to "all Namibian teachers—irrespective of their political leanings."[62] A former NUNW staff member agreed: "Now we have a situation where we have many members from the DTA, [other] people are coming in. It is a bread and butter issue. If you are working and you get dismissed, you go to a trade union to help you. You forget your political affiliation. In this way you have a lot of members from different parties and yet we are affiliated still [to SWAPO]."[63]

Former Mineworkers Union general secretary Ben Ulenga, in an interview just before the 1991 NUNW Extraordinary Congress and just before his departure to government, avoided taking an explicit position on the affiliation question. Rather, he pointed to the importance of defining the nature of the relationship between party and trade union: "I want to say, that the unions should work out a proper relationship with the political parties, with the government and with sister movements abroad. A relationship that leaves the trade union movement in a position to be sovereign over its own affairs and take its own decisions. In a position that does not weaken it or shift its responsibilities to other bodies. I want the union to be the union!"[64]

Others see no problem in the affiliation of trade union federation and political party. For example, in mid-1993, one Ministry of Labour official said: "If they [the unions] want to, they can disagree seriously with the ruling party and the government on their own and nobody is going to say anything and I think the affiliation as such, I think it's a paper affiliation . . . I haven't really seen the secretary general of SWAPO going to the NUNW for any other issues or . . . saying they should not say those things. What I know is that usually they say, 'well the union has got its own members, it has got its own views and they say what they want, whether they want the country to be directed to a certain degree.' That is their right to do so without really interfering in each other's affairs."[65] An MUN officeholder agreed: "We don't feel it [affiliation] is going to compromise our stand. If we feel that on a point we do not agree with SWAPO, we will say so. We are not agreeing with you. If we don't agree with the government we will say so and we have been saying so all along."[66]

Another general secretary pointed to SWAPO's affiliation to the NUNW as "a clear product of the nature of the trade unions of Namibia" and of the nature of the political party SWAPO: "And who is SWAPO? It is the workers." This general secretary strongly defended affiliation, so long as "you are affiliated through democratic procedures as our workers showed themselves." In this view, affiliation does not prevent the unions from defending workers' rights and interests; in fact, it can only help "to consolidate your political situation rather than just to say 'we workers, we [are] to just focus on labor issues.'"[67] NUNW general secretary in 1992 Bernhard Esau described affiliation as especially necessary in the early days of independence: "The situation is still such that there are still elements in society trying to destabilize the order, the social, the political . . . the cultural order of this country. And we feel that for us to maintain a stable order we need to be united. Now, we have realized that through affiliation we can counteract that sort of attempt to, by the enemy, to divide the whole society. So as workers, I think, it is quite vital for us certainly to have this link."[68]

Not surprisingly, SWAPO secretary for labor at the time Jeremiah Nambinga supported affiliation: "I think it is very important that SWAPO as a party, of course, does not dictate to the trade unions. The trade union is completely independent, on its own. But it is important that the leaders of the trade union are members of SWAPO and the trade union is affiliated to SWAPO, because there they can give their contributions to the ruling party, being members. Comrade Esau, for example, is a member of the Politburo. So he is able to convince the leadership of the ruling party from within, as a member of the Politburo and Central Committee. Whereas if he were not a member, I mean, his views could be judged from a distance and that could have a negative effect on the trade unions."[69]

At a tripartite labor consultation in February 1993, Prime Minister Hage Geingob described political affiliation for trade unions as a "beautiful thing." He argued that when senior people in the trade unions are also senior people in the party structures, they are part of the decision-making process. He noted that trade unions all over the world are affiliated to political parties and stressed that the more important issue is whether the unions are professional and are representing and providing adequately for their members. He recalled that most workers in Namibia are members of SWAPO anyway and that through affiliation party discipline could be promoted. Geingob warned the unions against losing their financial independence by taking money from foreign donors.[70]

The affiliation of the NUNW is clearly important to SWAPO. At the 1993 May Day rally in Katutura, SWAPO labor secretary Nambinga told the three hundred assembled workers that "foreign and local agents" were trying to get the NUNW to disaffiliate from SWAPO. He urged workers to tell anyone who might suggest disaffiliation to them "to go to hell." In March 1994, SWAPO stalwart and then deputy labor minister Hadino Hishongwa told an NUNW Central Executive Committee meeting in Walvis Bay, in a reportedly "aggressive tone": "If you divorce me, I will divorce you." According to the *Namibian*, Hishongwa referred to those who had left SWAPO, such as Andreas Shipanga and Mishake Muyongo, and also to what had happened to NANSO after 1991. Finally, he claimed that the unions would become puppets if they continued to accept external funds.[71]

A recurring theme since independence has been the need to distinguish among trade union, political party, and government. Over and over again trade unionists have stressed the urgent need to address this issue. According to an article in the *Namibian Worker*, the problems presented by this lack of clarity were outlined succinctly by a NAFAU regional organizer at a meeting in Luderitz: "We want to call a public meeting with some of the General Secretaries of our unions, representatives from the ruling party and from the government to explain what the aims and objectives are of a party, a trade union and a government. Today this is not clear. We find that workers sometimes go to SWAPO with a union problem—and sometimes the party will negotiate with the employer. This is wrong, if people have a problem at work they should follow the structures and go through the unions. If a person has a religious problem I leave it to the church to tackle it—not the unions!"[72] At the NUNW's October 1992 Economics Conference trade unionists confronted the issue of SWAPO's increasingly multiclass base, that government and the ruling party are compelled to represent a national and not just a worker interest, and that the trade unions are invited to participate in government initiatives and never initiate policy themselves. More than anything else, the trade unionists stressed the need to revisit the policy of national reconciliation.

What form has the NUNW's affiliation to SWAPO taken since independence? So far the most concrete evidence of the affiliation has come at election time, in particular the local and regional elections of November 1992, when the NUNW, through its general secretary, pledged that all members of the NUNW and its affiliates would vote SWAPO only. Two reasons were given: because of SWAPO's "unwavering support for the struggle of the workers and the total emancipation of our country" and because in the first two years of independence SWAPO had shown "that it is capable of running the country whereas in the past others had the opportunity to run the country but failed."[73] NUNW support for SWAPO candidates extended beyond mere pledges of support to the provision of equipment and the mobilization of potential voters.

Not all union members were in agreement with the NUNW general secretary, however; in early October the Rosh Pinah branch of the Mineworkers

Union of Namibia called on its members to boycott the elections "to protest the failure of the Government to address the problems of workers at the Rosh Pinah mine." In its statement the MUN branch said: "MUN at Rosh Pinah is tired of the Government and therefore warns political parties to stay away since all they are interested in is our votes. We have managed to become a strong trade union without the help of any political party and both the DTA and SWAPO can therefore gladly stay away."[74] In this instance the blurred lines of accountability between SWAPO and the unions were in evidence. Before he even knew about the Rosh Pinah action, the MUN general secretary was reportedly called into the SWAPO secretary general's office to explain the incident; the following day the *Namibian* carried an article in which the MUN distanced itself from the Rosh Pinah branch—calling on all its members to register and vote en masse to further the democratic cause denied them for centuries—although not recommending a particular political party.[75] Similarly, in March 1994, when NUNW general secretary Esau reportedly suggested that the trade union federation was considering forming its own political party to contest the 1994 elections (a position from which he quickly retreated), Esau was summoned to SWAPO headquarters to explain himself.[76]

Other examples indicate an ambiguous relationship between the two affiliates. A few examples from the mining industry illustrate the ambiguity: soon after independence, during negotiations with one of the major mining houses, MUN officials suggested that their workers might strike. At the close of the session, an official of the Ministry of Labour and Manpower Development suggested that if the union wanted to call a strike, its leaders should contact the deputy minister in the MLMD first. In late 1992, the government, in the form of the prime minister, intervened to mediate a strike at the Consolidated Diamond Mines, which was ultimately called off after only twenty-four hours. Although in the end MUN officials felt that they had won important concessions, they reported that workers were unhappy with the settlement and many refused to return to work immediately.[77] Again in November 1993 SWAPO secretary general Moses Garoeb and labor secretary Nambinga went to Oranjemund to intervene in deadlocked talks between the MUN and CDM management.[78]

A lack of communication or clear understanding between SWAPO and the trade unions has been identified by some in the unions as a cause for concern. At an NUNW Economic Workshop in April 1993 at which trade unionists discussed the relationship between trade unions and the government, Namibia's political economy, and the economic goals of the NUNW, trade unionists raised pertinent questions about government and SWAPO economic policy. Concern was expressed about the lack of proper consultation and communication, or any consultation and communication at all, between the unions and the political party to which they are affiliated.

The communications gap was in evidence in late November 1992, when workers in the public sector came up against the Prime Minister's Office as they learned, without prior warning, that it had applied to the Ministry of Labour for an exemption to certain provisions of the new labor legislation. The two public sector unions in the NUNW—NANTU and NAPWU—expressed "shock" at learning of government plans to apply for an exemption, especially because they expected government to be "a more progressive employer" than others and to grant better conditions of employment than those stipulated in the Labour Act, thereby setting a "good example" to the private sector.[79] Public sector workers were similarly dismayed during 1995 when the government "unilaterally declared" a wage increase offer very much below expectations despite the support that the ruling party receives from the labor movement, according to then acting NUNW general secretary Ranga Haikali.[80]

The NUNW's affiliation to SWAPO has clearly affected the issue of trade union or worker unity. As noted in Chapter 1, about 60 percent of total employed persons in Namibia are formal sector workers in the public or private sectors (about 230,000 people), and the remainder of the economically active population is estimated to be engaged in subsistence agriculture in the rural areas or in the informal sector in urban areas (about 270,000). Figures from 1995 for the two trade union federations—the NUNW and the NPSM—indicate an organized wage workforce in Namibia of just over 120,000, in other words, just over half of the formal sector workforce. But these 120,000 workers are divided among more than fifteen different trade unions in the two federations and a few independent ones.[81] Thus the organized workforce in Namibia is highly fragmented, and, without a doubt, one of the main issues dividing the two federations is the question of political party affiliation. Given that some of the unions of the NPSM originated in preindependence white staff associations, many trade unionists from the NUNW consider them to be firmly in the political camp of SWAPO's opposition and therefore unacceptable. At the same time, trade unionists from the NPSM insist that they are strictly nonpolitical and that the NUNW's affiliation to SWAPO is the main obstacle to increased cooperation or even unity between the two federations.[82] Still, in 1995, trade unions from the two federations came together for formal unity talks, issuing a document containing twenty points of agreement and six of disagreement. At the least, delegates agreed on the need for the establishment of a forum representing all Namibian unions so as to be able to discuss common socioeconomic concerns and provide input into national policymaking. According to the June 1995 *Namibian Worker*, most of the delegates to the talks indicated their wish to form a single umbrella body for Namibia's trade unions. Although for the unions political affiliation is not the only issue involved in "disentangling political activities from trade union activities," it is an obvious concern, in light of the propensity of political parties throughout Africa to absorb labor movements or trade unions after independence.

Another important aspect of the transition the unions are experiencing relates to questions of organizational and administrative, financial, leadership, and research and policy capacity. In all of these arenas, the young trade union movement—especially the NUNW and member unions—finds itself in difficulty, despite effective projects run by the NUNW in conjunction with the International Confederation of Free Trade Unions and donor agencies.[83] An opinion piece in New Era in late 1991 criticized the unions for having "lost the initiative in the process of struggle for improvement of workers' conditions." The piece attributed this "apparent apathy" prevalent in the labor movement to two factors: "its limited capacity to organise and the assumption that the long awaited labour code would solve all the problems at once."[84]

The unions confront a dire organizational and administrative situation. A confidential evaluation prepared for the NUNW in late 1992 found that it had no proper administration and never had. Reports were not given, proper accounts were not being produced, and there was no appropriate filing system. There were no policies regarding staff, and none of the staff had a contract. There were unfilled vacancies, and no clear recruitment policies existed; instead, all employment was decided on political grounds with little consideration for employees' skills or experience. Staff were not being trained. The general secretary was not delegating responsibility, administrative and staff meetings did not take place, and what administrative structure there was, was not adhered to. Even among member unions organizational issues have proved troublesome; in March 1993 the federation held a Demarcation Forum in a vain attempt to resolve jurisdiction disputes—which unions organize which workers—between member unions.

Such problems are not confined to the federation alone. Affiliated unions operate largely with skeletal staffs—usually with a general secretary, an administrative secretary, and perhaps a national educator or national organizer. Union general secretaries freely admit their own lack of knowledge and information about their industrial sectors, even about their own memberships.[85] A more profound problem, for all of the unions, remains workers' continued lack of understanding of what a trade union is and how it differs from other organizations. In 1983 Solomon Mifima found this to be the greatest obstacle to organizing unions in Namibia, and in the late 1980s Alpha Kangueehi found that workers had "no idea" what a union was—the only form of organization they knew about was a political party. In 1987 Ben Ulenga wrote that "most [workers] have never heard of trade unions, nor do they have any faith in them, for faith will have to be born out of experience and new forms of struggle."[86]

From their inception, the trade unions have had financial difficulties. Reports by Anton Lubowski to the Central Organisation of Finnish Trade Unions in 1986 and 1988 stated the lack of funds "to be a major stumbling block" to the ability to organize workers, open offices, print educational pamphlets, secure sufficient transport, and so on. And from the very beginning, as well, the unions and the federation have relied heavily on financial and in-kind contributions from foreign donor agencies, international trade union organizations, and the international trade secretariats in Europe and North America. At first this could be attributed to the trade unions' early development and then to the fact that so few employers complied with requests to provide check-off facilities for the unions. But despite independence and changes to the labor legislation, the heavy reliance on donor aid has continued and in some cases increased; in many instances the situation has been exacerbated by financial mismanagement. In an interview with the *Namibian Worker* just before his departure in March 1991, NUNW general secretary John Ya Otto admitted "the financial crisis and other problems the union is facing"; indeed, in the same issue the newspaper ran a separate story detailing the "financial crisis" plaguing the federation and member unions.[87]

The federation undertakes annual audited financial statements, has designed financial procedures, and created a computer-based accounting system in addition to setting up a Finance Committee. By September 1992, however, it could be reported that "the financial situation of the federation has not improved to the better." The reasons were many: "Lack of understanding of trade unionism, weak regional structures and poor wages are contributing to poor collection of union fees from the members. The hostile attitude of employers in reaching recognition and check-off agreements is also factor to that [*sic*]. Therefore, the unions are not in the position to contribute much to the federation's coffers."[88]

Leadership has been identified by many as a crucial concern facing the unions. The most well known and, in the view of many, the most capable trade union leader, Ben Ulenga, was lost to the unions when he was asked to join the government as deputy minister of wildlife, conservation, and tourism in March 1991. The move was seen by many as an outright attempt on the part of the government to weaken the trade unions by taking away one of their most outspoken and articulate leaders.[89] In the ensuing months and years dozens of middle-level cadres and even more from the leadership have left the unions for jobs in government and, in some cases, in the private sector. In the December 1994 elections, the NUNW and member unions lost more of their top leaders—Bernhard Esau, John Shaetonhodi, and Walter Kemba, and later Petrus Iilonga—to SWAPO seats in the National Assembly. Those who have remained behind acknowledge their own concern about their skills and capabilities as union officials, and most cite the need for more training for themselves, let alone for their members.[90]

The unions have only a very rudimentary research capacity, which has severely limited their ability to participate in national policy making and policy debates. Indeed, on several occasions the trade unions were essentially invited to participate in the policymaking process but were unable to do so in any meaningful way because of their lack of research and analytical skills. The NUNW unions were unable to offer any comments on such documents as the Draft Transitional National Development Plan or the 1993 proposed national budget. A research needs assessment for the NUNW, commissioned by the Friedrich Ebert Foundation, found that the unions face a wide range of research needs that are currently unmet.[91] The primary need was for support in the collective bargaining process and the second most important was for support for union interventions in the policy-making arena. In interviews for the report, union officials revealed an alarming lack of knowledge, which they readily admit, about their respective industries and sectors and about their own members and employers. Neither the federation nor the unions have their own researchers, nor do any research institutions in Namibia conduct research "from a union perspective." As NUNW general secretary Bernhard Esau noted, if the unions do not address the research issue, they will "become irrelevant."[92] In large part, this has also prevented the unions from articulating any clear vision for the future of the socioeconomic and political issues of particular importance to them.

Clearly, all of these factors make it difficult for the NUNW unions to participate in a significant way in the newly proclaimed tripartite relationship among employers, workers and their unions, and the government. As Corbett has noted, "The success of government initiatives to promote tripartism and the effective operation of labour legislation presupposes that workers are organised and have access to trade unions to advise them of their rights. Crucial also are the financial and human resources needed to challenge employer practices at the workplace through the courts."[93] Capital continues to wield inherently greater economic power, and the government, as labor commissioner in the Ministry of Labour and Manpower Development Bro-Matthew Shinguadja admitted in 1993, has a clear structural advantage over labor:

I think the government still has an upper hand in all issues, because—not only [the] Namibian government [but] worldwide—the government is also the ruling class of the country. It won't really have a balanced power with the unions because there is some information which has to be discussed first by the government personnel before it is taken to the Labour Advisory Council, or whatever body where the social partners will come together. And, again, when we go to the international meetings, usually the line which you take is that of the government . . . maybe at the homefront we may talk about a balanced structure but in the true sense it may not adhere that well. Although these partners are consulted, as I said, usually they are consulted after the government has looked for the issues at hand. The government will come there as actually a guiding partner, if I may say so.[94]

Labor relations in the early postindependence years in Namibia have been anything but harmonious.

LABOR RELATIONS AFTER INDEPENDENCE

At independence in Namibia collective labor relations hardly existed in any coherent and institutionalized fashion, despite the reform process under way from the late 1970s. A 1989 ILO report noted, for example, that "the registration, and hence official recognition, of trade unions has been a major cause of concern and grievance among the majority of black workers who have been denied representation and protection by organisations of their own choice."[95] Trade union federations could not be registered under the previous legislation, and some unions, such as NAPWU and MANWU, had had their applications for registration turned down at least twice. But even official recognition did not always provide legitimacy for trade unions, as the report continues: "Members of registered trade unions have been, for instance, harassed by employers and by their superiors; denied loans from employers and institutional sources; excluded from or overlooked for promotion; victims of unfair dismissal." According to the ILO, the situation weakened the trade unions' "partner" as well: "As far as employers are concerned there has been so far no compelling reason (for example, collective bargaining) for effective organisation on their part, since registered trade unions have been deliberately rendered weak and ineffective by existing labour laws and practices, and employers—in the absence of clear official guidelines and effective regulations—have at any rate dictated terms and conditions of employment. Existing employers' organisations are essentially trade associations, professional groups, chambers of commerce and industry and related research and advisory institutions."

For "economic development and social progress after independence," according to the ILO, "a good and harmonious industrial relations climate" was essential. Such an atmosphere, however, would "depend much on the existence of an independent, effective and responsible trade union movement alongside a strong, representative and efficiently-run national employers' organisation." Still, by the end of 1991, the ILO found that "the situation is fluid as regards workers' and employers' organisations."[96] Indeed, by June 1994, nearly twenty trade unions or federations were registered with the Office of the Labour Commissioner, while only six employers' organizations were registered.[97]

According to many in Namibia, while employers have, in many instances, openly discouraged the organization of trade unions, they have also been hostile to the formation of employers' organizations. Institutions such as the Namibia Institute for Economic Affairs—and even the ILO—have worked steadily to sensitize employers and to encourage them to organize themselves (as well as to tolerate the organization of their workers), but with little result. On 30–31 August 1990 the NIEA and the ILO sponsored a symposium in Windhoek named "The Role of Employers' Organisations in Africa."[98] On this occasion, a full array of employers' organization representatives was brought in from countries as diverse as Botswana, Kenya, the United Kingdom, Zimbabwe, and Denmark, as well as ILO representatives, to argue for the value and importance of employers' organizations. In early 1992 Akanimo Etukudo, from the ILO, was still arguing the merits of employer organizations in the pages of the *Business Spotlight* in Windhoek, in an article entitled "From Scepticism to Confidence: African Employers' Organisations as Partners in Development."

In Namibia, in sectors such as mining, agriculture, and construction, employers' organizations have a relatively long history—for example (with new names), the Chamber of Mines of Namibia, the Namibia Agricultural Union, and the Construction Industries Federation of Namibia—but these are the exception. In addition to encouraging industry or sector level organizations, the NIEA and others have been most concerned to establish an umbrella organization, the Namibia Employers' Federation, which was founded in 1993.[99] In 1990 the Namibia National Chamber of Commerce and Industry (NNCCI) was established as an umbrella organization to which all existing and newly created business organizations could affiliate. This was seen as an important step toward uniting Namibia's fragmented private sector and creating a strong and unified voice for business after independence. While initially seen as a chamber for "black business" only, this is changing over time.[100]

But while at independence and shortly thereafter workers were organized and employers were not, this did nothing, especially in the absence of the new labor legislation, to ameliorate the conditions of the enduring apartheid legacy in the workplace. At independence the situation was such that the Namibia Institute for Economic Affairs felt compelled to issue a press release warning that allegations of various unfair labor practices were influencing the "productivity, potential and motivation" of the Namibian workforce. The statement continued that the labor practices of Namibian employers were not conducive to the economic development so desperately needed in Namibia. Employers in the future would have to play "their rightful role" in the country's economic development, which included treating labor as "a valuable and key resource rather than as a cost factor."[101] The *Namibian Worker*, the *Namibian*, and *New Era* are rife with stories about unfair dismissals, ongoing racism and discrimination in the workplace, victimization of union members, violations of recognition agreements, inadequate accommodation, employers' refusal to adhere to provisions of the new labor legislation, and retrenchments.[102] Outgoing NUNW president John Shaetonhodi complained in May 1991 that employers were misusing reconciliation—that after independence they had only "intensified exploitation of the worker. . . . We see it in various industries; how people are being dismissed; how they are being denied trade union freedom in the workplaces."[103]

The lingering legacy, exacerbated by a series of retrenchments in the face of which the trade unions could seemingly do nothing, culminated in a tragic event in September 1992 when workers at MKU Enterprises, a furniture factory in Okahandja, beat unconscious their manager, Silvano Zapparoli, who later died in a hospital.[104] The beating was reportedly prompted when the manager revealed a gun to a group of enraged workers. The group was angry because 350 workers at MKU had been dismissed (following a strike which the MLMD and MKU determined to be illegal) and then reinstated after the union intervened—but with a 30 percent pay cut. To many, this event in Okahandja symbolized well the state of labor relations in Namibia two and a half years after independence.[105]

By 1996 the tensions and contradictions underlying labor relations in Namibia continued to surface, as could be seen in the way workers' interests were handled during the establishment of export processing zones (EPZs) and in the prolonged and acrimonious strike at TCL. In late 1995 and early 1996, the first moves to establish export processing zones were undertaken, including passage of the appropriate governing legislation. This quickly became the focal point of controversy between the unions of the NUNW and the government, however, when the original legislation proposed that Namibia's progressive labor law not apply in the EPZs. Union leaders objected strongly to this provision, threatening at one point to take the government to court over the matter. Ultimately, a compromise was reached, but not before much name-calling on both sides: the compromise provides for the implementation of the Labour Act in Namibian EPZs, but considers EPZs to be essential service areas, thereby prohibiting strikes and lockouts in them. The prohibition on strikes and lockouts is to apply for only five years, however; according to Trade and Industry Minister Hidipo Hamutenya, "if we discover there are no serious threats of strikes, we will relax the laws." Some trade unionists called Hamu-tenya's announcement that the no strike provision would disappear after five years if the unions "behaved themselves" a "joke." Indeed, other unionists predicted "'disaster' for both the workers and the EPZs with employees being forced into wildcat, illegal strikes and companies losing confidence in Nami-bia's EPZ programme."[106]

For some union leaders, the controversy surrounding the EPZs raised once again the issue of the NUNW's affiliation to SWAPO; in the view of some, the government was able to reach the no strike compromise with the unions "solely because of the NUNW's affiliation to SWAPO, which makes it almost impossible for the federation to vigorously oppose government policies." Moreover, for the unions, the government's decision on the EPZs represented another "betrayal of trust" and an example of its failure to consult with them.[107] Others sharply criticized union leaders for wanting to "have it both ways": wanting to give the impression that they have workers' rights at heart by opposing the early EPZ legislation and wanting to keep their relationship with the ruling party "sweet"—hence vacillating on the whole question and ultimately endorsing a compromise that pleased no one.[108] In the meantime, recent reports from Namibia suggest that "the government's drive to attract investment into the Export Processing Zone [in Walvis Bay] has begun to bear fruit." Initial commitments include a charcoal manufacturing plant and a clothing factory, each of which will initially provide four hundred jobs. By November 1996, N$40 million had reportedly been invested in the Walvis Bay EPZ, and seven companies had committed themselves to the zone.[109]

The strike at TCL rocked Namibia during August and September 1996. Before the strike of eighteen hundred mine workers was over, the contending parties—TCL management and the MUN—faced off over the right of nonstrik-ing workers to access to mine premises, threats to imprison union leaders, the legality of the strike, and contempt of court charges. At one point the water supply in Tsumeb was reportedly threatened when striking workers prevented essential service employees from analyzing water quality at the mine. Opera-tions at all three of TCL's mines—in Tsumeb, Otjihase, and Kombat—were brought to a halt by the strike and the company lost millions of dollars. The strike ultimately lasted nearly six weeks. During increasingly bitter negotiations, company management and the MUN leaders failed to reach any agreement, independent mediators failed to resolve the strike; indeed, a settlement was reached only with the intervention of Prime Minister Hage Geingob. As part of the settlement, between seven hundred and eight hundred workers at TCL's three mines would be retrenched (because some operations at all plants would be shut down), and a 10.5 percent wage increase would be given to category A1 to B2 workers (backdated to mid-July). MUN had originally sought a 13.5 percent wage hike and TCL had originally offered only 7 percent.[110]

Thus while a new labor relations framework has been put in place, in the form of the Labour Act No. 6 of 1992, labor relations since independence have hardly been harmonious. By 1992, forty-one strikes had been reported and workers in the mining industry, especially, had been hit hard by a series of debilitating retrenchments.[111] Indeed, despite the progressive new labor law, trade unions find themselves ill-equipped to use it. Organized labor is divided between two rival union federations, and the total organized workforce of approximately 120,000 is split among more than fifteen member unions. Moreover, the unions suffer from a lack of capacity in critical arenas such as organization and administration, finances, leadership, and research and policy. Kraus has identified several measures of union autonomy and strength, and on most of these counts trade unions in Namibia fall far short. These measures include "the size and strategic salience of the wage labour force; the age of the movement and thus prior inculcation of trade union or class values and consciousness among members and leaders; development of substantial organisational networks; levels of solidarity among union leaders and rank and file based on prior historical struggles; and the development of internal organisational norms, values and interests—all of which generate commitments to trade unions as working class organisations."[112]

Already in Namibia, as Linda Freeman has noted, one has the distinct impression that "the continuing support of workers has been taken for granted" by SWAPO and the government.[113] Indeed, criticism of the unions by party and government has been steady. In August 1991 Minister of Trade and Industry Ben Amathila chastised the unions for "opposing employers for the sake of it." He urged workers to take responsibility for the economic development of the country, while at the same time defending their own interests. He stressed that responsible unions and reliable workers were necessary to attract foreign investment. One year later Minister of Labour Hendrick Witbooi expressed his displeasure with the ongoing industrial unrest in Namibia, criticizing "the shortsighted and ill-considered actions" of certain employers as well as workers and their unions. In February 1993 one regional councillor accused trade unions of "neglecting their duties" and failing to meet the pressing needs of many of his worker constituents.[114] By mid-1994 the Office of the Labour Commissioner had sent a directive to trade unions reminding them of the provisions of the Labour Act, in particular as it pertains to strikes and dispute resolution mechanisms.

From a historical and comparative perspective, the relationship between trade unions and political party and state in the immediate post-independence period is crucial. Throughout Africa, nationalist movements turned ruling political parties "subverted and destroyed independent working-class activity" and, according to at least one observer, "Namibia is only the latest in a long list of countries that exemplify this pattern."[115] This judgment may be somewhat premature, but there is no doubt, as this book seeks to show, that trade unions in Namibia are at risk of being "subverted and destroyed."

Six

CONCLUSION

In many parts of Africa trade unions began to organize in earnest in the years following World War II. They were concentrated among railway workers and dock workers, in industries such as mining, and in the public service. African trade unions often grew out of industrial conflicts or already established ethnic associations and were occasionally assisted in their efforts by European labor movements. In little time, many of the nascent trade union movements had organized the nationalist movements that would lead the struggle for political independence throughout Africa. In Namibia, by contrast, the trajectory was quite different. Attempts were made in the 1920s and again in the 1950s to organize workers in the Luderitz fishing industry, but these early unions did not endure. Even the first surviving white staff associations in Namibia—the South West Africa Municipal Service Association and the South West Africa Mine Workers Union—were only truly organized from the 1950s and 1960s onward. Also in contrast to much of the rest of Africa, it was ultimately members of the nationalist movement in Namibia—waging an externally based war of liberation—who were key to the organization of the major trade unions, not the other way round.

Why were black trade unions in Namibia successfully organized forty years after they appeared in most other African countries? And when they finally did emerge, why were they so weak? Most important, what are the implications of the weakness of trade unions—in theory an important economic, political, and social force in Namibian society—for the prospects for the consolidation of democracy in Namibia? This book, in providing a historical account of the emergence and evolution of trade unions in Namibia, has attempted to answer these questions. This concluding chapter will elaborate the reasons for the late and weak emergence of unions in Namibia, namely, a fragile economy, a colonial legacy of repression and reform, and the unions' origins within the nationalist movement cum ruling political party and will consider the relationship between trade unions and democracy.

An Underindustrialized Economy

The debate over the relationship between economic and political development is of long standing. For Africa this issue has been revived of late, as many countries attempt to undertake, simultaneously, economic and political liberalization.[1] As elsewhere, Namibia's economic trajectory will continue to influence enormously the prospects for the consolidation of democracy, in general, and the fate of the trade union movement, in particular.

Namibia's economy has been called "potentially one of the most productive in sub-Saharan Africa"; it has an exceptionally high level of resources per capita, mainly because it has a variety of exploitable minerals, one of the world's richest offshore fishing grounds, and a climate that supports an extensive livestock industry. But the economy is also an open one—55 percent of GDP is exported—and therefore highly vulnerable to fluctuations in world price and demand. In addition, the land is susceptible to recurrent drought, and the country suffers from a narrow tax base and a shortage of skilled personnel.[2] From 1988 to 1994, real GDP growth averaged 3.3 percent, barely keeping ahead of the population growth rate for an average increase in per capita income of 0.4 percent over the period.[3] And though Namibia may have a potentially high level of resources per capita, at present and no doubt for a very long time to come, those resources are grossly maldistributed. The constraints and limitations of the Namibian economy are many.

More significant still for the trade union movement in Namibia, however, is the low level of industrialization. Manufacturing has, in recent years, increased its contribution to GDP to 9 percent (from about 6 percent in 1989), mainly because fish processing output has more than doubled; still, it continues to employ only about 6 percent of the labor force.[4] Food and beverage production dominates the manufacturing sector with the largest undertakings being meat packaging and fish processing factories, mineral processing plants, breweries, and confectionery manufacturers. Other activity includes the manufacture of metal, nonmetal mineral, wood, and furniture products.[5] Constraints on the future development of the manufacturing sector in Namibia include the fragmented nature of industry and marketing, finance, and management limitations. Many of these impediments result from regional economic relations, in particular those with South Africa.[6] Moreover, the formal sector labor force in Namibia is tiny—just over two hundred thousand workers (the minimum size for one of South Africa's "super unions")—while the majority of the economically active population is in the informal sector or in subsistence agriculture.

Concern about the nature and low level of industrialization in Africa was raised early on in writings about African workers that highlighted their small numbers and questioned their position as members of a fully proletarianized working class.[7] More recently, this concern about the level and nature of industrialization has been differently framed. For trade unionism in Africa, an important distinction can be made between the mining and agriculture sectors, on the one hand, and manufacturing, on the other. In South Africa, for example, skilled workers in the manufacturing sector were at the forefront of the effort to organize new unions in the late 1970s. Among other things, a growing manufacturing sector in South Africa led to the increased requirement for a more skilled and stable workforce, leading, in turn, to changes in employers' strategies that included the recognition of black trade unions.[8] While this does not discount the importance and potential for organization of workers in strategic export sectors (such as mining and commercial agriculture), there is little doubt that workers in key manufacturing sectors may be in the best position to form strong trade unions. Trade unionism in Namibia, then, remains at a potential disadvantage.[9]

Thus the very structure of the Namibian economy at present militates to a certain extent against a strong trade union movement. More broadly, the limitations of the economy pose formidable challenges to the consolidation of democracy. Despite a liberal investment code and generous incentives, the government has been unable to attract foreign or domestic investment on the scale that it would like. Formal sector unemployment is rising rapidly and has been exacerbated by the retrenchment of thousands of workers from the country's largest mines and the specter of more rationalizations in government. The land question remains intractable; the government apparently is unwilling to risk the wrath of the white commercial agriculture sector that contributes about 8 percent to GDP and whose continued presence provides an important marker of the country's political and economic stability. But as heightened expectations remain unmet, as resource constraints become evident, and as discrepancies in income, services, and opportunities continue, tensions will emerge. If no organizations exist for channeling grievances efficaciously, Namibia's nascent democracy could unravel quickly.

THE COLONIAL LEGACY: REPRESSION AND REFORM

Nearly everywhere in Africa the political legacy of the colonial state has taken its toll on the postcolonial state. Throughout Africa, according to Crawford Young, "a number of characteristics and behavioral dispositions which originate in the colonial era" have been shown to offer a partial explanation for the crisis of the contemporary African state. The colonial state left behind a legacy of bureaucratic, authoritarian rule marked by the imposition of alien institutions on a subject population, a reliance on military and security forces, the extraction of resources from the population, and a dearth of widespread social welfare services.[10] In Namibia colonial rule lasted for three decades longer than in most of the rest of Africa, and it was of a special variety confined largely to the settler colonies of southern Africa—one characterized by the formal institutionalization of a system of apartheid.

In the Namibian case, the colonial period was marked first by repression and then by reform. Both strategies go a long way toward explaining the situation of trade unions in Namibia today and threaten enduring legacies inimical to the project of democratic consolidation. At first, the highly repressive nature of South African colonial rule, manifest in a highly regulated contract labor system and restrictive security legislation, precluded the possibility of organizing black trade unions in Namibia. Later, a reform process that sought to encourage the development of "nonpolitical" trade unions that could easily be incorporated made available the space for the organization of unions, but with the result that organized labor in Namibia today is highly fragmented and disorganized.

One of the first ways in which colonialism touched the lives of Africans was through the "labor question." For migrant workers in Namibia this took the form of a highly controlled contract labor system, marked by a monopsonistic labor recruiting agency, strict rules and regulations governing living and working conditions, pass laws, the criminalization of breaches of contract, and so on. Even as the contract labor system began to break down during the 1970s, a phalanx of security legislation continued to restrict freedom of movement and of association. Even those in the business community at the time concede that "the oppressive situation and laws which existed, the whole apartheid situation and of course the [military] occupation of the country . . . made it very difficult for the trade unions to emerge."[11]

According to Ukandi Damachi, Dieter Seibel, and Lester Trachtman, "resistance against unions was particularly strong in the settler colonies," and Namibia certainly provides evidence for this assertion.[12] Indeed, part of the reason for the continuing repression of trade unions was the association, first of contract workers and later of the unions, with the nationalist struggle. Employers unequivocally associated unions with SWAPO and the resistance to colonialism: "employers . . . saw the unions as SWAPO, or if they saw them as unions they saw them as SWAPO unions"; "the idea was seen that the workers sided themselves [with SWAPO], belonged to SWAPO as a mass political organization."[13] Because union activity was perceived as SWAPO activity, every effort was undertaken to suppress the emerging union movement.

At the same time, this association with the nationalist movement ultimately served to distract workers from organizing for an economic as well as a political end. Workers subordinated their struggles in the workplace to the struggle for independence from South African colonial rule: "they viewed the struggle for worker rights as part and parcel of the broader struggle against the oppressive regime on the ground"; "people were more concerned about their political struggle and did not actually fully appreciate the nature of workers' struggle within that, or probably did appreciate it, but not as the potential of it internally."[14] With the independence struggle over, however, trade unions have found themselves in an awkward position from which to assert their economic rights and make their economic demands.

The particular dynamic of South African colonial rule influenced the emergence of unions in Namibia in another way. Whereas elsewhere in Africa trade unionists from the metropole often played a role in organizing workers, in Namibia there was no real impetus from South Africa to organize workers because in South Africa itself black trade unions began to organize on a mass scale only in the 1970s. When this did happen, of course, the influence on workers and a workers' movement in Namibia was significant. Nor was there a white trade union movement of any significance in Namibia, largely because there was no white working class. Rather, the original German settlers in Namibia became commercial farmers or went into retail trade and eventually small manufacturing, while the Afrikaner settlers brought in after World War I were channeled almost exclusively into commercial farming in central and southern Namibia. Other whites in wage labor were in carefully protected supervisory posts in industry or staffed in large numbers the bloated civil services of the colonial administrations.[15] Only during the 1980s would the inevitability of trade unionism become clear to the administrative authorities; then the strategy became one of reform and of the attempted incorporation of an emerging "nonpolitical" trade union movement, resulting in divided trade unions.

NATIONALISM AND THE LEGACY OF THE INDEPENDENCE STRUGGLE

Throughout Africa, mass-based nationalist movements were critical in the struggle for political independence, and Namibia has been no exception. In addition, these same nationalist movements, once transformed into ruling political parties, often turned on labor movements that had constituted so much of their early support. Once again, Namibia is unlikely to prove an exception. While some observers have sought to characterize SWAPO not as a nationalist movement but as "a liberation movement with impeccable proletarian credentials, largely free of the bourgeois elements so often to be found in the forefront of similar movements,"[16] SWAPO has consistently demonstrated itself to be a thoroughly nationalist movement, all socialist rhetoric aside. Nationalist impulses have strongly influenced the attitudes of SWAPO leaders toward labor and its organization in Namibia. The labor movement has apparently been seen as an alternative power base for potential rival political parties or the breeding ground for potential rival political leaders. Initially, at least, the organization of labor, like other preindependence "development" efforts, was seen as counterproductive to the nationalist struggle because it threatened to divert scarce resources or even to reduce the impetus to struggle. As Leys and Saul have noted, some have argued "that at the very least the preoccupations of SWAPO's external leaders led them to rein in excessively the kind of popularly-based 'politics of confrontation' that were feasible inside Namibia itself, with some significant negative consequences for post-independence political life."[17]

The relationship between nationalism and labor movements in Africa has been problematic. As Frantz Fanon has noted, nationalism was neither "a political doctrine, nor a program," although during the struggles for independence, nationalist movements highlighted the education and welfare needs of the masses, appealed to ideals of progress and self-government, and so on.[18] Once the primary objective was attained, however, the rationale for—and often the platform of—the nationalist movement disappeared. More important for labor, as Robin Cohen and associates have noted, "Most of the African nationalist or pseudo-socialist ideologies have never granted a specific place and role to the struggles of the working class, to those classes exploited by the capitalist system."[19] While some observers such as Jack Woddis and Thomas Hodgkin expected the "working class leaderships" of the nationalist movements to open the way to the "further radical reconstruction of African society" and to counteract national tendencies to present political independence as an end in itself, they were rarely accorded the opportunity to do so (if they even could have).[20] In places such as Namibia, policies of national reconciliation were quickly adopted by incoming governments—policies that could not privilege workers' interests and that quickly came to be viewed as preserving the privileges of the few.[21]

Moreover, in Africa at independence, nationalist leaders quickly became members of a "new elite" largely removed from their previous mass base.

Fanon was scathing in his criticism of the "national middle classes" that led their people to independence. Neither engaged in "production, nor in invention, nor building, nor labor"—and with "practically no economic power"—the national middle class was underdeveloped, narcissistic, and "convinced that it can advantageously replace the middle class of the mother country."[22] Conforming to this pattern, the national middle class that led the nationalist struggle and gained power at independence in Namibia has become part of an emerging new elite. In late 1991 Chris Tapscott claimed that in Namibia there was "evidence of growing stratification in class terms that transcends previous racial and ethnic boundaries. Key to this is the emergence of a new elite, with members of the pre-existing white settler elite now being joined by a new class of senior black administrators, politicians and business people."[23] Alex Davidson, in his review of democracy and human rights in Namibia in late 1991, noted with concern Namibia's rapidly expanding civil service and emerging new elite: "The expansion of ministries, and lavish salaries and benefits enjoyed by ministers and senior civil servants, has given rise to a new expression in ethnicity-conscious Namibia: 'the Mercedes tribe.' On one hand the embourgeoisement of the SWAPO elite as a result of this development defuses revolutionary enthusiasms for radical change, but on the other, the increasing discontent of grassroots SWAPO supporters, who see the growing wealth of the political leadership while little changes at village level, poses threats of division or apathy at the approaching [1992] election."[24] Indeed, in addition to the usual perquisites of office, in the first few years of independence numerous members of government appear to have obtained access to important economic resources through their access to political power—another familiar pattern in Africa.[25]

But still other factors beyond nationalist views and class aspirations have influenced SWAPO's attitudes toward labor and the prospects for democracy in Namibia. SWAPO was the officially sanctioned nationalist movement from Namibia. Throughout the years, SWAPO's status (ordained by the United Nations in 1976) as "sole and authentic representative of the Namibian people" effectively prevented other organizations and individuals from gaining significant international support and, in the view of many Namibian opposition leaders (and some in SWAPO itself), contributed markedly to a lack of accountability in SWAPO. This lack of accountability has been described as a particular "political culture" among the exiled SWAPO leadership. Leys and Saul, on the basis of their research into SWAPO's liberation struggle, conclude that in exile the SWAPO leadership "developed a political culture that frowned on spontaneity and debate, increasingly defined criticism as disloyalty, and eventually gave free rein to those in charge of the movement's 'security.'

Moreover, this political culture had a significant impact inside Namibia, too, as the external leaders gradually came to make 'internal SWAPO' into an instrument of their external strategy, and increasingly discouraged militant activism even in those parts of the country where it was still possible."[26]

A major concern of Leys and Saul and others has been to determine to what extent this "political culture" has carried over to the postindependence period and how it might influence Namibia's nascent democracy. In 1991 then Legal Assistance Centre director David Smuts was quoted in the *Namibian* as voicing a concern about a "culture of silence" that was developing in the newly independent nation, one that was reinforced when politicians implied that criticism of the government and ruling party was regarded as unacceptable behavior: "They thus imply that any person indulging in such behaviour must accept that they could be subject to sanctions—be this in the form of losing their employment with the state, suffering social ostracism and generally being regarded as persona non grata—or be this in the form of encouraging the development of a perception that real rewards will only come to those who stick to a party line."[27] Smuts added that in addition to constitutional guarantees of freedom of expression and association, a "culture where criticism of even the highest officials, including the President himself, is regarded as not only acceptable but essential to facilitate and promote democracy" was necessary in Namibia. Like Leys and Saul, Davidson sees "the culture left from the liberation struggle"—"violent and intolerant"—and the colonial legacy of authoritarianism as factors working against democracy in Namibia.[28] Events of 1996, surrounding demands that SWAPO account for the fate of its many detainees in exile, have only heightened many of these concerns.

LABOR AND THE PROSPECTS FOR THE CONSOLIDATION OF
DEMOCRACY IN NAMIBIA

Unlike many other countries in Africa, Namibia is not in the midst of a transition from an indigenous authoritarian rule to an indigenous democratic rule. Rather, in Namibia the transition has been part of a decolonization from one hundred years of colonial rule to political independence. The challenge confronting Namibia today concerns the consolidation of a still fragile democracy. Indeed, at first glance this process appears to be proceeding apace. In the first several years of independence Namibia has achieved a remarkable peace and stability. Namibia's much vaunted constitution enshrines an array of fundamental human rights and freedoms that have been carefully monitored since independence. Dozens of new, in many cases progressive, laws have replaced the previous archaic and highly discriminatory legal dispensation. Free and fair elections by universal franchise have been held three times since the transition to independence. In the National Assembly the Namibian people are represented by five political parties—although since the December 1994 elections SWAPO has held a two-thirds majority. A free press and even a partially government controlled radio and TV routinely initiate debate over postindependence policies and development.

And yet, there are increasing signs of movement toward at least a one-party dominant system, one that is increasingly less tolerant of dissenting voices. For example, the number of political parties has narrowed dramatically in recent years and the ruling party SWAPO now holds a better than two-thirds majority in both chambers of Parliament; second, while a position in favor of a one-party state has rarely been publicly articulated, there are constant exhortations by government and party leaders to build the nation, foster national unity, and so on—the same appeals made at independence thirty years earlier in much of Africa. Third, there has emerged a clear pattern of local, regional, and national leaders, often onetime SWAPO foes, joining the ruling party; fourth, a steady blurring of the distinction between ruling party and government and an effort to bolster the party's position vis-à-vis auxiliaries or wings (women, students, the unions) has taken place. Finally, there has been a kind of atrophying of the ruling party apparatus itself: a lack of funds to pay employees, minimal if any local level organization, a failure to attract large numbers of supporters to rallies, and a notable lack of party positions—as distinct from government—on most issues. These developments have been matched by a marked decline in the standing of opposition political parties, increased attacks on the media, an apparent reluctance to decentralize power to the local and regional levels, numerous allegations of corruption in government, and more.[29]

By examining the trade union movement in Namibia, this book has sought to evaluate more closely the prospects for democratic consolidation in Namibia. Assuming that organizations such as trade unions are integral to a process of political liberalization or democratization—acting as they do to articulate the preferences of their members and to serve as a counterpoise to state power—their fate must also offer some indication of the prospects for democracy in Namibia.

The centrality of social movements to efforts at political liberalization around Africa was noted in Chapter 1. Repeatedly, observers such as Ayesha Imam have stressed that "multipartyism is insufficient without the existence of substantial autonomy for civil society; that is to say, the increase in the capacity for social actors (trades unions, mass media, women, peasants, professional and other associations, entrepreneurs, etc) and individuals to act without undue restrictions, whether from the state or in authoritarian practices in their own organisations."[30] Like other Africans writing about democratization in Africa, Jimi Adesina emphasizes the importance of identifying those "social forces central to the struggle for democracy." According to Adesina, "this is where the labour movement comes in."[31] This association of labor movements with democracy can be found outside Africa as well. In their recent work on Latin America and Europe, Rueschemeyer, Stephens, and Stephens have argued that the growth of a working class—developed and sustained by trade unions, working-class political parties, and similar groups —is critical for the promotion of democracy. Similarly, Collier and Collier have suggested that in several Latin American countries the way in which worker protest and organized labor movements were first handled by governments and political parties had important implications for the future political trajectories of those countries.[32]

The potential roles for trade unions in democratization processes are many. As Gary Marks writes in his study of early British, German, and American trade unionism, "since the Industrial Revolution individual trade unions have been the chief organizational means for those towards the bottom of society to express their economic and political demands."[33] Indeed, many writing about African trade unions have noted their role in serving as a "voice" for a wide segment of African society beyond their individual memberships. Adrian Peace, in his refutation of the labor aristocracy thesis, argued that the political activity of wage-earning classes in Lagos had repercussions far beyond those classes because many others relied on those steadily employed. Peace identified Lagos workers as "populist militants": "militants in the sense that they have the organisational capacity and resolve to oppose firmly those actions of the ruling groups which they consider to be most iniquitous, populist in that they express through their class actions general grassroots sentiments of strong antagonism to the existing order." Similarly, in Ghana, Richard Jeffries found that "other urban mass groupings" looked to workers "for expressions of political protest against the increasingly inegalitarian socioeconomic structure" in that country. Jeffries found that, as in Nigeria, Ghanaian workers held "close social ties with other socioeconomic groups and identification with the grievances of the common people whose exploitation by the CPP [Congress People's Party] elite they were able to observe first hand." Like Peace and Jeffries, Michaela Von Freyhold sees labor movements in Africa as relying heavily "on moral and sometimes also material and political support from other strata, particularly the self-employed in the 'informal sector,' and more often than not demands were made not in the name of the working class, but the 'common man' . . . and his rights to a decent livelihood." Such "popular struggles" in Africa have, according to Von Freyhold, usually had a populist rather than a proletarian character and have very often focused on the contradiction between "the state and the common people rather than on the contradiction between capital and labour."[34] Thus the demands of trade unions in Africa tend to reflect more than merely those of their own members.

But trade unions can do more than simply articulate the grievances of their members and others. More important is the capacity of trade unions for collective action—a capacity that is generally greater among trade unions than any other organizations of civil society given their mass base and their ability to disrupt the national economy. Indeed, for many governments, one of the most significant aspects of trade unions is their ability to confer (or not) legitimacy on a regime. For states and political parties alike, the capacity to control a labor movement or to mobilize a labor movement's political support is a much sought after asset. In the absence of such an asset, governments, especially, run the risk of worker protest against their policies.[35] Thus an additional important vocation of trade unions in the quest for democracy is to ensure accountability in government. Yusuf Bangura and Bjorn Beckman argue that organized groups such as unions—through their demands for "the institutionalisation of collective bargaining, the independence of unions and associations and respect for the rule of law and civil liberties"—ultimately hold employers and state authorities accountable for their economic policies.[36] For the Nigerian case, Bangura and Beckman have argued for the role more recently of workers in "asserting the democratic aspirations" of the Nigerian people in the face of painful structural adjustment programs.[37]

Thus there is a potentially significant role to be played by trade unions in the consolidation of Namibian democracy. Still, one of the many dilemmas facing trade unions in Namibia today is what kind of trade unionism they will pursue. Eddie Webster has written of the "two faces" of trade unionism, in particular in South Africa. On the one hand, there is an economic dimension—"that of a union trying to win increases and improvements in living [and working] conditions"—and on the other hand, there is a social and political dimension—where unions act as a "voice institution," especially important in settings in which the majority may not have a "meaningful voice" in the political system. Of course, black trade unions in South Africa, as in Namibia, emerged in a situation that excluded workers from the central decision-making process. Although it focused initially on the economic dimension, by the mid-1980s the trade union movement in South Africa had come to focus as much on the political and social dimension—leading to the emergence of what Webster calls "social-movement unionism."[38]

Kim Scipes, meanwhile, differentiates among economic unionism (that accommodates itself to the prevailing industrial relations system and is most concerned with its members' well-being), political unionism (that is dominated by or subordinated to a political party or state and to which trade union leaders give their primary loyalty), and social movement unionism (that sees workers' struggles as merely one of many efforts to change society qualitatively and that "seeks alliances with other social movements on an equal basis and tries to join them when possible"). A new type of trade unionism emerging in such disparate places as Brazil, the Philippines, South Africa, and South Korea, social movement unionism is described by Scipes as a democratic trade unionism that "transcends the traditional economic-political divide of society" and acts in collaboration with other organizations.[39] In general, the literature on the role of social movements in democratization processes in Africa—with special reference to trade unions—implies that a social movement unionism holds the best prospects for a democratic future.

In Namibia at present, however, a political unionism seems to prevail, a result, no doubt, of the major unions' origins in the nationalist movement and their mobilizational role in the final years of the liberation struggle. Whereas unions in Britain and America, and elsewhere in Africa, preceded the formation of labor or other major political parties, this was not the case in Namibia; nor have trade unions in Namibia taken the step that party-created unions in Germany eventually took, emphasizing their political independence (and rapidly increasing their membership).[40] The relationship between the unions and the ruling political party or government in Namibia remains decisive. As long as the major trade union federation and affiliated unions remain tied to the ruling party—and Namibia's many unions remain divided—it seems unlikely that they will be able to play a major role in building and safeguarding democracy in Namibia.

By contrast, for the moment, an economic unionism eludes many Namibian trade unions, although the legislative framework is in place to facilitate such a path should they choose it. In Namibia, where many of the legacies of apartheid still reign in the workplace, a focus by trade unions on ameliorating harsh working conditions, increasing workers' wages and benefits, assisting in the training of members, servicing members' needs and grievances, and representing workers in national economic fora certainly would be warranted, at least for a time. Given that trade unions in Namibia were largely organized from above and primarily with a political objective in mind, more attention to the shop floor would do much to improve the living and working conditions of a sizable segment of the wage labor force—and by extension of many others.

Ultimately a social movement unionism of the type emerging in other developing countries might prove the most efficacious in Namibia. Indeed, Namibian trade unions—from both federations—have begun to work in alliance with each other and with other organizations, both formally and informally. Still, Namibian trade unions must overcome many obstacles—economic constraints, the enduring legacies of apartheid, uneasy relationships with party and government. Nevertheless, for the successful consolidation of democracy in Namibia, strong and autonomous trade unions, working in collaboration with a variety of other organizations, will be essential.

NOTES

CHAPTER ONE

1. *Africa Demos* 3, no. 5 (1996): 27; a democratic African political system is defined as one "enjoying wide competition between organized groups, numerous opportunities for popular participation in government, and elections that are regularly and fairly conducted. Constitutional guarantees of civil liberties and human rights are effectively enforced." The same definition of political democracy is given in Larry Diamond, Juan Linz, and Seymour Martin Lipset, eds., *Democracy in Developing Countries: Africa*, Vol. 2 (Boulder: Lynne Rienner, 1988), xvi. This definition draws on Robert Dahl's notion of polyarchy.

2. See, for example, Larry Diamond, "Is the Third Wave Over?" *Journal of Democracy* 7, no. 3 (1996): 20-37; Samuel Huntington, "Democracy for the Long Haul," *Journal of Democracy* 7, no. 2 (1996): 3-13; Guillermo O'Donnell, "What Makes Democracies Endure?" *Journal of Democracy* 7, no. 1 (1996): 39-55.

3. Julius Nyang'oro, "Critical Notes on Political Liberalization in Africa," *Journal of Asian and African Studies* 33, nos. 1-2 (1996): 120-21.

4. Julius Ihonvbere, "On the Threshold of Another False Start? A Critical Evaluation of Prodemocracy Movements in Africa," *Journal of Asian and African Studies* 33, nos. 1-2 (1996): 125-42.

5. See, for example, Mahmood Mamdani, "Africa: Democratic Theory and Democratic Struggles," *Dissent*, Summer 1992, 312-18; Mahmood Mamdani, Thandika Mkandawire, and Ernest Wamba-dia-Wamba, "Social Movements, Social Transformation and the Struggle for Democracy in Africa," *Economic and Political Weekly* 23 (1988): 973-81; Georges Nzongola-Ntalaja, "Prospects for Democratization in Africa," *African Perspectives* (New York: Africa Fund, 1991); Achille Mbembe, "Democratization and Social Movements in Africa," *Africa Demos* 1, no. 1 (1990): 4; Julius Nyang'oro, "Reform Politics and the Democratization Process in Africa," *African Studies Review* 37, no. 1 (1994): 133-49.

6. Celestin Monga, "Civil Society and Democratisation in Francophone Africa," *Journal of Modern African Studies* 33 (1995): 365-66.

7. For a variety of conceptions and uses of "civil society" in Africa see Jean Francois Bayart, "Civil Society in Africa," in *Political Domination in Africa: Reflections on the Limits of Power*, ed. Patrick Chabal (Cambridge: Cambridge University Press, 1986); Michael Bratton, "Beyond the State: Civil Society and Associational Life in Africa," *World Politics* 42 (1989): 407-39; Robert Fatton, *Predatory Rule: State and Civil Society in Africa* (Boulder: Lynne Rienner, 1992); Robert Fine, "Civil Society Theory and the Politics of Transition in South Africa," *Review of African Political Economy* 55 (1992):

71–83; Aili Mari Tripp, "Gender, Political Participation and the Transformation of Associational Life in Uganda and Tanzania," *African Studies Review* 37, no. 1 (1994): 107–31; John Harbeson, Donald Rothchild, and Naomi Chazan, eds. *Civil Society and the State in Africa* (Boulder: Lynne Rienner, 1994).

8. E. Gyimah-Boadi, "Civil Society in Africa," *Journal of Democracy* 7, no. 2 (1996): 122–26.

9. Michael Bratton and Nicolas van de Walle, *Democratic Experiments in Africa: Regime Transitions in Comparative Perspective* (Cambridge: Cambridge University Press, 1977), 255. Bratton and van de Walle cite "the deflation of popular political energy in the transition's aftermath" as the main reason for civil society's poorer performance during the consolidation of democracy.

10. Ruth Berins Collier and David Collier, *Shaping the Political Arena: Critical Junctures, the Labor Movement and Regime Dynamics in Latin America* (Princeton: Princeton University Press, 1991); Gay Seidman, *Manufacturing Militance: Workers' Movements in Brazil and South Africa, 1970–1985* (Berkeley: University of California Press, 1994); Margaret Keck, "The New Unionism in the Brazilian Transition," in *Democratizing Brazil: Problems of Transition and Consolidation,* ed. Alfred Stepan (New York: Oxford University Press, 1989); Leigh Payne, "Working Class Strategies in the Transition to Democracy in Brazil," *Comparative Politics* 23 (1991): 221–38; Dietrich Rueschemeyer, Evelyne Huber Stephens, and John Stephens, *Capitalist Development and Democracy* (Chicago: University of Chicago Press, 1992); Frederic Deyo, "State and Labor: Modes of Political Exclusion in East Asian Development," in *The Political Economy of the New Asian Industrialism,* ed. Deyo (Ithaca: Cornell University Press, 1987); Frederic Deyo, *Beneath the Miracle: Labor Subordination in the New Asian Industrialism* (Berkeley: University of California Press, 1989); Frederic Deyo, "Economic Policy and the Popular Sector," in *Manufacturing Miracles: Paths of Industrialization in Latin America and East Asia,* ed. Gary Gereffi and Donald Wyman (Princeton: Princeton University Press, 1990).

11. Samuel Valenzuela, "Labor Movements in Transitions to Democracy: A Framework for Analysis," *Comparative Politics* 21 (1989): 447. Glenn Adler and Eddie Webster ("Challenging Transition Theory: The Labor Movement, Radical Reform, and the Transition to Democracy in South Africa," *Politics and Society* 23 [1995]: 106) emphasize the "centrality" of the labor movement in South Africa's transition to democracy. Though they acknowledge the difficulties ahead, Adler and Webster remain optimistic that the labor movement can play the same central role during the consolidation of democracy in South Africa.

12. Collier and Collier, *Shaping the Political Arena,* 41–44, 48.

13. In many places, prominent nationalist leaders had their initial training and exposure in the early trade unions, for example, Sekou Toure of Guinea, Tom Mboya of Kenya, Siaka Stevens of Sierra Leone, Rashidi Kawawa of Tanzania, Simon Kapwepwe of Zambia, Cyril Adoula of Zaire, and Modibo Keita of Mali. See Thomas Hodgkin, *Nationalism in Colonial Africa* (New York: New York University Press, 1957), 115–38; Jack Woddis, *Africa: The Lion Awakes* (London: Lawrence and Wishart, 1961); Bill

Freund, *The African Worker* (Cambridge: Cambridge University Press, 1988), 91–109; Charles Orr, "Trade Unionism in Colonial Africa," *Journal of Modern African Studies* 4 (1966): 65–81.

14. Michaela Von Freyhold, "Labour Movements or Popular Struggles in Africa," *Review of African Political Economy* 39 (1987): 23–32.

15. Jon Kraus, "African Trade Unions: Progress or Poverty?" *African Studies Review* 19, no. 3 (1976): 95–108.

16. Ioan Davies, *African Trade Unions* (Harmondsworth: Penguin, 1966), 10, 12, 219.

17. Lloyd Sachikonye, "State, Capital and Trade Unions," in *Zimbabwe: The Political Economy of Transition, 1980–1986*, ed. Ibbo Mandaza (Dakar: CODESRIA, 1986); Pete Richer, "Zimbabwean Unions: From State Partners to Outcasts," *South African Labour Bulletin* 16, no. 7 (1992): 66–69; John Loxley and John Saul, "Multinationals, Workers and the Parastatals in Tanzania," *Review of African Political Economy* 2 (1975): 54–88; Manfred Bienefeld, "Trade Unions, the Labour Process, and the Tanzanian State," *Journal of Modern African Studies* 17 (1979): 553–93; Jon Kraus, "Strikes and Labour Power in Ghana," *Development and Change* 10 (1979): 259–86; Kwamina Panford, "State-Trade Union Relations: The Dilemmas of Single Trade Union Systems in Ghana and Nigeria," *Labour and Society* 13, no. 1 (1988): 37–53; Richard Sandbrook, "Patrons, Clients, and Unions: The Labour Movement and Political Conflict in Kenya," *Journal of Commonwealth Political Studies* 10 (1972): 3–27; Michael Chege, "The State and Labour in Kenya," in *Popular Struggles for Democracy in Africa*, ed. Peter Anyang' Nyong'o (London: Zed Press, 1987); Jack Parson, "The Working Class, the State and Social Change in Botswana," *South African Labour Bulletin* 5 (1980): 44–55. See also Jon Kraus, "The Political Economy of Trade Union-State Relations in Radical and Populist Regimes in Africa," in *Labour and Unions in Africa*, ed. Roger Southall (New York: St. Martin's Press, 1988).

18. Michael Bratton, "Testing Competing Explanations for Regime Transitions in Africa," 13, Paper presented at the Thirty-seventh Annual African Studies Association Meeting, Orlando, 1995.

19. Of course, these developments are just what African leaders and political parties have feared most. "Regimes have tended to view broadly based trade, student, professional, and civil rights associations as the greatest threats to their authority because these organizations have historically formed the launching pad for new political parties" (Naomi Chazan, "Africa's Democratic Challenge," *World Policy Journal* 9 [1992]: 295).

20. Michael Bratton, "Zambia Starts Over," *Journal of Democracy* 3, no. 2 (1992): 81–94; Babacar Kante, "Senegal's Empty Elections," *Journal of Democracy* 5, no. 1 (1994): 96–108; Dot Keet, "Zimbabwe Trade Unions: From 'Corporatist Brokers' Towards an 'Independent Labour Movement'?" *South African Labour Bulletin* 16, no. 4 (1992): 56–62.

21. Republic of Namibia, Central Statistics Office, *1991 Population and Housing Census: Basic Analysis with Highlights* (Windhoek: CSO, 1995), 49–56. See also Economist Intelligence Unit, *Country Profile: Namibia Swaziland, 1995–1996* (London: EIU, 1996), 17.

22. A list from the Office of the Labour Commissioner from July 1994 indicated that the following unions and federations were registered or had registrations pending: Namibia Public Workers Union, Public Service Union of Namibia, Namibia Transport and Allied Workers Union, Namibia Building Workers Union, Mineworkers Union of Namibia, Namibia Domestic and Allied Workers Union, Metal and Allied Workers Union, Local Authorities Union of Namibia, Namibia National Teachers Union, Namibia Wholesalers and Retail Workers Union, Namibia Food and Allied Workers Union, National Union of Namibian Workers, Namibian Pelagic Motorman Union, Namibian Telecommunications Union, Teachers Union of Namibia, Namibia Farmworkers Union, Society for Officials of Financial Institutions, South West Africa Mineworkers Union, Namibia People's Social Movement, and Bankworkers Union of Namibia.

23. Colin Leys and John Saul, "Introduction," in *Namibia's Liberation Struggle: The Two-Edged Sword*, ed. Leys and Saul (London: James Currey, Athens: Ohio University Press, 1995), 4. In their book, Leys and Saul (p. 5) explore the possibility that "the very process of struggling for liberation, especially by resort to force of arms, almost invariably generates political practices that prefigure undemocratic outcomes."

24. Dianne Hubbard and Colette Solomon, "The Many Faces of Feminism in Namibia," in *The Challenge of Local Feminisms: Women's Movements in Global Perspective*, ed. Amrita Basu (Boulder: Westview Press, 1995), 174–75; Gerhard Toetemeyer, Victor Tonchi, and Andre du Pisani, *Namibia Regional Resources Manual* (Windhoek: Friedrich Ebert Stiftung, 1994), 111.

25. See Heike Becker, *Namibian Women's Movement, 1980 to 1992: From Anti-Colonial Resistance to Reconstruction* (Frankfurt: Verlag für Interkulturelle Kommunikation, 1995); Hubbard and Solomon, "Feminism in Namibia"; Tessa Cleaver and Marion Wallace, *Namibia Women in War* (London: Zed Books, 1990), chap. 7. Also, author interviews with two members of Sister Collective, interview 119 and interview 127, Windhoek, 13 July 1994.

26. The Namibia National Students Organisation affiliated formally to SWAPO at its National Student Congress in 1989 and then repealed that affiliation when 96.3 percent of delegates voted against affiliation at NANSO's first Extraordinary National Student Congress in July 1991. See Sipho Maseko, "The Role and Effects of the Namibian Student Movement," in *Namibia's Liberation Struggle: The Two-Edged Sword*, ed. Colin Leys and John Saul (London: James Currey, Athens: Ohio University Press, 1995). Also, author interview with (NANSO) officeholder, interview 106, Khomasdal, 25 July 1994.

27. See Philip Steenkamp, "The Church and the Liberation of Namibia," in *Christianity and Democratization in Africa*, ed. Paul Gifford (London: James Currey, 1994). Also, author interviews with CCN officeholder, interview 118, Katutura, 15 July 1994, and Evangelical Lutheran Church in Namibia bishop, interview 92, Ongwediva, 8 July 1994.

28. Lori Ann Girvan and Chris Tapscott, "The Role of Farmers' Associations in Agricultural Policy Formulation and Implementation: A Look at Namibia," draft of a paper prepared for an International Conference on Governments, Farmers' Organizations, and Food Policy, Kadoma, Zimbabwe, 31 May–3 June 1993. Girvan and Tapscott cite an unidentified deputy minister who explained a "dependency paralysis" in the

rural areas as a remnant of the liberation struggle during which "it was frowned upon to act independently. . . . Now many people want to keep on waiting for leaders to decide; they can't deal with independence and taking action on their own." At the same time, my interviews with political party and regional and local government officials and representatives of nongovernmental and community organizations, small business associations, and cooperatives in Oshakati and Rundu in northern Namibia in July 1994 found a fair amount of community organization under way. Still, the complaint about the ongoing political tensions surrounding such activity continues.

29. As Charles Bergquist *(Labor in Latin America: Comparative Essays on Chile, Argentina, Venezuela, and Colombia* [Stanford: Stanford University Press, 1986], 10) points out for several Latin American cases, the influence and importance of strategic export sectors, such as mining, or sectors on which economic development depends such as transport, or the public service have always outweighed their small numbers.

30. Kaire Mbuende, *Namibia, the Broken Shield: Anatomy of Imperialism and Revolution* (Malmo: Liber Forlag, 1986); Peter Katjavivi, *A History of Resistance in Namibia* (Paris: UNESCO, 1988); Elia Kaakunga, *Problems of Capitalist Development in Namibia: The Dialectics of Progress and Destruction* (Abo: Abo Academy Press, 1990).

31. Zedekia Ngavirue, "Political Parties and Interest Groups in South West Africa: A Study of a Plural Society" (Ph.D. dissertation, Oxford University, 1972); Lohmeier Angula, "African Workers in the Mining and Fishing Industries—The 1978 Industrial Relations Framework and Beyond" (M.Sc. thesis, University of Strathclyde, 1986); Theo Angula, "The Law and Industrial Relations in Colonial Namibia" (LL.M. thesis, Warwick University, 1986); Simon Zhu Mbako, "The Development of Labour and Political Resistance in Namibia, 1890–1972" (M.A. thesis, Sussex University, 1986); Hiskia Angulah, "Legislative Control of Labour in Namibia: A Focus on the Migrant/Contract Labour System, 1910–1987," Mimeo, University of Warwick, 1988; Wolfgang Werner, "An Economic and Social History of the Herero of Namibia, 1915–1946" (Ph.D. dissertation, University of Cape Town, 1989); Vitura Kavari, "The Contract Labour System and the Process of Labour Control in Namibia" (M.Sc. thesis, University of Manchester, 1990).

32. Vinnia Ndadi, *Breaking Contract* (1974; rpt. London: International Defence and Aid Fund, 1989); John Ya Otto, *Battlefront Namibia* (Westport: Lawrence Hill, 1981); Hinananje Shafodino Nehova, "The Price of Liberation," in *Namibia: SWAPO Fights for Freedom,* ed. Namibian Support Movement (Oakland: LSM, 1978); Andreas Shipanga, *In Search of Freedom: The Andreas Shipanga Story* (Gibraltar: Ashanti Publishing, 1989); Helao Shityuwete, *Never Follow the Wolf: The Autobiography of a Namibian Freedom Fighter* (London: Kliptown Books, 1990); Helmut Kangulohi Angula, *The Two Thousand Days of Haimbodi Ya Haufiku* (Windhoek: Gamsberg Macmillan, 1990); Charles Kauraisa, "The Labour Force," in *South West Africa: Travesty of Trust,* ed. Ronald Segal and Ruth First (London: Andre Deutsch, 1967); James Kauluma, "The Migrant Contract Labor System in Namibia and the Response to It," Mimeo, Windhoek, 1977; Gerson Max, "Die Geestelike en Materiele Situasie van die Kontrakarbeiders," *Afrikanischer Heimatkalendar* (1977): 69–74; Ndeutala Hishongwa, *The Contract Labour*

System and Its Effect on Family and Social Life in Namibia (Windhoek: Gamsberg Macmillan, 1992); Robert Gordon, *Mines, Masters and Migrants: Life in a Namibian Mine Compound* (Johannesburg: Ravan Press, 1977). While both Gordon's and Hishongwa's books grow out of personal experiences, they were also originally doctoral dissertations.

33. Ray Simons, "The Namibian Challenge," Paper presented to Namibia Fights for Freedom Conference convened by SWAPO, Brussels, 26–28 May 1972; Ruth First, *South West Africa* (Harmondsworth: Penguin, 1963); Rauha Voipio, *Kontrak Soos die Ovambo Dit Sien* (Windhoek: Evangelical Lutheran Ovambo-Kavango Church, 1972); John Kane-Berman, "Contract Labour in South West Africa" (Johannesburg: South African Institute of Race Relations, 1972); John Kane-Berman, "The Labour Situation in South West Africa" (Johannesburg: South African Institute of Race Relations, 1973); Colin Winter, *Namibia: The Story of a Bishop in Exile* (London: Lutterworth Press, 1977); David Soggott, *Namibia: The Violent Heritage,* (London: Rex Collings, 1986).

34. Fritz Raedel, "Die Wirtschaft und die Arbeiterfrage Suedwest Afrikas" (Ph.D. dissertation, University of Stellenbosch, 1947); M. J. Olivier, "Inboorlingbeleid en Administrasie in die Mandaatsgebied van Suidwes Afrika" (D.Phil. dissertation, University of Stellenbosch, 1961); Peter Banghart, "Migrant Labour in South West Africa and Its Effect on Ovambo Tribal Life" (M.A. thesis, University of Stellenbosch, 1969); Richard Moorsom, "Colonisation and Proletarianisation: An Exploratory Investigation of the Formation of the Working Class in Namibia Under German and South African Colonial Rule Until 1945" (M.A. thesis, Sussex University, 1973); John Loffler, "Labour and Politics in Namibia in the 1970s" (M.A. thesis, University of York, 1979); Bettina Gebhardt, "Zur Sozialoekonomischen Lage der Farmarbeiter in Namibia: Entwicklung in Vergangenheit und Zukunft" (Ph.D. dissertation, Frankfurt University, 1983); Anthony Emmett, "The Rise of African Nationalism in South West Africa/Namibia, 1915–1966" (Ph.D. dissertation, University of the Witwatersrand, 1987); Alastair MacFarlane, "Labour Control: Managerial Strategies in the Namibian Mining Sector, 1970–1985" (Ph.D. dissertation, Oxford Polytechnic, 1990).

35. Keith Gottschalk, "South African Labour Policy in Namibia, 1915–1978," *South African Labour Bulletin* 4 (1978): 75–106; Robert Gordon, "A Note on the History of Labour Action in Namibia," *South African Labour Bulletin* 1 (1975): 7–17; Robert Gordon, "Variations in Migration Rates: The Ovambo Case," *Journal of Southern African Affairs* 3 (1978): 261–94; Gordon, *Mines, Masters and Migrants;* Robert Gordon, "Some Organisational Aspects of Labour Protest Amongst Contract Workers in Namibia," *South African Labour Bulletin* 4 (1978): 116–23; Richard Moorsom, "Underdevelopment and Class Formation: The Origins of Migrant Labour in Namibia, 1815–1915," in *Perspectives on South Africa: A Collection of Working Papers,* ed. Tuffy Adler (Johannesburg: University of the Witwatersrand, 1977); Richard Moorsom, "Underdevelopment, Contract Labour and Worker Consciousness in Namibia, 1915–1972," *Journal of Southern African Studies* 4 (1977): 52–87; Richard Moorsom, "Migrant Workers and the Formation of SWANLA, 1900–1926," *South African Labour Bulletin* 4 (1978): 107–15; Richard Moorsom, "Labour Consciousness and the 1971–72 Contract Workers Strike in Namibia," *Development and Change* 10 (1979): 205–31; Richard Moorsom, "Underdevelopment and Class

Formation: The Birth of the Contract Labour System in Namibia," in *Southern African Research in Progress: Collected Papers 5,* ed. Anne Akeryod and Christopher Hill (York: University of York Centre for Southern African Studies, 1980).

36. See, for example, SWAPO Department of Information and Publicity, *To Be Born a Nation* (London: Zed Press, 1981); SWAPO, *The Struggle for Trade Union Rights in Namibia* (Luanda: SWAPO Department of Labour, 1984); Brian Bolton, "The Condition of the Namibian Workers," Paper presented at the Seminar on the Activities of Foreign Economic Interests in the Exploitation of Namibia's Natural and Human Resources, Ljubljana, Yugoslavia, 16–20 April 1984; International Labour Organisation, *Labour and Discrimination in Namibia* (Geneva: ILO, 1977); Reginald Green, *Manpower Estimates and Development Implications for Namibia* (Lusaka: United Nations Institute for Namibia, 1978); Gillian Cronje and Suzanne Cronje, *The Workers of Namibia* (London: International Defence and Aid Fund, 1979); International Defence and Aid Fund, "Working Under South African Occupation: Labour in Namibia," *Fact Paper on Southern Africa No. 14* (London: IDAF, 1987); Pippa Green, "Cutting the 'Wire': Labour Control and Worker Resistance in Namibia," *Southern Africa Perspectives No. 2* (New York: Africa Fund, 1987).

37. Christine Von Garnier, *Katutura Revisited: Essays on a Black Namibian Apartheid Suburb* (Windhoek: Roman Catholic Church, 1986); Gerhard Toetemeyer, Vezera Kandetu, and Wolfgang Werner, eds., *Namibia in Perspective* (Windhoek: Council of Churches of Namibia, 1987); Cleaver and Wallace, *Namibia Women in War.* Other important works that deserve mention are the 1978 (Vol. 4, Nos. 1–2) special issue of the *South African Labour Bulletin,* "Focus on Namibia," and Roger Murray, Jo Morris, John Dugard, and Neville Rubin, *The Role of Foreign Firms in Namibia: Studies on External Investment and Black Workers' Conditions in Namibia* (Uppsala: Africa Publications Trust, 1974). Leys and Saul, eds. *Namibia's Liberation Struggle;* Becker, *Namibian Women's Movement;* Pekka Peltola, *The Lost May Day: Namibian Workers Struggle for Independence* (Helsinki: Finnish Anthropological Society, 1995).

38. In Namibia these include the following libraries: the National Archives of Namibia, the National [Estorff] Library of Namibia, the Parliamentary Library, the South West Africa Scientific Society library, the Namibia Economic Policy Research Unit library, the Namibian Institute for Social and Economic Research library, the United Nations Institute for Namibia collection at the University of Namibia and special collections from various trade unions and trade union federations and organizations such as the International Labour Organisation office in Windhoek, the Legal Assistance Centre, the Namibia Peace Plan 435, the Namibia Institute for Economic Affairs, the Private Sector Foundation, the Chamber of Mines, and others. In South Africa the following libraries were used: the South African Labour and Development Research Unit at the University of Cape Town (UCT), the Africana Library at UCT, the South African Institute of International Affairs library at the University of the Witwatersrand in Johannesburg, the William Cullen library at Wits, the John Dugard Documentation Centre at the Centre for Advanced Legal Studies at Wits, and the Africa Institute library in Pretoria.

39. These include the National Tripartite Seminar on the Labour Bill conducted by the Ministry of Labour and Manpower Development (MLMD), 13–14 February 1992; the National Tripartite Seminar on Employment and Development Planning in Namibia organized by the MLMD in cooperation with the National Planning Commission and the ILO, 6–8 April 1992; the First Annual Labour Law Seminar, 9 June 1992; the Prime Minister's Consultative Meeting on Labour Relations, 25–26 February 1993; and more informal meetings on labor relations initiated by the SWAPO secretary for labor and facilitated by the Friedrich Ebert Foundation in early 1993. In addition, I participated, with delegations of Namibian trade unionists and resource people, in two regional conferences on labor law and industrial relations: the Conference on Democracy and Trade Unions in Africa, 9–11 November 1992, Harare, Zimbabwe; and the First Regional Workshop on Labour Law and Industrial Relations in Southern Africa, 13–15 July 1993, Durban, South Africa.

40. I prepared written materials for events such as the NUNW Economics Conference, 10–12 October 1992 and the NUNW Demarcation Forum, 13 March 1993. In addition, I prepared a Research Needs Assessment for the NUNW and affiliated unions, at the request of the Friedrich Ebert Foundation, and attended monthly meetings of trade unionists and researchers.

Chapter Two

1. This description of the political status of South West Africa before 1971 is from Ernst Stals and Pieter Esterhuysen, "From Pre-Colonial Obscurity to International Prominence," in *Namibia 1990: An Africa Institute Country Survey,* ed. Erich Leistner and Pieter Esterhuysen (Pretoria: Africa Institute of South Africa, 1991), 35–37. See also Republic of South Africa, *South West Africa Survey, 1967* (Pretoria: Government Printer, 1967); *Financial Mail Special Survey,* "South West: Calm Amidst the Storm," 20 August 1965; and *Financial Mail Special Survey,* "Desert Deadlock," 2 March 1973.

2. Stals and Esterhuysen, "From Pre-Colonial Obscurity," 40.

3. Each of the nine members represented specific interests: four represented farming interests, two commercial interests, and one each mining, white labor, and "Native" administration. See Emmett, "Rise of African Nationalism," 167.

4. Stals and Esterhuysen, "From Pre-Colonial Obscurity," 31.

5. The South West Africa Native Affairs Administration Act of 1954 had made the state president of South Africa the supreme chief of South West Africa's indigenous peoples. This act was amended by Proclamation 87 of 1955 to delegate certain of the powers conferred upon him to the minister of Bantu administration and development. See Muriel Horrell, *South West Africa* (Johannesburg: South African Institute of Race Relations, 1967), 23.

6. Stals and Esterhuysen, "From Pre-Colonial Obscurity," 40. Also Republic of South Africa, *Report of the Commission of Enquiry into South West African Affairs, 1962–1963* (Pretoria: Government Printer, 1963 [Odendaal Report]); and First, *South West Africa.*

7. The South West Africa Constitution Act of 1968 essentially replaced the 1925 legislation. The act applied only to the "white areas" in Namibia, establishing an administration similar to that of provincial administrations in South Africa: a chief executive officer acted as territorial administrator, an Executive Committee was composed of the administrator as chairman and four members elected from the Legislative Assembly; the Legislative Assembly was composed of eighteen white members; and provision was made for a SWA Division of the Supreme Court of South Africa. While the powers conferred on the Legislative Assembly in 1968 were fairly wide-ranging, the South West Africa Affairs Act of 1969, which sought further to integrate the administration of SWA into that of South Africa, as per the recommendations of the Odendaal Commission, reduced the powers of the Legislative Assembly to that of a South African provincial council. See ILO, *Labour and Discrimination*, 9–12.

8. The Development of Self-Government for Native Nations in South West Africa Act of 1968 (amended in 1973) put into place further recommendations of the Odendaal Commission, namely, separate "nations" or "homelands" with separate systems of administration. The homelands were specified as follows: Damaraland, Hereroland, Kaokoland, Kavango, Caprivi, and Ovambo. Legislative Councils were to be established in each homeland with authority to deal with such matters as welfare services, education, roads, water, sanitation, imposition and collection of fees and taxes, registration of persons, and the establishment and management of labor bureaus. Any measures enacted were subject to the assent of the state president of South Africa. With prior approval of the state president, measures could also be made applicable to members of the "nation" resident outside the homeland. Coloured, Baster, and Nama peoples—falling outside the South African classification "African"—were governed by separate legislation (ILO, *Labour and Discrimination*, 13–15).

9. ILO, *Labour and Discrimination*, 17; see also 80–82.

10. Andimba Toivo ya Toivo, who was deported from Cape Town after a tape, in which he described the inequities of the contract labor system, smuggled to petitioner Mburumba Kerina at the United Nations, was discovered, says that the aim of the petitions was to have South West Africa fall under the auspices of the Trusteeship Council at the United Nations. In those days, he notes, no one was thinking about independence (Andimba Toivo ya Toivo, author interview, Windhoek, 16 June 1993). According to Emmett, "Rise of African Nationalism," 434, the petitions demanded that if the territory could not be part of the newly created United Nations Trusteeship System, it should be made a protectorate of Britain or the United States.

11. International Labour Organisation, *Special Report of the Director General on the Application of the Declaration Concerning the Policy of Apartheid in South Africa [and Namibia], 1968* (Geneva: ILO, 27). The UN Council for South West Africa later became the United Nations Council for Namibia.

12. This section relies heavily on Emmett, "Rise of African Nationalism," chaps. 3 and 8.

13. From the Administrator's Report of 1921 as quoted ibid., 166.

14. Ibid., 170. See also Wolfe Schmokel, "The Myth of the White Farmer: Commer-

cial Agriculture in Namibia, 1900–1983," *International Journal of African Historical Studies* 18 (1985): 93–108.

15. From the Administrator's Reports of 1920 and 1921, as cited by Emmett, "Rise of African Nationalism," 172.

16. See ibid., 186. "Locations" are residential areas for black and coloured persons, usually separate—and far—from "town"—the white residential area.

17. Emmett, "Rise of African Nationalism," 188.

18. Ibid., 189.

19. Ibid., 308.

20. Ibid., 312.

21. Ibid., 315.

22. Ibid., 323.

23. Ibid., 325.

24. Erich Leistner, Pieter Esterhuysen, and Theo Malan, *Namibia/SWA Prospectus* (Pretoria: Africa Institute of South Africa, 1980), 54.

25. Emmett, "Rise of African Nationalism," 328.

26. Ibid., 337–38.

27. Ibid., 333–36.

28. Ibid., 458.

29. Leistner, Esterhuysen, and Malan, *Namibia/SWA Prospectus,* 51.

30. Ibid., 52.

31. Ibid., 54.

32. Unpublished paper by Wolfgang Thomas as cited in ILO, *Labour and Discrimination,* 51.

33. RSA, *South West Africa Survey, 1967,* 89–93.

34. Jo Morris, "The Black Workers in Namibia," in *The Role of Foreign Firms in Namibia: Studies on External Investment and Black Workers' Conditions in Namibia,* ed. Roger Murray, Jo Morris, John Dugard, and Neville Rubin (Uppsala: Africa Publications Trust, 1974), 139.

35. *Financial Mail,* 1973, 49.

36. Horrell, *South West Africa,* 57.

37. Morris, "Black Workers in Namibia," 139.

38. *Financial Mail,* 1973, 49.

39. RSA, *South West Africa Survey, 1967,* 90.

40. Cited in Morris, "Black Workers in Namibia," 140.

41. Leistner, Esterhuysen, and Malan, *Namibia/SWA Prospectus,* 57.

42. Justin Ellis, *A Future for Namibia 4: Education, Repression and Liberation, Namibia* (London: Catholic Institute for International Relations, 1984), 83. See also Elizabeth Amukugo, *Education and Politics in Namibia: Past Trends and Future Prospects* (Windhoek: New Namibia Books, 1993).

43. ILO, *Labour and Discrimination,* 42.

44. Ibid., 49.

45. This description of the SWANLA system is from ibid., 55–56.

46. Free food and accommodation at the larger industrial centers such as Windhoek and Walvis Bay or on the mine meant staying in workers' compounds. The "Ovambo Compound" in Katutura was meant to house six thousand workers and was described in newspaper reports as "little less than a filthy ghetto." The beds consisted of concrete boxes in which the men kept their possessions, covered with wooden lids on which they slept. Employers paid forty cents per day for each worker eating and sleeping in the compound. In Walvis Bay the compound could house up to seventy-five hundred workers, mostly employed on a seasonal basis at the fish and canning factories; dormitory rooms consisted of eight sets of two-tiered bunks of concrete. Employers paid R10.75 per month per employee housed and fed in the compound (Kane-Berman, "Contract Labour," 14–15).

47. Ibid., 11–13.

48. ILO, *Labour and Discrimination,* 80; Kane-Berman, "Contract Labour," 11–12.

49. The criteria were that the person was born in the urban area or resided there permanently; had worked there continuously for fifteen years or for ten years for the same employer without being convicted of any crime more serious than a minor pass offense; was the wife, unmarried daughter, or minor son of a black person qualified as above and customarily resided with him; or had been granted official permission to remain (ILO, *Labour and Discrimination,* 80).

50. Ibid., 82. See also Horrell, *South West Africa,* 24–31.

51. This discussion neglects any mention of other nationalist organizations and precursors to those organizations such as the United Negro Improvement Association, the Otjiserandu, the African Improvement Society, the South West African Student Body, the South West Africa Progressive Association, the Herero Chiefs' Council, the Chiefs' Council (incorporating the Namas), and the South West Africa National Union. See Emmett, "Rise of African Nationalism," 378–552; Ngavirue, "Political Parties and Interest Groups," 292–341; First, *South West Africa,* 196–208; and Katjavivi, *A History of Resistance,* 24–54.

52. According to Emmett, "Rise of African Nationalism," 479–80, the launching of the OPO and the role of different leaders in its formation is "subject to both confusion and controversy." He maintains, based on interviews with, inter alia, Solomon Mifima, that the OPC as such never came into existence because it was thought imprudent to use the term "congress" in those days when South African congresses were increasingly under attack and the name might cause unnecessary attention from the police. Andreas Shipanga, another founding member, contends that the OPC did exist first, in 1957, but agrees that because of the perceived danger of the term "congress" at the time of the trial of members of the Congress Alliance in South Africa, the name was changed to Ovamboland People's Organisation in 1958 (Andreas Shipanga, author interview, Windhoek, 28 May 1993).

53. For example, Katjavivi, *History of Resistance,* 20; Ngavirue, "Political Parties and Interest Groups," 302; First, *South West Africa,* 199; Emmett, "Rise of African Nationalism," 476; Moorsom, "Labour Consciousness"; and Hidipo Hamutenya and Hage Geingob, "African Nationalism in Namibia," in *Southern Africa in Perspective:*

Essays on Regional Politics, ed. Christian Potholm and Richard Dale (New York: Free Press, 1972), 89.

54. Pekka Peltola, "The Role of the National Union of Namibian Workers in the Struggle for Independence," Mimeo, University of Helsinki, 1993, 6. Joachim Puetz, Heidi Von Egidy, and Perri Caplan, *Namibia Handbook and Political Who's Who* (Windhoek: Magus, 1989), 252, describe a gathering of thirty to forty SWA expatriate students and some two hundred casual laborers. Cronje and Cronje, *Workers of Namibia,* 102, refer to a group of students and workers gathered under the leadership of Toivo ya Toivo.

55. Jeremy Harding, *The Fate of Africa: Trial by Fire* (New York: Simon and Schuster, 1993), 91. Others in the leadership at the time included Solomon Mifima, Peter Mueshihange, Maxton Joseph Mutongulume, Paul Helmuth, Willie Kaukuetu, and Festus Isaak Newton.

56. Peltola, "Role of the NUNW," 6–8. According to one former contract worker, at the time that he worked at a canning factory in Walvis Bay in the early 1960s, "there were no trade union activities because SWAPO sort of embraced the trade union activities in the political organization. Trade union activities were not separately organized until much later. But SWAPO had the interests of the workers at heart, more than all the other political parties at the time" (Author interview 83, Windhoek, 22 March 1993).

57. Emmett, "Rise of African Nationalism," 481. According to Emmett, Emil Appolus copied the CPP constitution out of a book in a library in Cape Town. In his book, Ya Otto (*Battlefront Namibia* [Westport: Lawrence Hill, 1981], 45), in the same paragraph that he writes about "Sam and his OPO," reveals his hope that one day "Namibia's Nkrumah would emerge to give us leadership." Indeed, OPO's aims of "freedom" and "national independence" remained those of SWAPO president Sam Nujoma throughout the years of the liberation struggle; in speech after speech, Nujoma steadfastly affirmed these twin objectives.

58. Shipanga, interview. According to Ngavirue, the founders of the OPO "approached the labour question merely as an issue involving their kith and kin. The massive response they got from the migrant labourers was a clear demonstration of the accuracy with which the leaders of the OPO had located a subject which appealed to the northern people." Ngavirue adds that though initial membership figures may have been exaggerated, he, "as an on the spot observer . . . had no doubt that OPO had won the hearts of the migrant labourers" (Ngavirue, "Political Parties and Interest Groups," 302–3).

59. Toivo ya Toivo, interview.

60. Emmett, "Rise of African Nationalism," 483–86. Emmett notes that very little has been written on the political role of Nujoma in the pre-OPO period, and, indeed, this appears to be the case. He bases his information on interviews with Kozonguizi, Ngavirue, and Appolus, as well as with Shipanga and Mifima. The latter two, later arrested by SWAPO and imprisoned for two years in Tanzania before returning to Namibia in 1978 and founding SWAPO-D, contend that Nujoma played no significant role before 1959, while the others (whom Emmett considered more reliable sources)

describe a more important part. At the same time, Ngavirue ("Political Parties and Interest Groups," 298–99), in describing the second election of SWANU officeholders in late September 1959, relates how the "men from Pokkiesdraai" (the Ovambo Compound at the time) "were only following Sam Nujoma, whom they had to call by name whenever he disappeared in the crowd." Ya Otto (*Battlefront Namibia*, 41), in his chapter on the December 1959 "Windhoek Massacre," describes Nujoma as "already becoming a legend."

61. Shityuwete, *Never Follow the Wolf*, 23–26; see also Ndadi, *Breaking Contract*.

62. See Ya Otto, *Battlefront Namibia*, 44. The Main Location in Windhoek only became the "Old" Location after residents were forced to move to a new location—Katutura. The "Old" Location was officially closed on 31 August 1968. Sondagh Kangueehi ("From the 'Old Location' to Katutura," in *Katutura Revisited: Essays on a Black Namibian Apartheid Suburb*, ed. Christine Von Garnier [Windhoek: Roman Catholic Church, 1986], 29) points out that Katutura was the fifth location to which black Namibians in Windhoek were forcibly moved since white settlers first arrived in the territory; hence the meaning of the name in Otjiherero—"we do not have a permanent habitation." See also Dawn Ridgway, Milly Jafta, Nicky Kautja, Magda Oliphant, and Kapofi Shipinganga, *An Investigation into the Shooting at the Old Location on 10 December 1959* (Windhoek: University of Namibia, 1991); Wade Pendleton, *Katutura: A Place Where We Do Not Stay* (San Diego: San Diego University Press, 1974).

63. Quoted in Emmett, "Rise of African Nationalism," 542.

64. Ya Otto, *Battlefront Namibia*, 55–78; Ndadi, *Breaking Contract*, 96–120.

65. Tony Weaver, "The South African Defence Force in Namibia," in *War and Society: The Militarisation of South Africa*, ed. Jacklyn Cock and Laurie Nathan (Cape Town: David Philip, 1989), 91.

66. Helao Shityuwete and John Ya Otto, both of whom were among the thirty-seven to be tried, recount the experience in their respective books. Shityuwete was arrested in late March 1966 along with four others while on a SWAPO military incursion into Namibia. They were held in Pretoria and tortured until June 1966, when they were joined by four other Namibian prisoners. In September 1966 they were joined by the eight combatants arrested at Ongulumbashe; in April 1967 150 to 200 more Namibian detainees, including SWAPO northern region secretary Toivo ya Toivo, northern region chairperson Eliaser Tuhadeleni, acting president Nathaniel Maxuilili, secretary general John Ya Otto, information and publicity secretary Jason Mutumbulua, and Ongulumbashe base commander John Otto Nankudhu, were brought to Pretoria. According to Shityuwete, *Never Follow the Wolf*, 149, "they had all been rounded up and brought to Pretoria for interrogation for their 'part' in the armed struggle. We were really disturbed to find the entire SWAPO internal leadership in detention." See Shityuwete, *Never Follow the Wolf*, 124–79; Ya Otto, *Battlefront Namibia*, 87–119.

67. Colin Leys and John Saul, "SWAPO Inside Namibia," in *Namibia's Liberation Struggle: The Two-Edged Sword*, ed. Leys and Saul (London: James Currey, Athens: Ohio University Press, 1995), 70.

68. As is well documented, the 1971–72 strike was by no means the beginning of

labor resistance in the territory. As Robin Cohen ("Resistance and Hidden Forms of Consciousness Amongst African Workers," *Review of African Political Economy* 19 [1980]: 8–22) has indicated, labor protest and resistance in Africa must be understood in much broader terms than highly visible strikes or go-slows. Common worker responses—in Namibia as well—include desertion, community withdrawal or revolt, target working, efficiency and time bargaining, sabotage, creation of a work culture, accidents and sickness, drug use, belief in otherworldly solutions, and theft. In Namibia the first widely known act of organized labor resistance was the strike at the Gross Otavi mine in 1893. Keith Gottschalk ("South African Labour Policy," 90–91) lists almost annual strikes in Namibia from 1915 to 1972 among migrant workers on the mines, in the fish canneries, and, less frequently, on the farms. Labor protest in Namibia is discussed in detail, inter alia, in Cronje and Cronje, *Workers of Namibia;* Morris, "Black Workers in Namibia"; Moorsom, "Labour Consciousness"; Moorsom, "Underdevelopment, Contract Labour"; Gordon, "Note on the History of Labour Action"; Gordon, *Mines, Masters and Migrants;* Gordon, "Some Organisational Aspects"; Duncan Innes, "Imperialism and the National Struggle in Namibia," *Review of African Political Economy* 9 (1977): 44–59.

69. Ben Ulenga, author interview, Windhoek, 14 September 1992. Ulenga says he has yet to see any convincing evidence that the strike was formally organized by, for example, a SWAPO branch although SWAPO members were no doubt the catalyst. He attributes the strike rather to the workers in Walvis Bay, which, in any case, was a militant SWAPO stronghold. See also Brian Wood, "The Making of a Namibian Trade Unionist: An Interview with Ben Ulenga, 19 March 1987," *Review of African Political Economy* 39 (1987): 92, in which Ulenga says of the strike: "At that time there wasn't any organised union or such thing. SWAPO members I think were quite involved but you find that the whole thing was really a sort of spontaneous workers' upsurgence. It just started." A 1972 issue of the magazine *Africa* reported that fifteen arrests of "so-called strike leaders" had been made, "although the Ovambos insist that the strike has been spontaneous" ("The Ovambo Strike," *Africa,* July 1972, 37).

70. Ngavirue, "Political Parties and Interest Groups," 331.

71. Ya Otto, *Battlefront Namibia,* 140–41. In an interview with the author, Windhoek, 23 March 1993, Ya Otto said that "with the first national strike of 1970, these were spontaneous activities that people engaged in, you know, to collapse the economy of the regime, but not really well organized sort of a situation."

72. SWAPO, *To Be Born a Nation,* 191–97; SWAPO, *Struggle for Trade Union Rights,* 2.

73. *SWAPO Information Bulletin,* Luanda, September 1987, 17. In a 24 August 1977 interview with the *Guardian* newspaper, Sam Nujoma stated that the strike was organized by "SWAPO militants of the NUNW."

74. Shipanga, interview. Shipanga adds, however, that SWAPO claimed the strike as SWAPO work, as "a victory of SWAPO underground."

75. *Windhoek Advertiser,* 14 January 1972; Katjavivi, *History of Resistance,* 70.

76. Between March 1969 and July 1970 the United Nations Security Council had

passed four resolutions, the last of which called upon member states to isolate SWA by terminating all diplomatic, consular, treaty, and economic relations with South Africa wherever it acted on behalf of SWA. This then resulted in the request for yet another advisory opinion from the World Court, in particular, on the legal implications for member states of the continued South African presence in Namibia. The court ruled in June 1971 that Resolution 2145 (termination of the Mandate) was valid; it had been unnecessary to gain more information from South Africa on its administration of the territory because the policy of apartheid clearly violated fundamental human rights; South Africa's actions vis-à-vis the territory (such as the white referendum) were invalid because the Mandate had been terminated; as South Africa had created this situation, it was obliged to withdraw its administration from the territory (*Financial Mail,* 1973, 20).

77. The two church leaders were Bishop Leonard Auala of the Evangelical Lutheran Ovambo-Kavango Church and Paster Paulus Gowaseb, moderator of the Evangelical Lutheran Church of South West Africa. Their churches had memberships of 180,000 and 110,000, respectively, and the letter was widely disseminated in their churches throughout the land. The letter indicated various violations of human rights, such as the denial of freedom of movement, freedom of expression, and freedom of association. It called for an end to the contract system and for a peaceful solution to the problems of the territory, with independence as the ultimate end. South African Institute of Race Relations, *A Survey of Race Relations, 1971* (Johannesburg: SAIRR, 1972), 338–39; Peter Katjavivi, Per Frostin, and Kaire Mbuende, *Church and Liberation in Namibia* (London: Pluto Press, 1989), 12–15. The text of the letter is reprinted in Katjavivi, Frostin, and Mbuende, *Church and Liberation,* 134–36.

78. Following talks with church leaders, De Wet made a public statement denying the allegations that the contract system was a form of slavery. He said it was a purely voluntary arrangement and that men who objected to it did not have to enter into contracts (*A Survey of Race Relations, 1972,* 432). Gordon ("Notes on the History of Labour Action," 14) gives another precipitating factor: that the Population Group Classification Act was implemented in mid-1970, making photographic identification cards compulsory and thereby precluding the possibility of "identity switching" among workers. According to Gordon, "This act did much to heighten the sense of injustice the Ovambo workers felt and probably was a major factor in creating the necessary degree of worker consciousness needed for the 1971 strike to be as widespread as it was."

79. Max, "Die Geestelike en Materiele Situasie van die Kontrakarbeiders," 69. The dislike of the system culminated in the general strike of 1971–72 in Namibia: "Because the bad conditions had taught the workers, the difficulties had taught the workers, the history had taught the workers, the apartheid history had taught the workers to struggle to get out from the slavery system" (Gerson Max, author interview, Windhoek, 8 January 1993).

80. Helao Shityuwete, author interview, Windhoek, 5 February 1993. See also Shityuwete, *Never Follow the Wolf,* esp. 13–31.

81. Nehova, "Price of Liberation," 71–78, and Ya Otto, *Battlefront Namibia,* 141–45. Other accounts of the strike include Anonymous, "The Roads to Freedom in Nami-

bia: Strike and Political Protest," Paper presented to the Namibia Fights for Freedom Conference convened by SWAPO, Brussels, 26–28 May 1972; Simons, "Namibian Challenge"; SWAPO, *To Be Born a Nation;* SWAPO, *Trade Union Rights;* Cronje and Cronje, *Workers of Namibia;* Moorsom, "Labour Consciousness"; Marcelle Kooy, "The Contract Labour System and the Ovambo Crisis of 1971 in South West Africa," *African Studies Review* 16 (1973): 83–106; *South African Labour Bulletin,* "Focus on Namibia," 4, nos. 1–2 (1978): 1–194; *Special Report of the Director General, 1973; A Survey of Race Relations, 1972;* David De Beer, "The Ovambo Strike," *South African Outlook* 102 (1972): 25–27; Barbara Rogers, "Namibia's General Strike," *Africa Today* 19 (1972): 3–8; Loffler, "Labour and Politics;" *Namibia News,* November–December 1971, January– February 1972; *Sechaba,* "The Great Namibian Strike," 6, 4, April 1972, 19–24.

82. SWAPO's Consultative Congress at Tanga, Tanzania, 1969–70, had apparently made provision for the establishment of a Women's Council, a Council of SWAPO Elders, and a Department of Youth, according to the organisation structure as given in SWAPO, "Special Report from the Consultative Congress in Tanga, Tanzania," *Namibia News* 3 (January–March 1970): 7. Leys and Saul ("SWAPO Inside Namibia," 71) call the years 1971 to 1975 "the years of the SWAPO Youth League," though they give no date for its inception *inside* Namibia. Nehova, author interview, Windhoek, 29 June 1993, said that at the time of the strike the SYL was "not yet structured formally"; rather this followed the strike in 1972 or 1973. David Soggot (*Namibia,* 76), who acted as an attorney for many activists inside Namibia from the early 1970s, says that 1973 "ushered in a startling efflorescence of SWAPO and SWAPO Youth League activity" and that *after* the general strike "it [the Youth League] struck out on its own with growing confidence."

83. In SWAPO parlance, "youth" refers to anyone thirty-five or under, while "students" are those actually in school, more often secondary school, but also university. Jannie De Wet, "Bantu Commissioner" from 1970 to 1978, says he has "no doubt" that the strike was organized and that it was organized by SWAPO, in particular the youth who were "the biggest supporters of the idea" (De Wet, author interview, Windhoek, 12 July 1993).

84. Kandy Nehova says that there were no "formalized" trade unions at the time of the strike (Nehova, interview). John Ya Otto says there was not an NUNW presence in Namibia until the late 1970s (Ya Otto, interview). In an article about the 1971–72 strike in the first issue of the *Namibian Worker* to be published inside Namibia (1988, no. 1, no page), a question asks how it was possible for so many workers to come together ("saam te staan") in 1971, given that "hulle het nie eens vakbonde gehad nie" [they did not even have trade unions]. The origins of the NUNW inside Namibia will be pursued in the following chapter.

85. "It was not a spontaneous labor action against employers, it was an organized political act and it is us, the students, who organized it in our schools and then we came to implement it here [Windhoek, Walvis Bay]" (Nehova, interview). Much of the account given in the text comes from this same interview.

86. For more on the student strikes and the role of students in organizing the

general strike see Ya Otto, *Battlefront Namibia,* 141; Leys and Saul, "SWAPO Inside Namibia," 71–73; SWAPO, *To Be Born a Nation,* 187–92; De Beer, "Ovambo Strike," 25; Moorsom, "Labour Consciousness," 221; Cronje and Cronje, *Workers of Namibia,* 118; Soggot, *Namibia,* 47; NUNW and COSATU, *Namibian Workers Organise* (Johannesburg: COSATU, 1990), 26; *Namibian Worker,* no. 1, 1988.

87. Ben Ulenga, author interview, Windhoek, 28 July 1994.

88. Reporter J. M. Smith, of the *Windhoek Advertiser,* wrote on 13 December 1971: "Slowly through this year I saw the tension building up in that place [the Ovambo Compound]. In fact the Advertiser cautioned at the beginning of this year and at the end of last year that trouble was brewing in that place. Newsmen doing their beat knew what was coming." In fact, it seems it was not easy for newsmen to "do their beat" because special permission from the Municipal Offices was required to get anywhere near the Ovambo Compound; during the strike itself reporters had to face the "persistent refusal" of the authorities to say anything or allow them into Katutura.

89. De Wet says that from the moment he took over as commissioner general in 1970 the resentment of people toward the contract labor system was clear to him: "In the minds of these people they had one big grudge and that was the restriction. They had been part of the whole of Namibia . . . now they were restricted to the North, there was the fence and they couldn't go beyond that fence without permission and the only way they could get out—they were not even allowed to come out for shopping and to buy things down south—the only way they were allowed to come out was through the labor association, and through that organization." De Wet says that he told employers in Tsumeb in 1971: "I have heard the request of these people and their main complaint. They have referred to the 'draad'—'Odalate'—that's the fence that must be broken down and they must be allowed not to go through [SWANLA] because they say SWANLA made a lot of money out of them. The labor organization, they said it was a slave trade, that's what they said, they said it was a slave trade." De Wet further says he felt "at the time, this thing, it was a very fair request from their side, to be allowed to have freer movement to the South and come and negotiate their own contracts with their employers," but his appeals and warnings to the South African government went unheeded until it was too late (De Wet, interview).

90. In Nehova, interview, and in Nehova, "Price of Liberation," Nehova gives the date set for the start of the strike as 11 December (which was a Saturday). But he also refers to 10 December as a Monday. In fact, the strike started on Monday, 13 December, in Windhoek and appears to have begun only a few days later in Walvis Bay. Simons, "Namibian Challenge," 3, and *A Survey of Race Relations, 1972,* 433, give the date for the start of the strike in Walvis Bay as Tuesday, 14 December (what would have been Tuesday, 11 December, if Monday were 10 December). According to the *Windhoek Advertiser,* by 17 December ten thousand workers were on strike, half from Windhoek and most of the rest from different mines. The thirty-six hundred workers in Walvis Bay were expected to go on strike that day, after being paid. Divisional Commissioner of Police Brigadier E. de W. Brandt was reported as saying that the strike was well organized although he did not know what was behind it: the strike was "too well-timed

and too persistent to be attributed to mere chance" (quoted in Simons, "Namibian Challenge," 5).

91. "On our side, I think it [the comment] came at the right time. On their side, I think it came at the wrong time. He [De Wet] was not grasping the ability of the students to organize, not only the students, but to organize everybody in Namibia. He did not have that, you know, understanding . . . he was making a lot of these stupid remarks. We capitalized on that and we simply took it to the workers and said: 'Look this is what they are saying: If we come here on contract, it is because we want to. Now we must say that we don't want to come and work.' It was very easy for any worker to understand, very, very simple" (Nehova, interview).

92. See the "strike diary" of Leonard Nghipandulua in *Namibia News,* January–February 1972.

93. Nehova, "Price of Liberation," 75.

94. Simons, "Namibian Challenge," 3–5; *Windhoek Advertiser,* 13 December 1971.

95. *Windhoek Advertiser,* various issues, December 1971 and January 1972.

96. Kane-Berman, "Contract Labour," preface, gives the figure of 13,500 striking workers. Simons, "Namibian Challenge," 10, puts the total number of striking workers at 20,000 by the end of January. She says that the following industries or sectors were virtually paralyzed by the strike: mining, commerce, fishing, construction, railways, harbors, dairies, breweries, airports, and sanitation services.

97. *Windhoek Advertiser,* 17 December 1971.

98. The border was important to the territory not only because it was an international boundary but also because of its significance to the beef industry. Cattle producers feared that the lung sickness prevalent in the North (including Angola) would be more likely to spread if that border area were not properly controlled (De Wet, interview). The border fence was long a point of contention for the Ovambo people who lived on both sides of it. Within one week over one hundred kilometers of the fence were destroyed (De Beer, "Ovambo Strike," 25).

99. *Windhoek Advertiser,* various issues, January and February 1972. Gerhard Toetemeyer (*Namibia Old and New: Traditional and Modern Leaders in Ovamboland* [London: Hurst, 1978], 163) highlights the striking workers' "ill feelings against the traditional leaders which was already prevalent [and] received new impetus" with the general strike and the workers' return to the North. Toetemeyer writes that one SWANLA official in Grootfontein told returning workers "that the headmen and chiefs were really answerable for the poor wages, since the existing salary structure had been agreed on with them."

100. De Wet describes a situation of absolute chaos when suddenly ten thousand striking workers—"people without work, unemployed"—were unloaded in the North: "What they did, they started to get pangas . . . they started to cause a lot of problems in Ovambo, with homemade guns. They destroyed the fence between Ovambo and Angola . . . they broke down that whole thing . . . we had no control whatsoever and this lasted for December and January and then they started to shoot and kill some of the headmen, those headmen who were working with us. And they drew up lists, protest lists, and

complained about slavery and all that . . . I didn't know what to do . . . there was no law and order. Everything just went bang . . . there was no peace in Ovambo and of course the mines couldn't work, the fishing industry couldn't work." De Wet says that he insisted that law and order be restored and that the workers' demands then be given serious consideration. In a meeting with South African prime minister John Vorster it was decided to increase the police and military presence in the North but also to arm "the traditional power, the chiefs and headmen," which they then proceeded to do (De Wet, interview).

101. Kane-Berman, "Contract Labour," Appendix III, gives the full list of demands; see also *Windhoek Advertiser*, 12 January 1972; *A Survey of Race Relations, 1972*, 435.

102. Kane-Berman, "Contract Labour," 6; *Windhoek Advertiser*, 19, 20 January 1972. The text of the agreement is replicated in Simons, "Namibian Challenge," Annexure 3.

103. The newspaper reports are cited in *A Survey of Race Relations, 1972*, 435. According to Kane-Berman, "Contract Labour," 25–26, who was then a researcher for the South African Institute of Race Relations in Namibia just after the strike, this seemed unlikely given the unrest in Ovamboland and the fact that the new system differed so little from the old. In addition, according to many of those interviewed by Kane-Berman, Radio Ovambo was known for misleading people.

104. Kane-Berman, "Contract Labour," 7–11. He replicates the new and old contracts in Appendixes I and II, respectively.

105. Kane-Berman, "Labour Situation," 3.

106. De Wet, interview. Kandy Nehova puts great emphasis on the need to do away with the contract labor system so as to move more freely and thus be able to organize more freely: "We thought that once we have succeeded in doing away with or abolishing the contract labor system, then in that way we could have improved the movement of the people and in that way the movement of our political activities too. We would then be able to freely move around the country, organize workers, organize students, organize the people in order to broaden the scope of liberation. And that was to supplement of course the [military] arm of SWAPO" (Nehova, interview).

107. *Special Report of the Director General, 1973*, 31.

108. *A Survey of Race Relations, 1972*, 439–40; Kane-Berman, "Contract Labour," 32; *Windhoek Advertiser*, 16 January 1973.

109. *Windhoek Advertiser*, 24 January 1972.

110. *Windhoek Advertiser*, 27 January 1972; also other issues from January and February 1972.

111. *Special Report of the Director General, 1973*, 28.

112. *Windhoek Advertiser*, 7 July 1972; Toetemeyer, *Namibia Old and New*, 161–62.

113. *Windhoek Advertiser*, 14 July, 6 September 1972, 8 January, 16 August 1973.

114. Gottschalk, "South African Labour Policy," 93.

115. *A Survey of Race Relations, 1972*, 438.

116. Republic of South Africa, *South West Africa Survey, 1974* (Pretoria: Government Printer, 1975), 59–60.

117. Paul Hartmann, "The Role of Mining in the Economy of South West Africa, 1950–1985" (M.Sc. thesis, University of Stellenbosch, 1986), 321 (Table A.37).

118. While wages may well have been increasing, measured against the Household Subsistence Level they were not increasing fast enough. After April 1973 the Institute for Planning Research at the University of Port Elizabeth in South Africa began publishing household subsistence level figures twice a year for the major urban centers of South Africa and later for Windhoek (and still later for Tsumeb and Swakopmund) once a year. As well as a composite (monthly) Household Subsistence Level figure, the biannual reports would give housing, transport, clothing, food, and utility costs. For April 1976 the Household Subsistence Level figure for Windhoek blacks was R141.63; for coloureds it was R171.08.

119. The number of white secondary students peaked in 1976 at 7,550. The falling numbers most likely reflect the only real exodus of whites that took place in Namibia around 1978–80, during which time it appeared that independence for the territory was imminent. While the 1970 population census showed a white population of 89,917, the 1981 population census recorded a white population of 76,400. Education figures are from Leistner, Esterhuysen, and Malan, *Namibia/SWA Prospectus,* 57.

120. Ellis, *Future for Namibia 4,* 85.

121. *South African Labour Bulletin,* "Focus on Namibia," 32–35.

122. *A Survey of Race Relations, 1972,* 440.

123. *Windhoek Advertiser,* 6 June 1972.

124. *Windhoek Advertiser,* 20 June 1972.

125. *Windhoek Advertiser,* 29 May 1973.

126. *Windhoek Advertiser,* 29 March 1976.

127. *Windhoek Advertiser,* 23 March 1973.

128. *Windhoek Advertiser,* 8 October 1976, 22 December 1977.

129. Osita Eze, "Labour Regime and the Namibian Worker: Some Reflections on Human Rights," *International and Comparative Law* 9 (1976): 482.

130. Report quoted in *Special Report of the Director General, 1974,* 55–56.

131. Sporadic attempts had been made to organize black workers in Namibia before the 1970s, centered mostly around the Luderitz fishing industry. Katjavivi, *History of Resistance,* 19–20, cites a South African administrator's 1924 report that "several unions were in existence" in Luderitz at the time, including the "Cape Town Coloured institution known as the International and Commercial Workers' Union." During the 1950s, the Cape Town–based Food and Canning Workers Union attempted to organize canning workers, again in Luderitz Bay. After initial successes these efforts were prohibited through use of the Suppression of Communism Act. See also First, *South West Africa,* 196–97.

132. ILO, *Labour and Discrimination,* 71–73. The ordinance did not prohibit black workers from forming trade unions as such, but they could not be registered nor could they apply for the establishment of a conciliation board or participate in any other dispute resolution mechanisms. In addition, black workers were effectively prohibited from engaging in strikes.

133. Francois Adonis, author interview, Windhoek, 22 October 1992.

134. SWAPO, "Special Report from the Consultative Congress," 7. According to Shipanga, a close colleague of Mifima, there was a Labour Section of SWAPO, although not a department in full before the Tanga Congress. Shipanga says that Mifima, already in 1968, was traveling to Brussels and other European capitals on behalf of this Labour Section. Again, according to Shipanga, Mifima's labor activities were of long standing, dating from 1958 in Cape Town from where he would travel to Namibia and attempt to organize workers (Shipanga, interview).

135. SWAPO, *To Be Born a Nation,* 192.

136. Ya Otto, interview. Peltola, "Role of the NUNW," 11, notes that the congress documents "make no reference to the need for a trade union." He cites the documents to the congress contained in Y. Gorbunov, *Namibia—A Struggle for Independence: A Collection of Articles, Documents and Speeches* (Moscow: Progress Publishers, 1988). One of SWAPO's own histories (*SWAPO Information on SWAPO: An Historical Profile* [Lusaka: SWAPO Department of Information and Publicity, 1978]) makes absolutely no mention in its description of the Tanga conference of the Department of Labour or the NUNW although it devotes considerable space to other newly created structures. Nor does Katjavivi (*History of Resistance,* 104–5) make any reference to labor or trade unions in his brief summary of the Tanga congress.

137. Solomon Mifima, "The Labour Situation in Namibia," *Namibia Documentation 2* (East Berlin: SWAPO, 1972), no page number.

138. *Windhoek Advertiser,* 3 May 1974.

139. The same ILO publication to report this also noted in 1974 that "a National Union of Namibian Workers (NUNW), a trade union body affiliated to SWAPO, operates from Lusaka" (*Special Report of the Director General, 1974,* 56). Mifima, now deceased, could not be interviewed.

140. *Special Report of the Director General, 1976,* 38.

141. John Saul and Colin Leys ("SWAPO: The Politics of Exile," in *Namibia's Liberation Struggle: The Two-Edged Sword,* ed. Leys and Saul [London: James Currey, Athens: Ohio University Press, 1995]) provide the most comprehensive account of this crisis, which is usually misleadingly referred to as the "Shipanga crisis." In brief, according to Saul and Leys, this crisis was primarily about the demands from within the SWAPO rank and rile for more democratic procedures and greater leadership accountability and membership participation in the exile movement—demands that would ultimately not be met. The demands (for example, for the convening of a SWAPO congress) came, in particular, from SWAPO Youth Leaguers who were part of the mass exodus of youth from Namibia after the fall of the Portuguese in Angola in 1974 and from SWAPO military cadres—some belonging to the same exodus and others already fighting in the People's Liberation Army of Namibia (PLAN) before the exodus. See also Katjavivi, *History of Resistance,* 105–8, and Shipanga, *In Search of Freedom,* 98–144.

142. Up to two thousand SWAPO "dissidents" were detained in Mboroma in Zambia from mid-1976. Most of them were eventually "rehabilitated" although some two to three hundred chose protection of the United Nations High Commission for

Refugees and remained at a camp in Maheba in northwestern Zambia until they were repatriated with other Namibian exiles in 1989 (Saul and Leys, "SWAPO," 49–50).

143. See ibid., 50–52. Ya Otto chaired the commission and wrote the report for SWAPO's internal investigation into the affair: "Report of the Findings and Recommendations of the John Ya Otto Commission of Inquiry into Circumstances which led to the Revolt of SWAPO Cadres between April 1974 and June 1976." This report sought to portray the crisis as a bid for power by SWAPO dissidents, in particular, by Shipanga.

144. Ya Otto, interview.

145. *A Survey of Race Relations, 1973,* 382.

146. See Leistner, Esterhuysen, and Malan, *Namibia/SWA Prospectus,* 6–7; Pieter Esterhuysen, "The Decisive Years," in *Namibia 1990: An Africa Institute Country Survey,* ed. Erich Leistner and Pieter Esterhuysen (Pretoria: Africa Institute of South Africa, 1991), 44–50; RSA, *South West Africa Survey, 1974,* 29–32; *Windhoek Advertiser,* various issues, 1973–77.

147. These provisions were contained in the SWA Constitution Amendment Act No. 95 of 1977, which amended the SWA Constitution Act No. 39 of 1968 and the SWA Affairs Act No. 25 of 1969.

148. *Windhoek Advertiser,* various issues, 1975–77.

149. "I do not believe in social and racial discrimination. I feel that it should be voluntary. If people want to associate, let them associate" (Dirk Mudge, author interview, Windhoek, 30 June 1993). Mudge says that by the early 1970s many Namibians did not trust the motives of the South Africans in addressing the Namibian problem; indeed, they felt that "they misused, as a matter of fact, the Namibian problem in many ways to keep the attention away, to distract attention from South Africa." This, and a feeling that Namibians should determine their own destiny, led to his attempts at an internally directed resolution to the problem, for example, the Turnhalle Conference, according to Mudge.

150. *A Survey of Race Relations, 1973, 1974, 1975, 1976, 1977; Windhoek Advertiser,* various issues, 1973–77; Leys and Saul, "SWAPO Inside Namibia"; Soggot, *Namibia,* 76–111; Katjavivi, *History of Resistance,* 74–83.

151. *A Survey of Race Relations, 1973, 1974.* See also Soggot, *Namibia,* 61–69; *Namibia News,* September–October 1973.

152. Soggot, *Namibia,* 101; Katjavivi, *History of Resistance,* 78–81.

153. Richard Hyman, "Third World Strikes in International Perspective," *Development and Change* 10 (1979): 322–23.

154. Nehova says that from the strike workers and others became not only more conscientized but also more confident that they had the means to bring about their own liberation and that they could achieve independence (Nehova, interview). Interestingly, De Wet provides essentially the same assessment of the strike: "That strike did lead to a lot of changes and I would also say politically, it was the first success of SWAPO in this country, where they used the labor force in the first instance to establish their success and to broaden their support. Because those people claimed that after the strike, you see, we, we are forceful ourselves if we stand together and we do it in an organized

way we can achieve something. And one should never, never underestimate the influence of that strike on the whole development of the political scene since then—to where we find ourselves now and to the broadening of SWAPO's support" (De Wet, interview).

CHAPTER THREE

1. SWAPO, *To Be Born a Nation*, 268; SWAPO, *Struggle for Trade Union Rights*.

2. *South African Labour Bulletin*, "Focus on Namibia" 4, 1-2 (1978): 36-44.

3. Colin Leys and John Saul ("SWAPO Inside Namibia," 74-76) provide an account of this and the subsequent meeting in Katutura in 1977. According to Leys and Saul, the Walvis Bay congress was initiated by "younger and more highly educated [SWAPO] activists" still inside Namibia. One aim of the congress "was to reassert the organisation's vitality inside Namibia and, in particular, to confirm the internal party's identification with the external leadership, which South African propaganda was representing as having broken down; to elect a new internal leadership; and to reassert Namibia's claim to Walvis Bay by holding a congress there." See also Sue Cullinan, "The Namibian Dispute," *Work in Progress* 24 (1982): 36-39.

4. Jason Angula, author interview, Walvis Bay, 23 July 1993. At that point SWAPO in exile had the positions of secretary and assistant secretary for economic and legal affairs and secretary and assistant secretary for labor (as established at Tanga—although few of the original officeholders still held those positions); at the Central Committee meeting outside Lusaka 28 July to 1 August 1976 different positions of secretary for legal affairs and secretary for economic affairs were apparently created and a secretary for labor retained. See SWAPO, "Special Report from the Consultative Congress in Tanga, Tanzania"; SWAPO, *Constitution of the SWAPO of Namibia*, Adopted by the meeting of the Central Committee, Lusaka, Zambia, 28 July-1 August 1976.

5. Angula, interview. This splitting of the portfolio took place at a National Conference of SWAPO held in Katutura, 24-25 March 1977, where SWAPO's National Executive was enlarged in accordance with the revised constitutional proposals drawn up in February 1977 (creating the new positions as well as regional councils). The new positions were reportedly created, in part, to accommodate some of the southern political groupings that had recently joined SWAPO, such as Gaomab's Namibian African Democratic People's Organisation (NADPO). See Cullinan, "Namibian Dispute," 39.

6. Angula, interview.

7. Ibid.

8. Neville Rubin, then working at the ILO, recalls being approached by John Ya Otto, from exile, with a request to help write a constitution for "the workers' organization" (Neville Rubin, author interview, Windhoek, 13 January 1993).

9. *South African Labour Bulletin*, "Focus on Namibia," 190-94. The introduction to this special issue refers to "the embryonic general trade union, NAWU." Portions of the exact same draft constitution ("Windhoek, 1977") are reprinted in SWAPO, *To Be Born a Nation*, 269, as the draft constitution of the National Union of Namibian Workers.

10. SWAPO, *SWAPO Information on SWAPO,* 28.

11. Gerson Max, author interview, Windhoek, 8 January 1993. Gillian Cronje and Suzanne Cronje (*Workers of Namibia,* 106) cite a report to the Lutheran World Federation by Swedish journalist Eric Sjoquist of his 1977 visit with Pastor Max to a "trade union meeting in a church in Windhoek." At the meeting about twenty-five people reportedly discussed "proposals for a constitution for forming a trade union." Sjoquist called the meeting a "historic event" because "there have not been any trade unions in Namibia up until now."

12. Pekka Peltola, author interview, Windhoek, 2 January 1993. A member of the SWAPO National Executive Committee in Namibia at the time recalls "definitely some relationship" between especially the two secretaries for labor, Ya Otto and Angula (Author interview 50, Katutura, 5 November 1992). Certainly by 1979 there was fairly extensive contact between the two. According to Angula, Anton Lubowski, who made his first trip to Lusaka to meet SWAPO in exile in late 1979 (for other reasons) and who had a passport, later acted as a liaison (Angula interview). See also Molly Lubowski and Marita Van der Vyver, *Anton Lubowski: Paradox of a Man* (Strand: Queillerie Publisher, 1992), 49.

13. Cronje and Cronje, *Workers of Namibia,* 105; NUNW/COSATU, *Namibian Workers Organise,* 30.

14. This account is based largely on Pickering's own recollection of events in interviews with the author, Windhoek, 11 October 1992 and 25 July 1993, although the basic outline is known among Namibian trade unionists and others. See also "Inside Rossing Mine: An Interview with Arthur Pickering," *Action on Namibia,* November 1981. The account is confirmed, inter alia, by another employee at Rossing at the time, author interview 72, Windhoek, 26 March 1993; Angula, interview; John Ya Otto, author interview, Windhoek, 23 March 1993; and by MacFarlane, "Labour Control."

15. Barbara Rogers, "Notes on the Labour Conditions at the Rossing Mine," *South African Labour Bulletin,* 4, nos. 1–2 (1978): 140–44, documents working conditions on the mine at the time. Complaints among workers included living quarters of sixteen to twenty men per room, poor food which prompted a strike in November 1976, early morning raids by the police, discriminatory medical care, compensation policies in a highly dangerous working environment, and falling wages for black workers in comparison with those for coloured and white workers.

16. Carlsson was sent to Namibia by the Swedish LO/TCO. Using a model particularly inappropriate to Namibia at the time (and still today), Carlsson, who had never been out of Sweden, was supposed to help organize Namibia's largely illiterate workforce on the basis of "study circles." According to Pickering, Carlsson also had no appreciation for the political situation in Namibia at the time and therefore of the need to act discreetly. The Swedish LO continued to work with SWAPO and the NUNW in exile during the 1980s, for example, by sending instructors; the *Namibian Worker* of January 1984 notes that "the cooperation between NUNW and the Swedish LO/TCO Council for International Cooperation continues. It started in 1977–78 with attempts to establish trade union study circles inside Namibia." Pekka Peltola, interview, also remembers the Swedish involvement inside and outside Namibia.

17. Various reasons are put forward for the December 1978 strike. According to MacFarlane ("Labour Control," 210–16), the strike was sparked off on 20 December when workers received individual notification of their new job grades and pay rates resulting from a job evaluation exercise which had just taken place and refused to accept the envelopes containing the notification. The strike lasted until 28 December. MacFarlane, judging from the strikers' demands (for a basic minimum wage, a wage increase, no victimization of strikers, and full pay for the duration of the strike) calls the motivation for the strike "purely economic." Arthur Pickering found much confusion among the striking workers—"like most of these wildcat strikes"—and in ensuing discussions with workers about their grievances found the strike to reflect a pervasive anger and feeling of dissatisfaction that had existed on the mine for some time, in particular, concerning racial discrimination (Pickering, interview). Others link the strike to political developments at the time, in particular to the fact that Namibia did not gain its independence in December 1978 as had been so prominently assured. In addition, the new Paterson job grading system and the way it was implemented were sources of great tension.

18. Hilton Villet (like Pickering, trained at the University of the Western Cape), a personnel officer at Rossing and one of the mine workers' first shop stewards, went through Pickering's files after beginning work at the mine in 1985. He found, on the basis of the files, that indeed management had been "gunning for" Pickering: "They really worked him out." Villet was acutely aware of his predecessor's experience at Rossing, feeling that this was in large part why it was so very difficult for him (Villet) to get a job at the mine (Villet, author interview, Windhoek, 31 May 1993).

19. SWAPO, *Struggle for Trade Union Rights,* 35, reports that "through 1977 and 1978, NUNW branches in most of the major towns and mines played a leading role both locally and nationally in pressing employers to negotiate with their workers over basic issues, and in protecting workers against violent harassment by the police and hired thugs of the Turnhalle puppet parties." Similar reports appear in SWAPO, *To Be Born a Nation;* Anonymous, "Namibian Workers and the National Union of Namibian Workers," in *Trade Union Action on Namibian Uranium,* Report of a Seminar for West European Trade Unions organized by SWAPO of Namibia in cooperation with the Namibia Support Committee, 1982; and later publications (based on these).

20. According to John Ya Otto, interview: "At that time, 1978, the Turnhalle activities were in motion and they were organizing for elections and so we were to fight against these elections and so the activities to, among the workers, was that we should defy these elections and boycott these elections and so on. So it was from that point of view really that those sort of organizations, and Pickering and Boonzaaier and the rest of them, were very instrumental in the time that they were working at Rossing. That was also the time that we had also sort of succeeded in mobilizing for funds and clandestinely getting people to get out from Namibia and get into either some of the neighboring states, the Frontline States, to have them in a clandestine manner coming out and have discussions and then they went back and organized."

21. Pickering, interview.

22. As Gay Seidman (*Manufacturing Militance,* 184) notes, FOSATU "dominated the first phase of legalized black unionism" in South Africa and so was a natural choice for Namibian trade unionists seeking advice and assistance in the late 1970s. The distinct approach of the FOSATU unions was also important, namely, a "workerist" philosophy that emphasized factory-level organization and "rejected political alliances, insisting instead on forming an 'independent' working class organization" (p. 186) — not a philosophy that would likely have been embraced by SWAPO in exile. A matter of considerable concern to emerging black trade unionists in South Africa, according to Seidman (p. 187), was "what would be the role of the new labor movement in the national liberation movement?"

23. See Saul and Leys, "SWAPO," 52, and Katjavivi, *History of Resistance,* 108–9, for some details of this meeting.

24. Saul and Leys, "SWAPO," 52. Among other things, the Political Programme states SWAPO's determination to "unite all Namibian people, particularly the working class, the peasantry and progressive intellectuals into a vanguard party capable of safe-guarding national independence and of building a classless, non-exploitative society based on the ideals and principles of scientific socialism" (SWAPO, *Political Programme of the SWAPO of Namibia,* Adopted by the meeting of the Central Committee, Lusaka, Zambia, 28 July–1 August 1976, 6). Katjavivi, *History of Resistance,* 109, writes that the document "did not represent a sudden change in SWAPO's approach"; rather it had to be seen in the context of developments in southern Africa and of the inability or unwillingness of the United Nations and the Western powers to resolve the Namibian crisis.

25. SWAPO, *Constitution of the SWAPO of Namibia,* 22. The constitution (p. 5) also makes provision for affiliate membership to SWAPO, for example, by a trade union, student union, or professional organization, "which accepts the aims and objectives of SWAPO." The wings of SWAPO are given in the constitution (p. 33) as the People's Liberation Army of Namibia, the SWAPO Youth League, the SWAPO Women's Council, and the SWAPO Elder's Council. This constitution was amended and a new one adopted at the Second Enlarged Central Committee meeting, 17–20 April 1983 in Cabuta in Kwanza Sul. In the 1983 constitution the NUNW is added as one of four wings or affiliate organizations able to send representatives to a SWAPO congress. By 1983 the National Executive Committee had been transformed into the Political Bureau of the Central Committee. The duties of the secretary for labor remained the same from one constitution to the next, except that, as with all national officers, from the president down after 1983, he or she would "be accountable to the Central Committee and its Political Bureau" (SWAPO, *Constitution of the SWAPO of Namibia,* Amended and adopted by the Second Enlarged Central Committee meeting, Cabuta, Kwanza-Sul Province, Angola, 17–20 August 1983).

26. International Labour Organisation, *Special Report of the Director General on the Application of the Declaration Concerning the Policy of Apartheid in South Africa [and Namibia],* 1974 (Geneva: ILO, 1975).

27. *Special Report of the Director General, 1975, 1976.*

28. *Special Report of the Director General, 1977.*

29. Rubin interview; Ya Otto interview; Marita Koerner-Damman, "Labour in Namibia at Independence," Mimeo (Frankfurt: Goethe University, 1990), 7.

30. "Years of Struggle, Years of Support," *Namibian Worker*, 21 March–4 April 1990, 6–7; this article is an account, provided by John Ya Otto, of "international support to NUNW." Trade unions from China and Cuba also provided training, resources, and facilities for the future Namibian trade unionists in exile. British and French trade unionists showed their support by refusing to handle "illegally exported" minerals from Namibia and by spearheading campaigns for boycotts of South African products (in addition to providing resources and training). Portuguese trade unionists helped the NUNW in exile participate in annual sessions of the ILO. Unions from "as far afield as Japan, Indochina, India, Australia, New Zealand, Brazil, Nicaragua, Panama and so on made it possible for the NUNW to fulfill its task." Similarly, trade unions all over Africa, for example, in Angola, Zimbabwe, and the Congo, and regional organizations such as the Southern African Trade Union Coordinating Conference and the Organisation of African Trade Union Unity assisted the NUNW and SWAPO Department of Labour, according to Ya Otto.

31. Peltola interview; and author interviews with three participants in labor activities in exile: interview 29, Windhoek, 3 November 1992; interview 68, Windhoek, 25 June 1993; interview 69, Windhoek, 25 June 1993.

32. Author interviews in note 31. The main organisation involved was SAK, the Central Organisation of Finnish Trade Unions. Peltola was one of the early instructors sent to the SWAPO camps by SAK.

33. The first issue of the *Namibian Worker* ("Organ of the NUNW") was published in October 1983 by the NUNW (at the following address: Nduuvu Nangolo Trade Union Centre, Kwanza Sul, c/o [SWAPO] Department of Labour, Luanda). *Namibian Worker*, various issues, 1983–89. From 1988 another *Namibian Worker*, very different from this one, was published in Windhoek.

34. "Years of Struggle, Years of Support," *Namibian Worker*, 21 March–4 April 1990, 6–7; also Rubin, interview.

35. Ya Otto speaks of mobilizing the "world trade union movement" on behalf of the NUNW, in particular the ICFTU, the WFTU, and the WCL (World Confederation of Labour). Ya Otto, interview. One labor activist from exile, interview 69, recalls that the NUNW in exile was first affiliated to the ICFTU and then "switched" to the WFTU. From 1984 the *Namibian Worker* usually carried one story on the WFTU and its activities.

36. Pickering, interview. The issue of international affiliation became an important and divisive one after independence. At the March–April 1991 Extraordinary Congress of the NUNW, delegates voted in favor of a Mineworkers Union of Namibia resolution that the NUNW would "maintain its policy of non-alignment." The congress further expressed the view that "it does not feel that NUNW has ever been properly affiliated to the Eastern Block based World Federation of Trade Unions, WFTU. The decision to affiliate was taken by NUNW leaders in exile—not by Namibian workers themselves." At the congress there was also a resolution from the Namibian Food and Allied Union

"confirming the affiliation" to the WFTU which was, however, rejected (*Namibian Worker,* May 1991, 13).

37. Author interviews with participants in trade union activity in exile: interview 29, interview 68, interview 69, interview 80, Windhoek, 27 November 1992. Neville Rubin says, in talking about ILO fellowships: "This was SWAPO not NUNW, but they were all mixed up. There was no clear distinction in fact, certainly not in my mind" (Rubin, interview).

38. Peltola, interview.

39. Angula, "African Workers," 62, 64, 68. Angula has since strongly disavowed this model.

40. "Reactions Smashed in Poland," *Combatant,* 3, 7, February 1982, 7–8.

41. Saul and Leys, "SWAPO," 56, 55; see also Erika Thiro Beukes, Attie Beukes, and Hewat Beukes, *Namibia: A Struggle Betrayed* (Rehoboth: Akasia Drukkery, 1986); and David Niddrie, "Namibia: The Detentions," *Work in Progress* 61 (1989): 21–23.

42. Africa Watch (*Accountability in Namibia: Human Rights and the Transition to Democracy* [New York: Human Rights Watch, 1992], 68–91) has published a chilling account of SWAPO's "detainee" experience (as well as of South Africa's atrocities against Namibian refugees, detainees, and civilians, especially during the war period). In interviews with dozens of former detainees, the report tells of routine beatings and torture (beaten with salted sticks and tire strips, buried alive, and so on) until false confessions were extracted. After the "confessions," the accused were taken to camps in the vicinity of Lubango, where they were "housed" in dungeons ("pits dug in the earth, roofed with poles, leaves, tarpaulins, sand and sheet metal") and fed only meager amounts of water, cornmeal, and rice. The dungeons were dark and hot, had very poor to no ventilation, no toilet facilities, and sometimes held up to one hundred people at a time. Disease—including beri-beri, scurvy, malnutrition, and infection—was rampant, and many died. Women were held in separate dungeons, and even their children were imprisoned in the camps.

43. Saul and Leys, "SWAPO," 55. "Die gatte"—as the dungeons of Lubango are widely known in Afrikaans (meaning "the holes")—were certainly not directed only against the labor activists, as Saul and Leys and others demonstrate. This incident is usually interpreted in ethnic terms, with the feeling being that those arrested were predominantly Nama-Damara or Herero-speaking or indeed that they were "Ombuiti"—Ovambo-speaking people from central and southern Namibia, in other words, from the urban areas. More often than not it was also the more educated and politically progressive SWAPO cadres who found themselves in the "gatte." In the later years of the liberation struggle (from 1985) some of those who fled Namibia into exile, such as striking workers or students, went straight to the "gatte." Some SWAPO students being educated abroad, who realized what was happening, decided to prolong their studies until independence rather than return to the SWAPO camps. Indeed, some of those who attempted to clear their names of accusations against them and returned to Angola found themselves in the dungeons.

44. Peltola, "Role of the NUNW," 2. According to Peltola, such sentiments were

expressed by Hage Geingob, then director of the United Nations Institute for Namibia (UNIN), at the opening of a joint NUNW/SAK seminar in Lusaka on 4 August 1981. Peltola, interview, adds that there was another public discussion of this nature at which the SWAPO leadership expressed similar views at UNIN in 1988. One labor activist from exile, interview 68, who spent five years in the dungeons reports that "it was so that many people did not understand how a trade union [works] and what a trade union [is] . . . people were just labeled, if you are a trade union member you are one of the people who wants to go and organize strikes in Namibia and break the economy of Namibia and this type of thing."

45. Africa Watch, *Accountability in Namibia,* 74.

46. Peltola, "Role of the NUNW," 22–23, reports that "the SWAPO Deputy Secretary of Labour Pejavi Muniaro was probably killed by the people working for the [SWAPO] military security, as was the great friend of the Finnish trade unionists, the Director of SWAPO Settlements Abroad, Victor Nkandi."

47. Labor activist in exile, interview 68.

48. Labor activist in exile, interview 69.

49. Peltola, interview. See also Beukes, Beukes, and Beukes, *Namibia,* 2–3; Niddrie, "Namibia: The Detentions."

50. Labor activist in exile, interview 68.

51. Michael Mann, "The Giant Stirs: South African Business in the Age of Reform," in *State, Resistance and Change in South Africa,* ed. Philip Frankel, Noam Pines, and Mark Swilling (London: Croom Helm, 1988), 55. See also Jeremy Baskin, *Striking Back: A History of COSATU* (Johannesburg: Ravan Press, 1991); and Seidman, *Manufacturing Militance.*

52. On 27 September 1974 the United Nations Council for Namibia enacted "Decree No. 1 for the Protection of the Natural Resources of Namibia." This decree forbade the exploration, extraction, processing, or export of natural resources from Namibia without the permission of the UN Council for Namibia. It called any permission, commission, or license issued by the South African government or South West Africa "administration" as "null, void and of no force or effect." The decree vowed that "any person, entity or corporation which contravenes the present decree in respect to Namibia may be held liable in damages by the future Government of an independent Namibia" (United Nations, *Plunder of Namibian Uranium: Major Findings of the Hearings on Namibian Uranium Held by the United Nations Council for Namibia in July 1980* [New York: UN, 1982], 4–5).

53. MacFarlane, "Labour Control," 126.

54. Ibid., 167–68.

55. Chamber of Mines of SWA/Namibia, "A Working Paper on Labour Law and Labour Practices in SWA/Namibia," Mimeo, Windhoek, 1980.

56. Chamber of Mines of SWA/Namibia, *Annual Reports,* 1980–84.

57. Charles Truebody was the first executive director of the PSF; Miriam Truebody was the general manager in late 1992 (Author interviews with Charles Truebody, Windhoek, 29 October 1992, and Miriam Truebody, Windhoek, 13 October 1992).

58. Private Sector Foundation, *Constitution of the Private Sector Foundation,* Windhoek, March 1984.

59. Private Sector Foundation, *Annual Reports,* 1980–85.

60. Private Sector Foundation, *Statement of Employment Principles,* Windhoek, May 1981.

61. Private Sector Foundation, *Annual Reports,* 1980–85.

62. Miriam Truebody, interview.

63. Charles Truebody, interview.

64. Henk Schoeman, founder of the NIEA, author interview, Windhoek, 19 February 1993.

65. Karl Kuhrau, who worked on the Labour Relations Project in later years, says that the aim was to "get the employers together, sensitize them, because changes were coming." He describes how they initially went to employers to speak with them about employment practices, trade unions, and collective labor relations: "Most of the companies listened, I would think. But a lot of companies thought, especially smaller employers, they said 'what communist stuff are you talking?' They labeled us. In fact, at one stage, the Institute, which was basically started by businessmen which I would normally consider conservative, was considered a very liberal orientated organization. But we, the project, had a good effect, I mean a lot of people listened." An Industrial Relations Executive Club was even established and met one evening a week for an hour (Kuhrau, author interview, Windhoek, 25 November 1992).

66. Suidwes Afrikaanse Landbou Unie, *Jaarsverslae,* 1977–86.

67. *Windhoek Advertiser,* 23 August, 28 September 1984.

68. These included the Namibia Institute for Economic Affairs, the Chamber of Commerce and Industries, the Master Builders' Association, the Business and Professional Women's Association, the South West Africa Agricultural Union, the Guild of Carpenters, and residents' associations in Katutura and Khomasdal. See *Windhoek Advertiser,* 9 October 1984, 10 January 1985.

69. *Windhoek Advertiser,* 2 July 1985; Ottilie Abrahams, author interview, Windhoek, 21 June 1993.

70. Esterhuysen, "Decisive Years," 50–51. See also *A Survey of Race Relations in South Africa, 1978–1984.*

71. One of the most significant acts of this "government" was the administrator general's Proclamation No. 8 of November 1980, known as AG 8, which provided for the establishment of nine different "second tier" or ethnic "Representative Authorities" for "ethnic self-government."

72. In fact, the conscription for SWATF was a universal conscription applicable to all men in Namibia. Conscription was not applied in Ovambo and the Kavango, however, according to the military, because they had "enough volunteers" from these areas; indeed, the monthly salary for a "recruit without rank" in the mid-1980s was about R800, many times that of most workers. According to Tony Weaver ("South African Defence Force," 96), however, the real reason for recruiting mostly in central and southern Namibia was the high level of support for SWAPO in the North and a fear that

military training for SWATF soldiers would be military training for potential SWAPO combatants.

73. In the 1950s and the 1960s considerable legislation had been promulgated with the intention of "ensuring the security of South Africa." It included the Defence Act No. 44 of 1950, the Internal Security Act No. 44 of 1950, Sections of the General Law Amendment Acts of 1963 and 1986, the Terrorism Act No. 83 of 1967, the Prisons Act No. 8 of 1959, the Police Act No. 7 of 1958, the Post Office Act No. 44 of 1958, the Official Secrets Act No. 16 of 1956, and the Criminal Procedures Act No. 16 of 1956. From the appointment of the first administrator general in 1977 new security legislation served to constrict further political and other activity within the territory. This included Proclamation No. AG 9—Security Districts Proclamation, 1977 of 11 November 1977, which provided for detention for interrogation for periods of up to thirty days at a time, renewable by the AG; Proclamation No. AG 26—Detention for the Prevention of Political Violence and Intimidation Proclamation, 1978, of 18 April 1978, which provided for indefinite detention for the prevention of violence and intimidation; Proclamation No. AG 50, 1978, which authorized the AG to deport persons considered by him to be threatening the peace or good government of the territory; Proclamation No. AG 117, Promulgation of Prohibition and Notification of Meetings Act, 1981 (Act 22 of 1982) of the National Assembly of SWA, which provided for written notice to be given of certain political meetings, which might then be banned; and the Residence of Certain Persons in SWA Regulation Act, 1985 (Act 33 of 1985). See Hartmut Ruppel, "Namibia: Security and Its Consequences," in *Namibia in Perspective,* ed. Gerhard Toetemeyer, Vezera Kandetu, and Wolfgang Werner (Windhoek: Council of Churches of Namibia, 1987); *A Survey of Race Relations in South Africa, 1983,* 607. See also Elizabeth Landis, "Security Legislation in Namibia: Memorandum of the South West Africa (Namibian) Bar Council," *Yale Journal of International Law* 11, no. 1 (1985):48–103.

74. *Windhoek Advertiser,* 2 June 1979.

75. *Windhoek Advertiser,* 21 February 1984.

76. The 1952 law was based on the South African Industrial Conciliation Act No. 36 of 1937 and provided for the registration of trade unions and employer organizations and for the control of their activities. Section 4 of the Wage and Industrial Conciliation Amendment Proclamation No. 45 of 1978 amended Section 48 of the original ordinance, which had excluded black workers from the definition "employee" (Koerner-Damman, "Labour in Namibia," 42–43).

77. *Windhoek Advertiser,* 6, 12 July 1978.

78. *Special Report of the Director General, 1983,* 45.

79. *Windhoek Observer,* 18 August, 1 September 1979. SWAPO-D was formally founded in June 1978 in Sweden after initial agreement among some of those held by SWAPO in Tanzanian prisons from 1976 to 1978, including Andreas Shipanga and Solomon Mifima. Other founding members included Kenneth and Ottilie Abrahams, although Mifima and the Abrahams all later left the SWAPO-D. "SWAPO-D defined its policy as remaining faithful to the original political, military and diplomatic strategy of forcing South Africa to accept Namibian independence but re-emphasised the

democratic principles of the party" (Puetz, Van Egidy, and Caplan, *Namibia Handbook,* 290–91).

80. *Windhoek Observer,* 24 November 1979. One black mine worker who worked at the TCL's Otjihase mine outside Windhoek joined and began to work for SWAMU in Tsumeb from October 1978, when the union became multiracial. He had originally been interested in establishing a new black trade union but was encouraged by government officials to join an existing union. According to the SWAMU officeholder, a "white" union such as SWAMU (which had first been established in 1953) had difficulty recruiting black workers, who assumed that because it was white it was also DTA. He says that workers at the Tsumeb mine at the time faced real problems and that one of the union's achievements was to establish grievance procedures, which did improve the situation. According to the union official, by 1982 SWAMU had three thousand members, though thereafter it lost members at a rapid rate, again for "political" reasons (SWAMU officeholder, interview 4, Tsumeb, 10 May 1993).

81. Mifima is reported to have received support from the United States labor federation the AFL-CIO and the African American Labour Centre, in setting up the NTUC (IDAF, "Working Under South African Occupation," 41).

82. *Financial Mail Special Survey,* "Namibia," 1983, 25.

83. Author interviews with Sammy Lawrence, Windhoek, 20 October 1992 and 12 August 1993, and Francois Adonis, Windhoek, 22 October 1992. Lawrence was the secretary general of the Public Service Union of Namibia (PSUN), successor to the GSSA, during 1992 and 1993, and Adonis was the president of the Local Authorities Union of Namibia (LAUN), successor to SWAMSA, during 1992. The GSSA was long perceived to be, or at least labeled as, a "white" or "white and coloured" association. According to Lawrence, this is in part because the executive of the association was originally all white.

84. IDAF, "Working Under South African Occupation," 41. Brian Bolton, "The Condition of the Namibian Workers," Paper presented at the Seminar on the Activities of Foreign Economic Interests in the Exploitation of Namibia's Natural and Human Resources, Ljubljana, Yugoslavia, 16–20 April 1984, 12.

85. IDAF, "Working Under South African Occupation," 1987, 41; Bolton, "Condition of Namibian Workers," 12–13. According to Neville Rubin, who at the time worked in the southern Africa program at the ILO, there were various attempts by the "internal regime" and organizations such as SWACOL to be recognized at the ILO (Rubin, interview). This was especially important to them because the UN Council for Namibia had been recognized by the ILO as the "government" of Namibia and employers and workers were represented at the ILO by SWAPO members from exile.

86. Barry Streek, "Unions in Namibia," *South African Labour Bulletin* 9 (1984): 14. In addition, there were other staff associations, for example, for railway workers and teachers.

87. Streek, "Unions in Namibia," 14; IDAF, "Working Under South African Occupation," 41.

88. Seidman, *Manufacturing Militance,* 125.

89. Dozens of small strikes reportedly occurred in Namibia between June 1973 and June 1975; in addition, there were strikes at Rossing in November 1976 and March and December 1978 and others at CDM and the Krantzberg, Uis, and Tsumeb mines in 1979. Strikes and walkouts occurred at the Oamites mine and at Damara Meatpackers in 1981, at Table Top in Walvis Bay in 1982, and at Otjihase mine, Rossing, and CDM in 1983 (IDAF, "Working Under South African Occupation," 38).

90. Mifima found that the response of most workers to a grievance was to strike rather than to negotiate, an observation that Mifima's interviewer found tallied with the experience of "the Namibian Workers Union (NAWU), founded by SWAPO. Organisers found workers willing to pay for and carry membership cards as a gesture of support but shopfloor organisation is virtually non-existent" (*Financial Mail*, 1983, 25).

Chapter Four

1. Valenzuela, "Labor Movements in Transitions to Democracy," 449: "Periods of crisis of authoritarianism, liberalization, and transition normally lead to increased rank-and-file activation and participation in unions, a widespread restructuring of labor organizations, and the re-establishment or recomposition of union links to parties."

2. This characterization of the NUNW during the late 1980s is from Richard Pakleppa, former researcher, educator, and media coordinator for the NUNW, in author interview, Windhoek, 29 April 1992.

3. Community activist Rosalinde Namises: "I remember early '80s, late '70s there was the last rally and after that rally people were arrested and the whole Terrorism Act came in and things became very tough. So it was the time when people were forced to go underground. And things were so quiet . . . until I think 81/82" (Author interview, Windhoek, 7 February 1993).

4. Weaver, "South African Defence Force," 80. See also International Defence and Aid Fund, "Apartheid's Army in Namibia: South Africa's Illegal Military Occupation," *Fact Paper on Southern Africa No. 10* (London: IDAF, 1982); Tony Weaver, "The War in Namibia," in *Namibia in Perspective*, ed. Gerhard Toetemeyer, Vezera Kandetu, and Wolfgang Werner (Windhoek: Council of Churches of Namibia, 1987).

5. Helao Shityuwete, author interview, Windhoek, 5 February 1993.

6. Andre Strauss, "Community Organisations in Namibia," in *Namibia in Perspective*, ed. Gerhard Toetemeyer, Vezera Kandetu, and Wolfgang Werner (Windhoek: Council of Churches of Namibia, 1987), 185.

7. Andre Strauss, "Community Based Organisations (CBOs) in Katutura," in *Katutura Revisited: Essays on a Black Namibian Apartheid Suburb*, ed. Christine Von Garnier (Windhoek: Roman Catholic Church, 1986), 35; Strauss, "Community Organisations," 187.

8. Strauss, "Community Based Organisations," 37–39; Strauss, "Community Organisations," 193–95.

9. A university education inside Namibia was not really an option, so most black students went to South Africa. German-speaking whites often went to West Germany, and Afrikaans-speaking whites also went to South Africa. According to the *Special Report of the Director General, 1983*, "By 1977 only 5,000 Africans had attended a secondary school. In 1980 an Academy for Tertiary Training, open to all races, was established in Windhoek offering training of the type provided at technical colleges, and certain university courses. The syllabi and examinations for the latter courses were provided by the University of South Africa at Pretoria. But the Academy was reported by the International Defence and Aid Fund to be seriously overcrowded and ill-equipped, whilst in contrast a teacher training college in Windhoek, built for 1,500 at a cost of R80 million and controlled by the second-tier white administration, was in 1981 being used by fewer than 200 students." A part of the academy gained university status in 1985. For more on education in Namibia before independence, see Amukugo, *Education and Politics*.

10. Lindy Kazombaue, author interview, Windhoek, 20 April 1993.

11. "We also worked in the Single Quarters [in Katutura] a lot. . . . Sometimes workers were beaten up. . . . Next to the Single Quarters there was this police quarters and Koevoet quarters, so sometimes they just went in and they started harassing the informal sector. . . . They came to us and we got them legal representation because the church had legal advice funds, not a bureau, but a fund from which you could get lawyers. . . . So we got a name that at least [we] could help. . . . Also we worked a lot with single parents, especially domestic workers, so when they were fired, they also came to see us. . . . So we were actually responding to a situation where we found . . . a large number of people were fired or abused by the employers" (Kazombaue, interview).

12. Around the same time, from about 1984 to 1986, another community organization, the Legal Aid and Community Advice Bureau (LACAB) in Katutura, provided legal advice and assistance to workers (about half of their complainants) and others. Established in part by Ottilie and Kenneth Abrahams, LACAB's director was Advocate Vekuii Rukoro. According to Rukoro, most of the complaints concerned unfair labor practices or unfair dismissals by employers "who exploited the complete ignorance of workers as to their rights, their entitlements under law," usually by dismissing workers without notice and without payment in lieu of notice and withholding accrued leave pay (Rukoro, author interview, Windhoek, 4 February 1993). The problems and hardships facing workers at the time, according to Rukoro, were "compounded by the absence of effective trade unions capable of safeguarding their rights against cowboy employers" (Vekuii Rukoro, "Legal Aid and Community Advice Bureau," in *Katutura Revisited: Essays on a Black Namibian Apartheid Suburb*, ed. Christine Von Garnier [Windhoek: Roman Catholic Church, 1986], 40). See also *Windhoek Advertiser*, 3 December 1985, and *Namibian*, 21 February 1986, for reports on LACAB's activities.

13. Namises, interview.

14. Author interviews with Bob Kandetu, Windhoek, 3 September 1992; Namises; Kazombaue. On 28 November 1985 the *Namibian* reported "WAC Chairman" Bob Kandetu's opposition to some new proposed labor legislation. The article noted that the

WAC had been formed recently "by a group of Namibians with the principal aim of 'educating, enabling and facilitating conditions for workers in Namibia to organise themselves to protect and defend their rights.'"

15. It was on this basis that NUM first approached CDM and not other mines in Namibia such as Rossing or Tsumeb Corporation (Howard Gabriels, author interview, Windhoek, 5 October 1993). See also *Special Report of the Director General, 1986,* 59. According to Ben Ulenga (in Brian Wood, "Interview with Ben Ulenga," *Action on Namibia,* Spring 1987, 9), while NUM was trying to negotiate an access agreement with CDM concerning South African workers at the mine, NUM's organizers "had a chance of meeting our workers informally; and of course they discussed unions and so on."

16. Because there was a strong SWAPO branch in Oranjemund, the level of political consciousness among workers was very high. There had been some industrial action on the part of workers, but it had not led to the formation of trade unions, according to Gabriels: "There had been a host of activities on the mine throughout the '70s, where workers were asserting their power, asserting themselves, because it was a highly mobilized body of workers. So there had been stoppages and various forms of engaging the employers in some form of struggle. But I don't think it was transformed in a lasting trade union structure" (Gabriels, interview).

17. MUN shop steward, interview 31, Oranjemund, 21 January 1993. The Mineworkers' Union of Namibia's 1989 *Shop Steward Training Manual* states that during the mid-1980s mine workers at CDM "were in the process of forming the Diamond and Allied Workers Union," the idea for which had been generated during strikes at the mine in 1979 and 1982. See Mineworkers Union of Namibia, *Shop Steward Training Manual,* compiled with the assistance of the NUM (National Union of Mineworkers in South Africa) and IMF (International Miners Federation) (Windhoek: MUN, 1989), 20.

18. Gabriels, interview.

19. Hilton Villet, Rossing Personnel Department employee during the mid-1980s, author interview, Windhoek, 31 May 1993.

20. MacFarlane, "Labour Control," 322–23. Management, however, was apparently wary of the consequences of unionization. In September 1985, managing director of Rossing Uranium Colin Macaulay told a newly constituted branch of the Institution of Mining and Metallurgy in Windhoek [according to the *Namibian,* 16 September 1985] that "it would be tragic if the present 'excellent relations' were damaged in the process of unionisation of mine employees." According to the *Namibian,* Macaulay was not opposed to the formation of unions and "regularly reminded his employees that they were free to join a union if they wished," but he did not feel that current channels for direct communication between employees and management should be replaced by "communication through union officials only."

21. Villet, interview.

22. *Namibian,* 25 April 1986, 8.

23. *Namibian,* 4 September 1987. Of course, by this time the Mineworkers Union of Namibia had already been established. Indeed, it does seem that for some time there was confusion about the relationship between the two, although the same people, such

as Asser Kapere and Winston Groenewald, held leadership positions in both. In an 11 September 1987 article in the *Namibian,* RMU chairman Groenewald is quoted as saying that the RMU was unmistakably a part of the MUN; at the time that the negotiations for a recognition agreement with Rossing had started, however, MUN was not a registered union but the RMU was. The recognition agreement made provision for an eventual change in the agreement when the status of MUN changed. In fact, a new recognition and procedural agreement was signed with Rossing and MUN on 14 November 1988 *(Namibian,* 18 November 1988). On 29 June 1988 MUN had signed a recognition agreement with CDM *(Namibian,* 1 July 1988).

24. According to Howard Gabriels, "Another crucial development that took place was that a number of comrades came off of Robben Island, amongst them John Pandeni and Ben Ulenga . . . they came into the union movement, which obviously gave the union movement a lot of strength because they brought with them a lot of skills, a lot of resources and a lot of understanding of how to build an organization from their own past political experiences. And from that time, when these comrades came out, the Namibians took more charge of the organization and we [NUM] were merely providing a support base for that" (Gabriels, interview).

25. See Ulenga's interviews with Brian Wood: Wood, "Interview with Ben Ulenga"; Brian Wood, "Ben Ulenga Interview Part II," *Action on Namibia,* Summer 1987, 10–14; Wood, "Making of a Trade Unionist"; also NUNW/COSATU, *Namibian Workers Organise,* 36–38. Says Ulenga: "I think we generally agreed that, well, definitely we should get into the local SWAPO structures . . . we didn't instruct each other, we just had consensus. For example, those that left Robben Island before us in 1984, when they came here most of them were taken to Ovamboland . . . but we consciously refused to do that, we wanted to be together with the people who were very active players on the ground. So we went . . . and just joined the structures, the Youth League structures, the branch structures" (Ulenga, interview).

26. Ulenga, interview. Others recall the same prison meeting and the discussion that took place. See also NUNW/COSATU, *Namibian Workers Organise,* 36, and Wood, "Making of a Trade Unionist," 100.

27. Ulenga, interview; trade union fieldworker, interview 46, Windhoek, 1 March 1993. See also Wood, "Interview with Ben Ulenga," and Wood, "Making of a Trade Unionist."

28. Author interviews with Ulenga; trade union fieldworker, interview 46; and WOSC officeholder, interview 74, Windhoek, 28 July 1993. In a chapter in a book published in 1987, Ben Ulenga wrote that "earlier last year two Katutura based workers' committees merged to form the Workers Steering Committee (WOSC). Both [committees] had aimed to inform workers of matters related to their rights and assisting workers to organise amongst themselves. WOSC has field workers who work in close contact with the workers in Windhoek but also countrywide" (Ben Ulenga, "The Exploited Worker in Namibia—A Testimony," in *Namibia in Perspective,* ed. Gerhard Toetemeyer, Vezera Kandetu, and Wolfgang Werner [Windhoek: Council of Churches of Namibia, 1987], 123).

29. The names of officeholders are given in Anton Lubowski's December 1986 Progress Report of the NUNW to the Central Organisation of Finnish Trade Unions. Ben Ulenga recalls that the Steering Committee consisted of about eight to ten people, including himself, Anton Lubowski, George Kaiyamo, Gabriel Ithete, Jappie Nangolo, Ruben Itengula, and Barnabus Tjizu.

30. Lubowski, Progress Report.

31. *Namibian,* 26 September 1986. See also Wood, "Interview with Ben Ulenga," 9.

32. *Namibian,* 28 November 1986. See also Wood, "Interview with Ben Ulenga," 9.

33. *Namibian,* 11 December 1987. The first general secretary of MANWU was Steering Committee chairperson Barnabus Tjizu. Steering Committee official and fieldworker Gabriel Ithete was appointed acting general secretary of NAPWU at its launching in Windhoek. In January 1988 former Robben Islander Petrus Iilonga, who was also involved with the Steering Committee, was elected NAPWU general secretary.

34. Pakleppa, interview; WOSC officeholder, interview 74. According to Ben Ulenga, the JUC was formed as a "stepping stone for the full scale restructuring of NUNW." The JUC consisted of three representatives from each industrial union and three officials from the former Steering Committee and itself consisted of three committees: administrative, transport, and finance. See *Namibian,* 26 June 1988. See also NUNW/COSATU, *Namibian Workers Organise,* 41.

35. An article in the *Namibian Worker* in August 1988 (no. 5, pp. 22–27) acknowledged that the NUNW "is egter nog nie 'n regte Federasie van Vakbonde nie" [is not, however, yet a real federation of unions], but was on the way to becoming one, and explained why this was necessary. The January–February 1989 issue of the *Namibian Worker* (no. 8, pp. 3ff.) reported on a 14–15 January 1989 meeting in which members of MUN, NATAU, NAPWU, NAFAU, MANWU, and the JUC gathered to discuss federation structure, policy, and name.

36. *Windhoek Advertiser,* 22 November 1985.

37. Kazombaue, interview. According to Tessa Cleaver and Marion Wallace, *Namibia Women in War,* 94, Namibian Women's Voice was voluntarily disbanded in March 1989 "for the sake of maintaining peace and good relations" and "in order to unify resources for preparation for the election." According to Dianne Hubbard and Colette Solomon ("Many Faces of Namibian Feminism," 170), "One frequently cited factor [for NWV's dissolution] is the opposition engendered by its challenge to male authority in church and political party hierarchies. The autonomy and success of the group were apparently threatening." Heike Becker (*Namibian Women's Movement,* 226) largely confirms this account of external SWAPO attitudes toward NWV and autonomous organizing inside Namibia at the time.

38. Namises, interview.

39. Kazombaue, interview; Kandetu, interview. Also Namises, interview. Community activist and physician Dr. Kenneth Abrahams observed in an August 1991 Namibia Peace Plan conference on NGOs that during the late 1980s SWAPO was hostile to community-based organizing efforts, claiming that they would "sap the revolutionary potential of the people."

40. Ulenga, interview. When Ulenga first heard about the WAC, for instance, he was discouraged from approaching it: "Some people were aware of it, in the SWAPO circles, and I think quite a number of people were quite negatively disposed to it . . . when I heard of it, I had this interest, I tried to raise the issue of the workers with some of the leaders of the [SWAPO Windhoek] branch. . . . And almost everybody I talked to was very negative and warned me against this other group."

41. Ulenga, interview. Indeed, Namises and Kazombaue felt themselves "worked out" of the Steering Committee, and other observers agreed. According to Lindy Kazombaue, there were some substantive disagreements over procedure between members of the two committees: "I think one of the biggest problems for me was that the general secretaries of SWAPO, of the unions, were never elected, coming from the workers' mandate. It was more political appointments. So you will see all the high powered people there at the top . . . counteracting the workers' power. It means those people were more accountable to the party than to the workers. . . . Most of the Robben Islanders were never workers before they started into this. So our idea was we really need to elect our own general secretary. So that was a principle we couldn't compromise on. The other was that you can't start with the umbrella first. First you have to organize individual trade unions . . . and then afterward these unions organize the umbrella but not the umbrella first" (Kazombaue, interview). Rosalinde Namises: "There was too much mingling of the [SWAPO] branch . . . when we started we didn't really want political things to play a role. We said every worker must just participate and maybe that's why they took it over from us, to put it into that line of the party" (Namises, interview).

42. Strauss, "Community Organisations," 188–89.

43. Namises, interview.

44. As Ben Ulenga wrote in "The Exploited Worker," 119: "The workers' struggle for the advancement of their interests as a class cannot but be part and parcel of the wider anti-colonial national liberation struggle. There is thus no way the workers can win an equitable dispensation than by passing through the gate of national self-determination and independence."

45. *Namibian*, 8 January 1988.

46. *Namibian Worker*, no. 6, October 1987, 10–11 (from Luanda), carried an article titled "Trade Unions and Political Struggle," which addressed "the two diametrically opposed views to what ought to be the nature and character of this relationship [between a trade union and a national liberation movement]." One view, represented by "ardent freedom fighter of yesterday, now in the lap of the CIA" Solomon Mifima, was characterized by a "vulgar-narrow workerist and crude economistic tendency" beneath which lay "a misplaced, if not misleading, concern for the interest of the working class." The other view, represented by SWAPO and the NUNW, "following closely the principles that 'one cannot separate politics and the way in which people are governed from the bread and butter questions,'" argued that "the struggle for trade union rights is intertwined with the struggle for national independence, freedom, and democracy."

47. Leys and Saul, "Introduction," in *Namibia's Liberation Movement*, 14.

48. NUNW trade union activist, interview 52. Various studies have observed the deterioration of SWAPO's organization and capacity by the mid-1980s inside Namibia and a certain weariness or apathy among its supporters. Thus the new trade unions emerged at an auspicious moment. See Leys and Saul, "SWAPO Inside Namibia"; Max du Preez, "Namibia: A Future Displaced," in South African Research Service, *South African Review III* (Johannesburg: Ravan Press, 1986).

49. John Ya Otto, author interview, Windhoek, 23 March 1993.

50. Peltola, "Role of the NUNW," 24.

51. See, for example, *SWAPO Information Bulletin*, June, August, and September 1987.

52. See "New Year Message by Comrade Sam Nujoma, President of SWAPO to the Namibian People, January 1st 1986" and "1988: Year of Unity and Popular Action—SWAPO Central Committee New Year Message to the Namibian People, Luanda, December 1987."

53. Author interviews with former trade unionists, interviews 81 and 74.

54. *Namibian*, 11 January 1985.

55. *Namibian*, 9 December 1985.

56. Alpha Kangueehi, author interview, Windhoek, 10 February 1993.

57. For example, *Namibian*, 19 September 1986, 6 March, 2 October 1987, 17 May 1991. On 30 October 1987 the *Namibian* reported that the Automobile and Metalworkers Union, an affiliate of the NTU, had signed a recognition with the engineering company Southwest Engineering (SWASTAHL).

58. The NTU is loosely affiliated with the Workers' Revolutionary Party in Namibia together with whom it published, until recently, *Workers' News*. The NTU claims the following affiliated unions: Automobile and Metal Workers Union, Transport and Allied Workers Union, Sweepers and Cleaners Union of Namibia (a committee), Domestic Workers Union of Namibia (a committee), Farmworkers Union of Namibia, Transport Corporation Workers Union, and a National School Workers Union, although there is little, if any, public evidence of the existence of these unions (Kangueehi, interview). In a 1987 interview Ben Ulenga said that "the *only* evidence of its [the NTU's] existence is an office where Alpha Kangueehi works from and they make some booklets. The booklets generally consist of them trying to attract the attention of the Multi-Party government to the situation of the workers" (Wood, "Ben Ulenga Interview Part II," 11).

59. Internal NNTU documents, dated 22 March and 15 September 1986.

60. *Namibian*, 28 February 1986.

61. Internal NNTU document, 15 September 1986. See also *Namibian*, 11 July 1986, for an announcement of the establishment of the Drivers, Transport and Allied Workers Union as the second affiliate union of the NNTU.

62. *Namibian*, 5 June 1987. R4,000 was allegedly given to the NNTU to support May Day activities, such as purchasing T-shirts. This only served to confirm accusations from other trade unionists, such as those of the nascent NUNW, that "these are people who are generally supporters of the MPC [Multi-Party Conference or interim government]" (Ben Ulenga in Wood, "Ben Ulenga Interview Part II," 11). As "SWANU exiles"

who had sided with Moses Katjioungua when SWANU split in the early 1980s, people such as Ngaujake were even more susceptible to accusations of collusion with the interim government in which Katjiuongua was "Minister of Manpower and National Health and Welfare."

63. The charges of a smear campaign are cited in Wolfgang Werner, "Namibia Update: Trade Unions and Labour Action, May–August 1987," *South African Labour Bulletin* 12 (1987): 60–73. Theo Ngaujake, author interview, Windhoek, 11 February 1993: "The fact was that our own main objective was to create a trade union body that would bring about changes in labor relations in the country, but of course it was difficult for us to operate without funds. So we were given funds by the interim government at the time. An interim government had decided with its ministers and so on to give us some kind of support; to us it was not a secret but of course the interim government wanted it to be a secret for their own reasons . . . so we had received funds from them."

64. *Namibian,* 5 June 1987, 1 July 1988; Werner, "Namibia Update, May–August 1987," 64. There are reports, however, that an NNTU did continue to exist, run by Veripi Kandenge, one of the founding members of the NNTU. Wolfgang Werner, "Namibia Update: Trade Unions and Labour Action, September–October 1987," *South African Labour Bulletin* 13 (1987): 97, cites articles in the *Namibian,* 4 September 1987, and *Die Republikein,* 10 September 1987, to this effect. See also *Namibian,* 1 July 1988.

65. The Executive Committee of NANAU consisted of Aloysius Yon (president), Henoch Handura (vice-president and founding member of NNTU), Reginald Van der Hoven (treasurer), Theo Ngaujake (general secretary), G. F. Brendell (administrative secretary), Maria Mokomele (education secretary), and Sarel Louw (organizing secretary). Member unions included the Namibia Building Workers Union (NBWU), the Namibia Wholesale and Retail Workers Union (of the NNTU), the Namibian Women's Support Committee, and the Drivers, Transport and Allied Workers Union (also of the NNTU). See Werner, "Namibia Update, May–August 1987," 64.

66. Henoch Handura, author interview, Windhoek, 6 January 1993. Also Ngaujake, interview, and Aloysius Yon, interview, Windhoek, 20 November 1992.

67. Handura, interview; Ngaujake, interview; Yon, interview. According to Yon and the others, the name for the NCSTU and some funding came from Austrian trade unions. Jason Angula, SWAPO secretary for labor during these years, gives little credence to the efforts of Mifima, Ngaujake, and others, but takes more seriously the now rival federation: "It is only by 1987 that the trade union to which Aloysius Yon is a member now started to get a little bit of momentum, because they started with the coloured section and they had some backing there. That was a first, I must say, because they had quite a following" (Angula, author interview, Walvis Bay, 23 July 1993).

68. According to a "Report of the Secretary to the Congress of NCSTU," delivered at the First Congress of the Namibian Christian Social Trade Unions, held at Brakwater in October 1992, the membership of affiliated unions in April 1992 was as follows: NBWU, 3,000; NWRWU, 1,500; PSUN, 20,000; NAMSA, 1,700; SWAMU, 482.

69. At the First Congress of the NCSTU, attended by the author, Yon gave this brief

overview of the history of the NCSTU. At that same congress it was decided that the NCSTU would be transformed into the Namibian People's Social Movement (NPSM), and a new constitution to that effect was approved. NAMSA became the Local Authorities Union of Namibia (LAUN) in early 1993.

70. Aloysius Yon, interview: "Now I had had enough experiences with SWAPO and I wouldn't affiliate myself with a political party. On the one hand was SWAPO and I couldn't affiliate myself with it and on the other hand was the DTA which I didn't like in any case. So we stayed outside politics; all along knowing full well what the political implications of a trade union can be." Alpha Kangueehi, interview: "When we started off as a trade union we had to tell workers what a trade union was all about. Some people were organizing this on a political ticket and people like us . . . we weren't aligned with SWAPO, with DTA, with SWANU, our aim was to organize a very strong working class movement in this country and I am sure that to some extent we did achieve that."

71. Aloysius Yon, interview: "1985 was also the year that everybody that wasn't a SWAPO supporter was regarded as a puppet. They were using this type of term in order to brand people." See also Brian Wood, "The Battle for Trade Unions in Namibia," *South African Labour Bulletin* 12 (1987): 56–61, for similar language vis-á-vis these and other unions.

72. Handura, interview. In March 1987, Johann Van Rooyen of the Department of Manpower and Civic Affairs reported that eleven trade unions were registered at the time in Namibia, five of which had registered in 1986. He stated further that four applications for registration were pending, including from the MUN and NAFAU (*Namibian*, 6 March 1987).

73. In South Africa an extensive debate over whether to register trade unions with an illegitimate apartheid state, on its terms, took place during the late 1970s and early 1980s. See, inter alia, Bob Fine, Francine de Clerq, and Duncan Innes, "Trade Unions and the State: The Question of Legality," *South African Labour Bulletin* 7 (1981): 39–68; Baskin, *Striking Back;* Johann Maree, ed., *The Independent Trade Unions, 1974–1984* (Johannesburg: Ravan Press, 1987); Friedman, *Building Tomorrow Today.* As Baskin, *Striking Back,* 37, notes, the "registration debate" "mirrored political debates between the 'non-collaborationist' and the 'participationist' traditions of resistance politics." In Namibia the issue does not appear to have received the same level of discussion.

74. Moses Katjiuongua, author interview, Windhoek, 11 February 1993. Katjiuongua left Namibia in 1959 to attend school in Botswana and from there lived in exile in Africa, Europe, and North America, active in SWANU; he returned to Namibia in 1981 and "got involved in SWANU again politically." For Katjiougua and many others, returning to Namibia was the only way to participate in the liberation struggle: "At that time abroad, there were some of us who turned back, it was that if you are not SWAPO, you had no platform outside where you could be politically active. You come to the UN, SWAPO had observer status. You just went around the corridors there and nobody would listen to you. They would tell you to go and join SWAPO. . . . So there came a time when the UN decided now that SWAPO was the sole and authentic

representative for Namibia. Then it became more difficult for our political parties to operate from outside. So people were trying to create a local political base here [in Namibia]." Ottilie Abrahams, who returned to Namibia in 1978 with her husband, Kenneth, expressed the same sentiments: "This is something that we have been fighting for years and years and years and years. Because what we couldn't understand is that the Western powers who preached to us about freedom and democracy and all the rest of it, how they could invent 'sole authenticity' and try to shove it down our throats . . . one day when we have time we should actually write about the birth and effect of 'sole authenticity' because for people outside who were not in SWAPO, it was the biggest problem outside and it is still the biggest problem here" (Abrahams, author interview, Windhoek, 21 June 1993).

75. *Namibian,* 4 October 1985. Henk Schoeman, at the time of the Namibia Institute for Economic Affairs and an appointed member of the National Labour Council, attributes the new legislation to two factors: "I think it was twofold, one was what was happening in South Africa [the Basic Conditions of Employment Act of 1983], the other was the realization that particularly the employers were doing what they wanted, they had an open playing field, no rules, they could do what they wanted" (Schoeman, author interview, Windhoek, 19 February 1993). Former NIEA project manager and now employer consultant Karl Kuhrau provides an example: "It was so easy, I mean a lot of employers in those days, it was quite easy to phone the police and say 'I've got a riot outside'—it's not a strike—it's a 'riot'" (Kuhrau, author interview, 25 November 1992).

76. Koerner-Damman, "Labour in Namibia," 43.

77. See, for example, *Namibian,* 2 May, 26 September 1986.

78. Koerner-Damman, "Labour in Namibia," 43. The consequences of this were significant, according to labor consultant Karl Kuhrau: "If you look at the '86 legislation, you could give a guy notice and say 'thank you very much.' That was the labor relations up to the first of November this year [1992] . . . you paid to get rid of sometimes his [the manager's] bad management . . . so you avoided labor relations . . . there was no provision for an unfair labor practice, that is why I say labor relations were non-existent" (Kuhrau, interview).

79. David Smuts, author interview, Windhoek, 30 March 1993.

80. Charles Truebody, then executive director of the Private Sector Foundation, author interview, Windhoek, 29 October 1992.

81. *Namibian,* 19 November 1985.

82. *Namibian,* 31 December, 28 November 1985.

83. *Namibian,* 11 April, 2 May 1986.

84. For a while, organizers of the Steering Committee simply refrained from telephone calls with trade unionists in South Africa; instead they would meet outside Namibia in places such as Springbok, just over the border, or in Johannesburg. NUM organizer Howard Gabriels reports no problems coming into Namibia for short periods and, although he was aware of being followed around, he says he was never detained or "anything like that" (Gabriels, interview).

85. *Namibian,* 8 May 1987, 6 May 1988, 2 May 1989.

86. Werner, "Namibia Update, September–October 1987," 94–95.

87. South West Africa, *Report of the Commission of Inquiry into Labour Matters in Namibia* [Wiehahn Report] (Windhoek: Office of the Administrator General, 1989), 78.

88. Werner, "Namibia Update: May–August 1987," and Werner, "Namibia Update: September–October 1987"; NUNW/COSATU, *Namibian Workers Organise,* 42–57.

89. Baskin, *Striking Back,* 26. See also *South African Labour Bulletin,* "Focus on Wiehahn" 5 (1979): 1–126. Clearly, in appointing Professor Wiehahn as chair, authorities in Namibia knew well what the outcome of the commission's investigation would be. Author interviews with commission members Henk Schoeman and Johann Van Rooyen confirm this.

90. *Namibian,* 18 September 1987; *SWA/N Ekonoom* 1, no. 11 (1987).

91. Katjiuongua, interview.

92. Author interviews with Johann Van Rooyen, Aloysius Yon, and Charles Kauraisa, Windhoek, 27 January 1993, and Dave Smuts. Charles Truebody notes that such a sentiment had been growing in Namibia: "There was a move to suggest that let's accept that we're going to have trade unions in this country after all and let's try and do things to make sure that the trade unions that come are going to be soft and they're going to be considerate and they're going to be cooperative and so on and so forth" (Truebody, interview).

93. *Namibian,* 18 December 1987. Dave Smuts: "Progressive people in the communities obviously realized that it is very important to have a much more, a legal framework where you could assert rights. It was one of the real problems, we had no [legal] basis whatsoever and when you are removed from the political, the democratic process, really essentially from asserting rights and the executive process, then you often have to use the courts of law to assert certain rights . . . certainly in this context it was very important that more rights should be attained" (Smuts, interview).

94. *Namibian,* 3 March, 15 December 1989.

95. *Namibian,* 11 April 1986.

96. Van Rooyen, interview.

97. Theo Mey, "Report: Exploratory Study on Labour Relations in SWA/Namibia" (Windhoek: The Academy, 1986).

98. Bob Meiring, "Industrial Relations in an Impoverished, Politicized and Polarized Society—A Discussion of the Fundamentals," Mimeo (Windhoek: Private Sector Foundation, 1988).

99. Cited in the *Special Report of the Director General, 1989,* 86.

100. *SWA/N Ekonoom,* various issues, 1986–88.

101. For more on the transition to independence, see Lionel Cliffe et al., *The Transition to Independence in Namibia* (Boulder: Lynne Rienner, 1993); Christopher Saunders, "Transition in Namibia, 1989–1990: And the South African Case," *Transformation* 17 (1992): 12–24; Linda Freeman, "Contradictions of Independence: Namibia in Transition," *Transformation* 17 (1992): 25–47.

102. SWAPO secretary for information and publicity Hidipo Hamutenya ex-

pressed "no doubt that the workers will rally behind SWAPO." The interests of the Namibian workers, he continued, were inseparable from those of SWAPO, and workers' interests occupied a central position in SWAPO's election campaign. Indeed, he said, "It will be your democratic right to hold SWAPO accountable for promises it made to workers" (*Namibian,* 26 June 1993).

103. Agenda and Resolutions from the 1989 NUNW Consolidation Congress, Katutura, 23–25 June 1989. Also *Namibian,* 28 June 1989. Cassinga Day, 4 May, now a nationally observed holiday in Namibia, marks the day in 1978 when several hundred SWAPO exiles—mostly women and children—were killed during a bombing raid by the South Africans in Angola.

104. *Namibian,* 26 June 1989.

105. Resolutions from the 1989 NUNW Consolidation Congress, Katutura, 23–25 June 1989. Also *Namibian,* 28 June 1989.

106. *Namibian,* 26, 27 June 1989. In January 1990 a conflict between SWAPO and the NUNW was reported in South African newspapers, over an alleged demand by the NUNW that the Constituent Assembly's draft constitution be made available for public scrutiny and comment and that certain of the NUNW's demands concerning workers' rights be included in the constitution. According to the South African newspaper article, NUNW representatives were told in a meeting with Constituent Assembly chair Hage Geingob to end their public criticism; further, the NUNW members were reportedly told that the NUNW should support SWAPO and work hard for the next election to ensure a two-thirds majority for SWAPO, which would enable SWAPO to write the constitution it wanted. While NUNW leaders apparently acknowledged that a meeting took place with Geingob, John Ya Otto and others denied vehemently that there was a conflict between the NUNW and SWAPO (*Namibian,* 25 January 1990). See also *Namibian Worker,* 1–14 February 1990.

107. *Namibian,* 5 December 1989. Subsequently, John Ya Otto was appointed ambassador to the People's Republic of Angola and so left the National Assembly. Ben Ulenga remained a member of Parliament and was appointed deputy minister of wildlife, conservation, and tourism, and Marco Hausiku, member of Parliament, was appointed minister of lands, resettlement, and rehabilitation (later minister of works, transport, and communication).

108. Kraus, "Political Economy of Trade Union–State Relations," 180.

109. Fine, "Civil Society Theory," 76.

110. Collier and Collier, *Shaping the Political Arena,* 3.

CHAPTER FIVE

1. See, for example, World Bank, *Namibia: Poverty Alleviation with Sustainable Growth* (Washington, D.C.: World Bank, 1991); Overseas Development Institute, "Economic Prospects for Namibia," *ODI Briefing Paper* (London: IDAF, 1989); United Nations Development Programme, *Base Studies on Financial, Economic and Social Aspects*

for the Arrangement for Independence in Namibia: A Macroeconomic and Sectoral Overview of the Economy of Namibia (Windhoek: UNDP, 1989); Richard Moorsom, *Namibia's Economy at Independence: Report on Potential Norwegian-Namibian Cooperation* (Bergen: Chr. Michelsen Institute, 1990).

2. In greater detail: the World Bank report noted that 5 percent of the population received 70 percent of GDP while the poorest 55 percent received only 3 percent; 25 to 30 percent of the formal sector labor force was unemployed and perhaps two-thirds of those in subsistence agriculture were underemployed; the tax base for the government was narrow and highly dependent on diamond and uranium revenues; the wage bill for general government was excessive; and current expenditures were high with services for the majority of low quality.

3. Fanuel Tjingaete, "Set the Market Free," *Optima* 37 (1989): 71–78.

4. *Namibia Brief,* "Namibia Welcomes Investors as Partners," no. 13, March 1989. See also the interview with Prime Minister Hage Geingob, "Partnership with Business to Create Wealth," and the interview with Ben Amathila, "Added Value Equals Greater Prosperity," both in *Courier* 127 (1991): 35–41.

5. "Statement of the Honourable Ben Amathila, Minister of Trade and Industry," read by Permanent Secretary of the Ministry of Trade and Industry, Tsudao Gurirab; and "Opening Address by the President of Namibia, Sam Nujoma," delivered on the opening day of the National Union of Namibian Workers Economic Conference, Katutura, 2–4 October 1992.

6. SWAPO, *Namibia's Economic Prospects Brighten Up,* An Economic Policy Position Document of the Political Bureau of the Central Committee of SWAPO, 28 November 1988 (Luanda, May 1989), 5–6.

7. SWAPO, *SWAPO Election Manifesto, Towards an Independent and Democratic Namibia: SWAPO's Policy Positions* (Windhoek: SWAPO Directorate of Elections, 1989), 8. For a short while after independence some SWAPO leaders seemed to indicate that the mixed economy option might be only an interim measure because African countries, in general, were "in a stage of insufficient degree of economic and cultural development . . . for bringing about socialist transformation" at present. See Hidipo Hamutenya, in an address to the NANSO Central Region Consultative Conference, as reported in *Namibian,* 15 January 1990; see also interview with Ben Amathila in *Namibian,* 21 November 1989.

8. See, for example, United Nations Institute for Namibia, *Namibia: Perspectives for National Reconciliation and Development* (Lusaka: UNIN, 1986). An introductory chapter to this UNIN publication, "Macro Economic Structures, Trends and Perspectives," cites SWAPO's 1976 Political Programme and notes that "the basic mode of production set as a goal is socialist" (although during a transitional period other forms of ownership may prevail), "comprehensive agrarian reforms aimed at giving the land to the tillers are seen as precondition for rural development," and so on. The entire thousand-page volume continues in this vein.

9. Lauren Dobell, "SWAPO in Office," in *Namibia's Liberation Struggle: The Two-Edged Sword,* ed. Colin Leys and John Saul (London: James Currey, Athens: Ohio

University Press, 1995), 171. Per Strand ("SWAPO and Nation Building in Namibia, Transfer of Power in a Post-Communist Era," *Discussion Paper No. 8* [Windhoek: NISER, 1991]), based on his interviews with several SWAPO leaders, considers that some in the SWAPO leadership were genuinely convinced of "the supremacy of socialism over capitalism" and suggests that if independence had been attained a few years earlier, SWAPO's policies might not be so "pragmatic." As such, events in the East were decisive.

10. This view is held especially strongly among members of a still anxious business community in Namibia. (Windhoek) Chamber of Commerce and Industry general manager Harald Schmidt: "I think international events overtook their [SWAPO's] whole plan. I truly believe that if our independence would have been five years or two years earlier we would have seen different policies. I am so convinced about that. Mainly because it does come up, that conviction comes up, that in a weak moment you would find that without exception, without exception, they still believe socialism is the right model. It was just not applied properly in the East" (Schmidt, author interview, Windhoek, 1 February 1993).

11. For discussions of SWAPO's "ideology" over the years, see Sue Cullinen, "SWAPO and the Future of Namibia," *South Africa International* 15 (1985): 141–49; Stanley Uys, "Namibia: The Socialist Dilemma," *African Affairs* 81 (1982): 569–76; Kimmo Kiljunen, "Namibia: The Ideology of National Liberation," *IDS Bulletin* 11 (1980): 65–71; Hamutenya and Geingob, "African Nationalism in Namibia"; Katjavivi, *History of Resistance;* Randolph Vigne, "SWAPO of Namibia: A Movement in Exile," *Third World Quarterly* 9 (1987): 85–107; Mbuende, *Namibia, the Broken Shield.:*

12. "Interview: Sam Nujoma," *Africa Report*, March–April 1975, 12–13. See also "Comrade Sam Nujoma Talks to an American Correspondent About SWAPO," *SWAPO Information Bulletin*, no. 2, 1981.

13. "Sam Says No Compromise: Nujoma Speaks Out in Anniversary Interview," *Windhoek Advertiser*, 25 April 1985. In an interview with Gwen Lister in Paris, printed in the *Windhoek Observer*, 30 April 1983, Nujoma said that SWAPO was not a communist-dominated movement and that SWAPO would not implement a "communist blueprint" in Namibia. One of the founders of the Interessengemeinschaft Deutschsprachiger Suedwester (Organisation of German Speaking Namibians) who met on several occasions with Nujoma and others in the SWAPO leadership during their exile described Nujoma as a "Sonntags Kommunist," or "Sunday communist." This IG member says he once asked Nujoma whether he was a communist, to which Nujoma replied he was first a Namibian, second a patriot, and third had many friends in the East (Author interview 35, Windhoek, 22 June 1993).

14. "Sam Says No Compromise: Nujoma Speaks Out in Anniversary Interview," *Windhoek Advertiser*, 25 April 1985.

15. "Priority Number One: Reconciliation, Sam Nujoma Speaks on Detainees, Namibians Still Abroad and the Priorities of an Independent Government," *Namibian*, 19 September 1989. SWAPO had always been fairly clear in its nonracialism with Nujoma repeating, as he did in many interviews, that "SWAPO is not anti-white. It

never has been and never will be. Our fight is against a system which denies us our birthright, which is to govern ourselves in our own country" ("Interview: Sam Nujoma," *Africa Report*, March–April 1975, 13).

16. Opening Address by the Honourable Minister for Broadcasting and Information [*sic*] (Namibia) Minister Hidipo Hamutenya. In *Reconstruction and Reconciliation: Critical Choices for Southern Africa*, Proceedings, 15–19 November 1990 (Windhoek: Friedrich Ebert Foundation, 1990). See "Extending an Olive Branch," *New Era*, 21 March 1991, for Prime Minister Hage Geingob's view of national reconciliation as "a cornerstone of the SWAPO government."

17. In general, the Foreign Investment Act's liberal provisions were well received with the emphasis seen as "facilitating investment rather than putting up obstacles in the form of burdensome and complex regulations." Among other things, the act provides for the equal treatment of foreign and local investors with no joint venture or minimum local equity requirements. In addition, the act guarantees the right of investors to remit capital, loans, and after-tax profits and provides for compensation in the event of expropriation. See Republic of Namibia, *Foreign Investment Act No. 27 of 1990* (Windhoek: Office of the Prime Minister, December 1990). Also *Namibian*, 1 February 1991; *Africa Analysis*, 22 February 1991.

18. The Interessengemeinschaft (IG) was formed in August 1977 by a group of German-speaking Namibians who were opposed to apartheid, who realized that the existing situation inside Namibia was not politically sustainable, and who recognized that SWAPO was the "kommende Kraft" (future power), according to one founding member, interview 35. Founders of the IG considered that political parties participating in the different interim governments in Namibia were too ethnically oriented and were, in any case, "castrated" by the administrator general. In the view of the IG, these governments achieved no real improvements for the majority and were seen merely as South African puppets. Although the IG members were not SWAPO sympathizers, they were realistic enough to know that SWAPO was the party of the future and should be dealt with accordingly. The Namibia Peace Plan 435 (NPP 435) was launched in November 1986 by a group of (mostly professional) white Namibians (in part in response to conversations held with the SWAPO leadership in August 1986 in Lusaka) who were concerned about the disinformation campaign being waged by the South Africans about United Nations Security Council Resolution 435 and who saw the implementation of Resolution 435 as the most satisfactory way of bringing peace to Namibia. The group published a pamphlet called *The Choice* in numerous Namibian languages which summarized all of the documentation concerning 435 and detailed the political process to date inside Namibia and the unwillingness of the South African and interim governments to go forward with the resolution. NPP 435 used the press, seminars and conferences, public statements, and meetings abroad to conscientize people, primarily the Namibian white community, about 435 (Christo Lombard, author interview, Windhoek, 30 March 1993; and Peter Koep, author interview, Windhoek, 10 February 1993).

19. See "SWAPO Meets White Namibians" and "Namibia Peace Plan Study and Contact Group: Superficial or Real Reconciliation?" *SWAPO Information Bulletin*,

March 1987. See also various reports on the Kabwe and Stockholm trips supplied by Christo Lombard from NPP 435 and press reports from earlier trips by Interessengemeinschaft members.

20. See "Summary of Minutes Taken During Consultations Between SWAPO and Members of the White Community of Namibia, 19–21 June 1988, Stockholm" (Windhoek: Namibia Peace Plan 435).

21. Interview 35.

22. Schmidt, interview.

23. Frederic Fritscher, "Government Maintains Reconciliation Policy," *Le Monde,* 21 March 1991.

24. Koerner-Damman, "Labour in Namibia," 28.

25. Ibid., 67–68.

26. Republic of Namibia, *National Policy on Labour and Manpower Development* (Windhoek: GRN, July 1990). See also *Namibian,* 2 August 1990.

27. Compare Republic of Namibia, *Labour Act No. 6 of 1992* (Windhoek: Office of the Prime Minister, April 1992), with South West Africa, *Report of the Commission of Inquiry into Labour Matters in Namibia* . This observation was also made during interviews with the author by members of the Wiehahn Commission including Johann Van Rooyen, Windhoek, 22 January 1993; Charles Kauraisa, Windhoek, 27 January 1993; and Aloysius Yon, Windhoek, 20 November 1992.

28. Nic Wiehahn, "Industrial Relations in Namibia," *Optima* 37 (1989): 62.

29. Wiehahn Report, ii.

30. See Wiehahn Report; Wiehahn, "Industrial Relations," 63.

31. See "A Collection of Papers Presented at the NIEA Symposium on the Report of the Commission of Inquiry into Labour Matters in Namibia," 1–2 June 1989 (Windhoek: NIEA).

32. In an article in the *Namibian,* 25 February 1990, Da'oud Vries reported that the Wiehahn Report, while "commendable," seemed to be collecting dust on shelves in offices. The article continued: "Considering the amount of work and money spent on researching and producing the report, the document should be at least studied by concerned parties and be considered for forming the basis for an independent labour code." The article reported that numerous attempts to obtain comments from the trade unions or employers on the report were unsuccessful, as "they had not studied it as yet."

33. *Namibian,* 18 December 1987. Similarly, in a public address in 1988, Nic Wiehahn said that sound labor relations must be based on six fundamental principles: the right of every person in the country to work, the right of workers to organize themselves, the right to withhold labor, the right to protection in the work situation, the right of management and workers and their trade unions to negotiate, and the right to development through education and training for the labor market *(Namibian,* 11 March 1988).

34. See Cheadle, Thompson, and Haysom, "Preliminary Written Representations Before the Commission of Inquiry into Labour Matters at Windhoek," Mimeo (Windhoek: Legal Assistance Centre, 1987); and Thompson, Cheadle, Jacobus, and

Lubowski, "Before the Commission of Inquiry into Labour Matters at Windhoek: Supplementary Written Representations" (Windhoek: Legal Assistance Centre, 1988).

35. At the request of the Ministry of Labour and Manpower Development, the ILO produced studies on the labor situation in Namibia, including "Report of Exploratory Mission to Namibia," 25–29 September 1989; "Report of the ILO Employment Advisory and Training Policy Mission," January 1991; "Namibia: Country Strategy Paper," December 1991; "Development of a Modern National Labour and Social Policy Administration System: Technical Memorandum to the Government of Namibia," 1992. Koerner-Damman, "Labour at Independence," was also commissioned by the ILO.

36. ILO, "Technical Memorandum."

37. *Namibian Worker,* 23 May–6 June 1990, 1–14 August 1990.

38. Comments given during the National Tripartite Seminar on the Labour Bill conducted by the Ministry of Labour and Manpower Development, 13–14 February 1992, SKW Hall, Windhoek. See also "The NUNW Comment on the Labour Bill as Read the First Time to the National Assembly of the Republic of Namibia," Mimeo (Windhoek: NUNW, March 1992). The *Namibian Worker,* April 1992, reported that "the recent National Tripartite Seminar held in Windhoek's SKW Hall turned into a 'fury-flow' of blows when the National Union of Namibian Workers spoke out sharply because their key demands were ignored in drafting the bill." The tone of this article was in marked contrast to an earlier article in the *Namibian Worker,* 1–14 August 1990, in which was written: "The Ministry of Labour has opened his doors for a pro-active process of worker participation in the formulation of the laws which are going to regulate the relationship between workers and owners of the industries—capitalists. This is a most progressive step from an equally progressive and farsighted Ministry of our country."

39. Comments given during the National Tripartite Seminar on the Labour Bill conducted by the Ministry of Labour and Manpower Development, 13–14 February 1992, SKW Hall, Windhoek. These issues are also touched upon in Karl Kuhrau, "Trade Unions: To Recognise or Not to Recognise," *Business Spotlight* 3 (1992): 9–11; Karl Kuhrau, "Guidelines for Fair Retrenchment," *Business Spotlight,* October 1991, 18–20; and "The New Labour Act and Labour Relations in Namibia—Prospects for Investment," Address by Karl Kuhrau to the Namibia Working Group Meeting organized by the Namibian International Business Development Organisation, Windhoek, 30 July 1992.

40. Hyman, "Third World Strikes," 330.

41. See Gretchen Bauer, "The New Labour Act: Best Compromise Achievable," *Namibia Review* 1, no. 6 (1992): 18–24; John Ford, "The Labour Act—How It Affects Your Business," *Namibia Business Journal* 3, no. 1 (1993) 1–2, 8–9; Andrew Corbett, "Capital, Labour and Government," *Namibia Yearbook 1992–93,* no. 3, 52–55.

42. Corbett, "Capital, Labour and Government," 55.

43. *Debates of the National Assembly,* Vol. 18, Fourth Session, First Parliament, 18 February–5 March 1992, 274.

44. Gretchen Bauer, "Tripartism and Workers in Namibia," *South African Labour Bulletin* 17 (1993): 65.

45. Indications of the tension surrounding this first May Day since independence were made public in the pages of the *Namibian*. Then NUNW president John Shaetonhodi is quoted on 3 April 1990 as saying, "May Day is not going to be hijacked by anybody," following previous newspaper reports of Deputy Minister of Labour Hadino Hishongwa's proposal that the rally be held at the Independence Stadium in the distant white suburb of Olympia and that a "tripartite" committee consisting of the ministry, employers' organizations, and the unions organize it. On 25 April 1990 it was reported in the *Namibian* that "grand plans go ahead despite the controversy." In addition to the shift of the celebration from Katutura to the Independence Stadium, a dinner banquet for dignitaries, foreign guests, and business people would be held in Windhoek. The May Day rally would be addressed by President Sam Nujoma, NUNW president Shaetonhodi, and the minister of labor. On 2 May 1990 Rajah Munamava, writing in the *Namibian*, reported the event "a fiasco": "Missing was the usual workers' militancy and the colourfulness which characterised past festivities. Spades and other workers' tools carried by workers at rallies were also absent. Overalls and other garments worn by workers to mark their day were scarce, while for some trade union officials it was bow-ties and nice suits. But above all, it was the failure to have the speeches translated from English into some of the local vernaculars that made the occasion appear 'elitist.'"

46. See *Namibian*, 5 November 1990, 8 May 1992.

47. Editorial in *NUNW News*, a publication of the *Namibian Worker*, June 1992.

48. See *Namibian*, 20 January, 17 April, 18 August 1989.

49. Mark Verbaan, "NUNW in Constituent Assembly," *Namibian*, 5 December 1989.

50. *Namibian Worker*, March 1991, 6.

51. *Namibian Worker*, May 1991, 2.

52. Lauren Dobell, "The SWAPO Congress," *Southern Africa Report* 7, no. 5 (1992): 23.

53. *Namibian*, 22 September 1993.

54. *Namibian*, 24 September 1993.

55. Christelle Terreblanche, "Namibian Trade Unions in Tatters," *South*, 29 October–2 November 1993, 7.

56. *Namibian*, 27 September 1993.

57. Community activist, interview 30, Windhoek, 20 April 1993.

58. Former trade unionist, interview 74, Windhoek, 28 July 1993.

59. Former trade union activist, interview 66, Windhoek, 28 October 1992.

60. Trade union general secretary, interview 28, Windhoek, 5 November 1992.

61. Markus Kampungu, author interview, Windhoek, 5 November 1992.

62. *Namibian*, 14 October 1992. The statement was released in response to a speech by Prime Minister Hage Geingob at a conference of the independent Teachers'

Union of Namibia in which he said that he found "the division of a profession along political lines—with one union pledged to SWAPO and the other to the DTA—totally unnecessary and I daresay harmful." NANTU rejected the implication that it was "pledged to SWAPO."

63. Former NUNW staff member, interview 48, Katutura, 11 December 1992. A former NUNW official, interview 22, Katutura, 23 November 1992: "I don't know why they [the workers] decided it [affiliation], it could be that that time it was too early for them to think of leaving SWAPO just like that. Because the whole thing [the unions], it was initiated by SWAPO, it was formed as the Department of Workers, of Labour, that is how it got started. . . . But anyway, I hope that as time goes they will realize that for NUNW to get all workers involved, maybe we also need to change. But that is for the workers themselves to decide."

64. *Namibian Worker*, March 1991, 5. In a different interview before the 1991 NUNW congress, Ulenga said, according to the *Namibian*, 28 March 1991, that "it would be in the interest of SWAPO to have a 'strong independent and militant trade union movement.'" Ulenga continued: "Because if SWAPO can weaken or destroy the trade union movement, I think it would be destroying itself."

65. Ministry of Labour official, interview 63, Windhoek, 22 June 1993.

66. MUN officeholder, interview 62, Katutura, 13 February 1993.

67. Trade union general secretary, interview 18, Katutura, 17 November 1992.

68. Bernhard Esau, author interview, Katutura, 2 November 1992.

69. Jeremiah Nambinga, author interview, Windhoek, 2 March 1993. In mid-1993, NUNW general secretary Bernhard Esau was a member of the twenty-one-member Politburo of SWAPO; Walter Kemba and John Shaetonhodi, both of MUN and NUNW, were members of the Central Committee, as was John Pandeni, who was the general secretary of NAFAU until elected a regional councillor and governor of the Khomas region ("List of Members of the Central Committee of SWAPO Party," from SWAPO Headquarters, Windhoek, July 1993).

70. Author observation and notes from the Prime Minister's Consultative Meeting on Labour Relations, 25–26 February 1993, Cabinet Chambers, Windhoek.

71. Author observation, May Day rally, Katutura, 1993; *Namibian*, 4 March 1994.

72. *Namibian Worker*, November 1991, 15.

73. *Namibian Worker*, October 1992, 3.

74. *Namibian*, 7 October 1992.

75. *Namibian*, 8 October 1992.

76. *Namibian*, 16 March 1994. Esau reportedly could not make the meeting with SWAPO official Thomas Nekomba, however, because of a previous commitment. According to the article, "NBC radio had quoted Esau as saying the NUNW was considering participating in the vote because workers' problems were not being properly addressed in Parliament. According to several sources, the radio report was greeted with consternation in union, SWAPO and even state security circles."

77. *Namibian*, 17, 18, 21 September 1992.

78. *Namibian*, 22 November 1993.

79. *Namibian,* 27 November, 1 December 1992. See also *Namibian Worker,* December 1992, 9.

80. *Namibian Worker,* June 1995, 9.

81. In early 1995, the NUNW claimed a total membership of eighty-eight thousand signed-up workers (*Namibian Worker,* January–February 1995); according to Peltola, *Lost May Day,* 281, the NPSM in 1994 claimed a total signed-up membership of about thirty-three thousand.

82. Author interviews with, for example, Sammy Lawrence, secretary general of the Public Service Union of Namibia, Windhoek, 20 October 1992, and Francois Adonis, president of the Local Authorities Union of Namibia, Windhoek, 22 October 1992.

83. Although the NUNW is not affiliated to the ICFTU, the ICFTU still funds and organizes projects together with the NUNW. In the years since independence these have included projects in the areas of basic trade union education, training in the new labor legislation, human resource development including literacy and organizational skills, research and information, and women's activities (Markku Vesikko, NUNW-ICFTU project coordinator, author interview, Windhoek, 27 November 1992, and various NUNW project reports). Projects with other donors include leadership seminars and economics workshops with the Friedrich Ebert Foundation, health and safety seminars with the Trades Union Congress of Britain, and training of media workers with WUS of Denmark. Together the three Italian trade union federations—the CISL, the CGIL, and the UIL—built regional offices for the NUNW in Tsumeb, Keetmanshoop, and Swakopmund, as well as the national center in Katutura. Member unions also have their own projects with foreign donors and the International Trade Secretariats and other sister trade union bodies.

84. Hafeni Nghinamwami, "Unions Urged to Meet Challenges," *New Era,* 28 November–4 December 1991, 11.

85. Author interviews with NUNW general secretaries, May 1993, conducted for Gretchen Bauer, "Research Needs Assessment for the National Union of Namibian Workers (NUNW) and Affiliated Unions," report prepared for the Friedrich Ebert Foundation, Windhoek, May 1993.

86. See *Financial Mail Special Survey,* "Namibia," 22 July 1983, 25; Alpha Kangueehi, author interview, Windhoek, 10 February 1993; Ben Ulenga, "Exploited Worker," 122.

87. *Namibian Worker,* March 1991. In the same issue, Ben Ulenga stated that the federation's finances were "in a mess," in part because of "a very, very deplorable mentality," namely, "the hat in the hand mentality." Ulenga continued: "People think that there are other people who must give us the money, donor countries and organisations. . . . But this actually perpetuates a very bad relationship which is neo-colonialism . . . we shall get money from Europe, but it makes people very much dependent. Actually the donors end up ruling everything."

88. NUNW project reports.

89. In an interview published in the *Namibian Worker,* March 1991, Ulenga was asked: "Some newspaper reports have indicated that you were becoming too

troublesome to the government, and to make you quiet they appointed you. What do think of such allegations?" Ulenga noted that "there is nothing to indicate" such an allegation might be true. According to Sipho Maseko ("Role and Effects of the Namibian Student Movement," 127–28), part of the reason that the national student organization NANSO chose to disaffiliate from SWAPO was a "suspicion that SWAPO was attempting to weaken NANSO as an independent structure"—in part by assigning away, without prior consultation, some of its most capable leaders.

90. For example, one general secretary, in an interview for Bauer, "Research Needs Assessment," said that he did not have the theoretical background of trade unions that he would like, nor did he have the management skills he would like to be a trade union general secretary. At a meeting at the NUNW national center in Katutura, 12 May 1993, to evaluate the 1993 May Day, another general secretary commented (in a discussion about the party, government, and unions) that though he knows how to be a party member, he does not know how to be a trade union leader. Such sentiments have been echoed by other trade union leaders as well.

91. Bauer, "Research Needs Assessment." Specific research needs were identified as basic information on trade unions and their members and employers, education on basic trade unionism and the economy, collective bargaining, legal issues including the new labor legislation, health and safety issues, and national policy making.

92. Esau, interview.

93. Corbett, "Capital, Labour and Government," 55.

94. Bro-Matthew Shinguadja, author interview, Windhoek, 22 June 1993.

95. ILO, "Exploratory Mission."

96. ILO, "Namibia: Country Strategy Paper."

97. These included the Construction Industries Federation of Namibia, the Chamber of Mines, the Namibian Employers Federation, the Agricultural Employers Association, the Motor Industries Federation of Namibia, and the Namibia National Farmers Union.

98. See "A Collection of Papers Presented at the ILO/NIEA Symposium on the Role of Employers' Organisations in Africa," held on 30 and 31 August 1990 in Windhoek, Namibia.

99. *Namibian*, 20 September 1993.

100. Joel Barkan, Gretchen Bauer, and Carol Lynn Martin, "The Consolidation of Democracy in Namibia: Assessment and Recommendations," Final report prepared for Associates in Rural Development, Washington, D.C., and USAID, Windhoek, 1994, 41.

101. *Namibian*, 20 April 1990.

102. For example, *Namibian Worker*, March, June, July–August, September 1991, October, December 1992. See also, for example, "Swearing Becomes a Problem for Otjihase Mine Workers," *Namibian*, 22 October 1992; "TCL Accused of New Apartheid," *Namibian*, 5 November 1992; John Pandeni, "The Workers' Struggle Must Continue," *New Era*, 19–25 September 1991; and "NAFAU Blasts Negligent Bosses," *New Era*, 16–22 April 1992.

103. *Namibian Worker,* May 1991. Many interpreted the situation as one in which employers were abusing the policy of national reconciliation. According to then deputy minister of labor Hadino Hishongwa, the policy was being misconstrued as a sign of weakness on the part of the government: "Some employers, therefore, apparently feel free to abuse the government's attempts at nation-building by what amounts to irresponsible conduct towards their employees." Hishongwa predicted an improvement in the situation with the new labor legislation *(Namibian,* 8 June 1990).

104. *Namibian,* 29 September 1992.

105. Employer consultant Karl Kuhrau called the death of Zapparoli "a sad day for labour relations in general." He essentially blamed the unions for failure to control their members during a labor dispute, thus resulting in lack of a proper mandate. He charged that the incident would negatively affect potential investors as well as the overall attitude of employers toward collective relations. According to the *Namibian,* 14 October 1992, MANWU (the union representing workers at MKU) general secretary at the time, Gabriel Shikongo, described the labor relations situation as one in which "many employers still refused unions entry to workplaces to educate and inform workers on trade union related issues."

106. *Namibian,* 10, 17 May 1996.

107. *Namibian,* 17 May 1996; *Namibian Worker,* June 1995.

108. *Namibian,* Editorial Comment, 12 April 1996.

109. Economist Intelligence Unit, *EIU Country Report: Namibia Swaziland 4th Quarter 1996* (London: EIU, 1996), 14; *Namibian,* 12 November 1996.

110. *Namibian,* 25 October 1996, and various other issues during August and September.

111. According to the Ministry of Labour and Manpower Development, there were forty-one strikes in Namibia during 1990–92, lasting from one day to one week. In most cases, according to the MLMD, "industrial action involved disputes over wages and conditions of employment, although in some cases retrenchments were also a reason." In all cases trade unions were involved. The MLMD assumes that there were also "a number of smaller work stoppages which did not come to the attention of the Ministry." The strikes occurred in the following sectors: four in mining, five in construction, fourteen in engineering and manufacturing, five in wholesale and retail trade, two in agriculture and fishing, three in catering and accommodation, one in transport, five in the public sector, and two in other sectors. Cited in Republic of Namibia, *Draft Transitional National Development Plan, 1991/92–1993/94* (Windhoek: National Planning Commission, December 1992), 196.

112. Kraus, "Political Economy of Trade Union–State Relations," 180.

113. Freeman, "Contradictions of Independence," 43.

114. *Namibian,* 19 August 1991, 10 August 1992; also "Trade Unions Sleeping on the Job?" *New Era,* 18–24 February 1993.

115. Bill Freund, "The Unions of South Africa," *Dissent,* Summer 1992, 378.

CHAPTER SIX

1. See, for example, Thomas Callaghy, "Political Passions and Economic Interests: Economic Reform and Political Structure in Africa," in *Hemmed In: Responses to Africa's Economic Decline*, ed. Thomas Callaghy and John Ravenhill (New York: Columbia University Press, 1993); and Crawford Young, "Democratization in Africa: The Contradictions of a Political Imperative," in *Economic Change and Political Liberalization in Sub-Saharan Africa*, ed. Jennifer Widner (Baltimore: Johns Hopkins University Press, 1994).

2. Economic Intelligence Unit, *Namibia Country Profile, 1992–93* (London: EIU, 1992), 13; Economist Intelligence Unit, *Namibia Swaziland Country Profile, 1995–1996* (London: EIU, 1996), 13.

3. EIU, *Namibia Swaziland Country Profile*, 14.

4. Ibid., 15, 17.

5. EIU, *Namibia Country Profile*, 33.

6. Steve Curry and Colin Stoneman, "Problems of Industrial Development and Market Integration in Namibia," *Journal of Southern African Studies*, 19 (1993): 49.

7. See Victor Allen, "The Meaning of the Working Class in Africa," *Journal of Modern African Studies* 10 (1972): 169–89; Robin Cohen, "From Peasants to Workers in Africa," in *The Political Economy of Contemporary Africa*, ed. Peter Gutkind and Immanuel Wallerstein (Beverly Hills: Sage, 1976); Robin Cohen, Jean Copans, and Peter Gutkind, "Introduction," in *African Labour History*, ed. Peter Gutkind, Robin Cohen, and Jean Copans (London: Sage, 1978).

8. See Seidman, *Manufacturing Militance*.

9. Moreover, unions in Namibia are faced by many of the same negative trends affecting unions throughout the world. All over the developing (and developed) world, trade unions confront increasing challenges to their organization and effectiveness, resulting, in many places, in "confusion and a lack of clarity with respect to roles and possibilities" according to Henk Thomas. Trade unions have been particularly hampered by a general lack of industrialization (and more recently an actual deindustrialization in Africa), accompanied by massive urban informal sectors, significant rural underemployment, and large-scale labor migration. With the implementation of structural adjustment programs in the last decade, the resulting casualization of work, falling wage rates, public sector retrenchments, and privatization of state-owned enterprises and consequent job losses have all greatly aggravated an already untenable situation. In many places, unions have been weakened by authoritarian political regimes, too close an association with ruling political parties, insufficient attention to internal democratic structures, serious deficiencies in organizational and financial capacity, and an almost total male dominance of union structures. See Thomas, ed. *Globalization and Third World Trade Unions: The Challenge of Rapid Economic Change* (London: Zed Books, 1995), 3, 193.

10. See Crawford Young, "The African Colonial State and Its Political Legacy," in *The Precarious Balance: State and Society in Africa*, ed. Donald Rothchild and Naomi

Chazan (Boulder: Westview Press, 1988); Crawford Young, *The African Colonial State in Comparative Perspective* (New Haven: Yale University Press, 1994).

11. Author interviews with members of the business community, interview 27, Windhoek, 27 January 1993; interview 59, Windhoek, 1 February 1993.

12. Ukandi Damachi, Dieter Seibel, and Lester Trachtman, "Introduction," in *Industrial Relations in Africa,* ed. Damachi, Seibel, and Trachtman (London: Macmillan, 1979), 7.

13. Author interviews with former trade union activist, interview 66, Windhoek, 28 October 1992; and trade union general secretary, interview 28, Windhoek, 5 November 1992.

14. Author interviews 57, Windhoek, 4 February 1993; 67, Windhoek, 30 March 1993.

15. Kaire Mbuende (*Namibia, the Broken Shield,* 172–200) characterizes class formations in Namibia in the 1980s as follows: a white bourgeoisie in mining, agriculture, and commerce; a black working class consisting of contract workers; a white bureaucratic bourgeoisie including managers, supervisors, civil servants, police officers, and army officers; a minute intelligentsia; a predominantly white and numerically weak petty bourgeoisie consisting of retail shop owners and traders; and the black peasantry.

16. Vigne, "SWAPO of Namibia," 94.

17. Colin Leys and John Saul, "Introduction," in *Namibia's Liberation Struggle,* 14.

18. Frantz Fanon, *The Wretched of the Earth* (1961; rpt. New York: Grove Press, 1968), 203.

19. Cohen, Copans, and Gutkind, "Introduction," 18.

20. Woddis, *Africa,* 291; Hodgkin, *Nationalism in Colonial Africa,* 137–38.

21. In 1990 Chris Tapscott and Ben Mulongeni (*An Evaluation of the Welfare and Future Prospects of Repatriated Namibians in Northern Namibia,* Research Report No. 3 [Windhoek: NISER, 1990], 22) found among a small group of returnees in northern Namibia the belief "that national reconciliation had gone too far, and that whites and former supporters of the South African regime were benefitting more from independence than those who had fought hardest for it." In 1991 Andre du Pisani ("Rumours of Rain: Namibia's Post-Independence Experience," *Africa Insight* 21 [1991]: 171) wrote that "for an increasing number of Namibians—the peasantry, trade unionists, millenarian ideologues, students, members of the SWAPO Youth League and the growing army of the unemployed—the government's national reconciliation policy seems opportunistic. They tend to regard the SWAPO leadership's efforts here as merely harmonizing the new political elite's interests with those of local and foreign capital." And in 1993 one former People's Liberation Army of Namibia combatant told *New Era* ("The Ups and Downs of Reconciliation," 8–14 April 1993): "All I see is that we liberated this country for the Boers [Afrikaners] to have a free entry into the world, to have their sports teams participate in world sports and to continue exploiting us." In the same article a white Namibian was reported as saying that "reconciliation had worked in that he had lost none of his belongings, neither was any harm done to him by SWAPO, contrary to the propaganda he was fed on by the colonial administration."

22. Fanon, *Wretched of the Earth,* 149–50.

23. Chris Tapscott, "Namibia: A Class Act?" *Southern Africa Report* 6 (1991): 3–4. See also Freeman ("Contradictions of Independence," 37, 40); Chris Tapscott, "National Reconciliation, Social Equity and Class Formation in Independent Namibia," *Journal of Southern African Studies* 19 (1993): 29–39.

24. Alex Davidson, "Democracy and Development in Namibia: The State of Democracy and Human Rights, 1989–1991," *Studies in Democracy 2* (Uppsala: Uppsala University, 1991), 39.

25. See, for example, Issa Shivji, *Class Struggles in Tanzania* (New York: Monthly Review Press, 1976); Richard Sklar, "The Nature of Class Domination in Africa," *Journal of Modern African Studies* 17 (1979): 531–52.

26. Leys and Saul, "Introduction," 5.

27. *Namibian,* 25 February 1991, cited in Davidson, "Democracy and Development in Namibia," 47.

28. Davidson, "Democracy and Development in Namibia," 58. Such a political culture—and for similar reasons—has also been identified in Zimbabwe: "The liberation struggle also left a significant mark on Zimbabwe's political culture. The commandist nature of mobilization and politicization under clandestine circumstances gave rise to the politics of intimidation and fear. Opponents were viewed in warlike terms, as enemies and, therefore, illegitimate. The culture from the liberation struggle was intolerant and violent" (Masipula Sithole, "Zimbabwe: In Search of a Stable Democracy," in *Politics in Devei ,ping Countries: Comparing Experiences with Democracy,* ed. Larry Diamond, Juan Linz, and Seymour Martin Lipset [Boulder: Lynne Rienner, 1990], 481).

29. Gretchen Bauer, "Prospects for the Consolidation of Democracy in Namibia," revised version of paper originally presented at the Thirty-seventh Annual African Studies Association Meeting, Toronto, 1996.

30. Ayesha Imam, "Democratization Processes in Africa: Problems and Prospects," *Review of African Political Economy* 54 (1992): 103.

31. Jimi Adesina, "Labour Movements and Policy-Making in Africa," *Working Paper 1/1992* (Dakar: CODESRIA, 1992), 53.

32. Rueschemeyer, Stephens, and Stephens, *Capitalist Development and Democracy*; Collier and Collier, *Shaping the Political Arena.*

33. Gary Marks, *Unions in Politics: Britain, Germany and the United States in the Nineteenth and Early Twentieth Centuries* (Princeton: Princeton University Press, 1989), xiii.

34. Adrian Peace, "The Lagos Proletariat: Labour Aristocrats of Populist Militants?" in *The Development of an African Working Class,* ed. Richard Sandbrook and Robin Cohen (London: Longman, 1975), 289; Richard Jeffries, "The Labour Aristocracy? Ghana Case Study," *Review of African Political Economy* 3 (1975): 60, 66; Von Freyhold, "Labour Movements or Popular Struggles," 29–30.

35. See Collier and Collier, *Shaping the Political Arena,* 48; Valenzuela, "Labor Movements in Transitions to Democracy," 447.

36. Cited in Adesina, "Labour Movements," 53.

37. Yusuf Bangura and Bjorn Beckman, "African Workers and Structural Adjustment: The Nigerian Case," in *The IMF and the South: The Social Impact of Crisis and Adjustment,* ed. Dharam Ghai (London: Zed Books, 1991), 160–62.

38. Eddie Webster, "The Rise of Social-Movement Unionism: The Two Faces of the Black Trade Union Movement in South Africa," in *State, Resistance and Change in South Africa,* ed. Philip Frankel, Noam Pines, and Mark Swilling (London: Croom Helm, 1988), 175–76, 194.

39. Kim Scipes, "Understanding the New Labor Movements in the 'Third World': The Emergence of Social Movement Unionism," *Critical Sociology* 19 (1992): 86–87, 97.

40. Marks, *Unions in Politics,* 3–4.

BIBLIOGRAPHY

Government Documents

Republic of Namibia. 1990. *The Constitution of the Republic of Namibia*. Windhoek: GRN.

———. 1990–92. *Debates of the National Assembly*. Vols. 1–20. Windhoek: GRN.

———. July 1990. *National Policy on Labour and Manpower Development*. Windhoek: GRN.

———. December 1990. *Foreign Investment Act No. 27 of 1990*. Windhoek: Office of the Prime Minister.

———. March 1991. *White Paper on National and Sectoral Policies*. Windhoek: GRN.

———. June 1991. *National Conference on Land Reform and the Land Question*. Windhoek: Office of the Prime Minister.

———. April 1992. *Labour Act No. 6 of 1992*. Windhoek: Office of the Prime Minister.

———. August 1992. *White Paper on Industrial Policy*. Windhoek: GRN.

———. March 1993. *Working for a Better Namibia, Sectoral Development Programmes: Review of 1991–93 and Plans for the Future*. Windhoek: Office of the Prime Minister.

———. Central Statistics Office. 1992. *Statistical Abstract 1992*. Windhoek: National Planning Commission, Central Statistics Office.

———. Central Statistics Office. 1995. *1991 Population and Housing Census: Basic Analysis with Highlights*. Windhoek: Central Statistics Office.

———. Ministry of Finance. 1990–92, 1994. *Economic Review*. Windhoek: Ministry of Finance.

———. Ministry of Labour and Manpower Development. August 1990. Proposed Labour Code. Consultative Document. Mimeo. Windhoek.

———. Ministry of Labour and Manpower Development. September 1992. *The Status of the Economically Active Population of Namibia: Report of a Labour Force Sample Survey, August 1991*. Windhoek: MLMD.

———. National Planning Commission. September 1992. *1991 Population and Housing Census: Preliminary Report*. Windhoek: NPC.

———. National Planning Commission. December 1992. *Draft Transitional National Development Plan, 1991/92–1993/94*. Windhoek: NPC.

Republic of South Africa. 1963. *Report of the Commission of Enquiry into South West African Affairs, 1962–1963*. [Odendaal Commission] Pretoria: Government Printer.

———. Department of Foreign Affairs. 1967. *South West Africa Survey, 1967*. Pretoria: Government Printer.

———. Department of Foreign Affairs. 1975. *South West Africa Survey, 1974.* Pretoria: Government Printer.

South West Africa. 1948. *Report of the SWA Native Labourers Commission, 1945–1948.* Windhoek: Unie-Volkspers Beperk.

———. 1978. *The Economy of SWA/Namibia: Problems, Future Prospects and Required Policy Measures.* Windhoek: Department of Finance.

———. 1980. *South West Africa/Namibia Survey.* Windhoek: Office of the Administrator General.

———. 1989. *Report of the Commission of Inquiry into Labour Matters in Namibia.* [Wiehahn Commission] Windhoek: Office of the Administrator General.

———. Department of Economic Affairs. 1988. *Manpower Survey.* Windhoek.

———. Department of Finance. 1982–89. *Statistical/Economic Review.* Windhoek.

———. Department of Governmental Affairs. 1984. *Manpower Survey.* Windhoek.

PERIODICALS AND OTHER SERIES

Action on Namibia. 1981–90. London: Namibia Support Committee.

Africa Confidential. London.

Africa Demos. 1990–96. Bulletin of the African Governance Program. Carter Center of Emory University.

Africa Research Bulletin. Economic and Political Series. London.

Africa South and East. 1991–93. Johannesburg.

Business Spotlight. 1992–93. Windhoek: Chambers of Commerce and Industry.

Household Subsistence Level for the Major Urban Centres of the Republic of South Africa [including Windhoek]. 1976–91. Port Elizabeth: University of Port Elizabeth Institute of Planning Research.

IDAF Briefing Paper on Southern Africa. London: International Defence and Aid Fund.

IDAF Focus on Political Repression in South Africa and Namibia. London: International Defence and Aid Fund.

International Newsbriefing on Namibia. 1986–90. London: Namibia Support Committee.

Investor. 1992–93. Windhoek: Investment Centre of the Ministry of Trade and Industry.

Namibia, Botswana, Lesotho, Swaziland: Country Report. London: Economist Intelligence Unit.

Namibia Brief. 1985–93. Windhoek: Namibia Foundation.

Namibia Business Journal. 1991–93. Windhoek: Namibia National Chamber of Commerce and Industry.

Namibia: Country Profile. London: Economist Intelligence Unit.

Namibia Economist. 1990–93. Windhoek.

Namibia Review. 1992–95. Windhoek: Ministry of Information and Broadcasting.

Namibia Yearbook. 1990–91, 1991–92, 1992–93. Windhoek: Windhoek Printers.

Namibian. 1986–96. Windhoek.

Namibian Review. 1976–84. Stockholm and Windhoek.
Namibian Review Publications. 1983–85. Windhoek.
Namibian Worker. 1988–95. Windhoek: National Union of Namibian Workers.
New Era. 1991–96. Windhoek: Ministry of Information and Broadcasting.
Race Relations Survey. [*A Survey of Race Relations*] 1971–92. Johannesburg: South African Institute of Race Relations.
South West Africa Annual. 1945–86. Windhoek: South West Africa Publications.
Special Report of the Director General on the Application of the Declaration Concerning the Policy of Apartheid in South Africa [and Namibia]. 1965–90. Geneva: ILO.
SWA/N Ekonoom Economist. 1986–89. Windhoek.
Windhoek Advertiser. 1971–78, 1982, 1984, 1985. Windhoek.
Windhoek Observer. 1978–81, 1983. Windhoek.

SWAPO OF NAMIBIA PUBLICATIONS:

Combatant. Organ of the People's Liberation Army of Namibia (PLAN). 1981–89. Luanda.
Information and Comments. 1979–84, London; 1980–88, Luanda; 1978–82, Lusaka; 1976–84, New York; 1977–82, Stockholm.
Information Bulletin. 1980–88. Luanda.
Informations-Bulletin. 1983–89. Bonn.
Mifima, Solomon. 1972. "The Labour Situation in Namibia." *Namibia Documentation* 2. East Berlin: SWAPO.
Namibia News. 1968–76. London.
Namibia Today. Official Organ of the SWAPO. 1970–73, Dar es Salaam; 1973–79, Lusaka; 1980–85, Luanda.
Namibian Worker. 1983–89. Luanda: SWAPO Department of Labour.
SWAPO. 1961. *The Programme of the South West Africa People's Organisation.*
―――. 1970. "Special Report from the Consultative Congress in Tanga, Tanzania." *Namibia News.* Vol. 3, January–March 1970. [London.]
―――. 1976. *Constitution of the SWAPO of Namibia.* Adopted by the meeting of the Central Committee, 28 July–1 August 1976, Lusaka, Zambia.
―――. 1976. *Political Programme of the SWAPO of Namibia.* Adopted by the meeting of the Central Committee, 28 July–1 August 1976, Lusaka, Zambia.
―――. 1978. *SWAPO Information on SWAPO: An Historical Profile.* Lusaka: SWAPO Department of Information and Publicity.
―――. 1980. *20th Anniversary of the Founding of SWAPO: 1960–1980: Two Decades of Heroic Struggle.* Luanda: Central Committee of SWAPO.
―――. Department of Information and Publicity. 1981. *To Be Born a Nation.* London: Zed Press.
―――. 1983. *Constitution of the SWAPO of Namibia.* Amended and adopted by the

Second Enlarged Central Committee meeting, 17–20 August 1983, Cabuta, Kwanza-Sul Province, Angola.

———. 1984. *The Struggle for Trade Union Rights in Namibia.* Luanda: SWAPO Department of Labour.

———. 1985. *SWAPO Guidelines to Patriotic Allies Inside Namibia.* SWAPO Central Committee, 11 September 1985, Luanda.

———. May 1989. *Namibia's Economic Prospects Brighten Up.* An Economic Policy Position Document of the Political Bureau of the Central Committee of SWAPO, 28 November 1988, Luanda.

———. 1989. *SWAPO Election Manifesto. Towards an Independent and Democratic Namibia: SWAPO's Policy Positions.* Windhoek: SWAPO Directorate of Elections.

SWAPO Party. 1991. *Constitution.* Adopted by the First Congress of SWAPO Party in an Independent Namibia, 6–12 December 1991, Windhoek.

UNITED NATIONS AGENCY PUBLICATIONS

International Labour Office. 1983. *Report on the Seminar Concerning Discriminatory Legislation in Namibia Relating to Labour Matters, 2–5 December 1981, Lusaka.* Geneva: ILO.

———. March 1991. "Revised Draft: Republic of Namibia Labour Code." Mimeo. Windhoek.

———. 1991. *Report of the ILO Employment Advisory and Training Policy Mission.* Vol. 1. Geneva: ILO.

International Labour Organisation. 1953. *Report of the Ad Hoc Committee on Forced Labour.* Geneva: ILO.

———. 1964. *Programme for the Elimination of Apartheid in Labour Matters in the Republic of South Africa.* Geneva: ILO.

———. 1977. *Labour and Discrimination in Namibia.* Geneva: ILO.

———. October 1989. "Report of Exploratory Mission to Namibia, 25–29 September 1989." Geneva: ILO.

———. December 1991. "Namibia: Draft Country Strategy Paper." Geneva: ILO.

———. 1992. "Technical Memorandum to the Government of Namibia: Development of a Modern National Labour and Social Policy Administration System." Geneva: ILO.

United Nations Development Programme. 1989. *Base Studies on Financial, Economic and Social Aspects for the Arrangement for Independence in Namibia: A Macroeconomic and Sectoral Overview of the Economy of Namibia.* Windhoek: UNDP.

United Nations Institute for Namibia. 1986. *Namibia: Perspectives for National Reconciliation and Development.* Lusaka: UNIN.

THESES AND DISSERTATIONS

Angula, Lohmeier. 1986. "African Workers in the Mining and Fishing Industries—The 1978 Industrial Relations Framework and Beyond." M.Sc. thesis, University of Strathclyde.

Angulah, Hiskia. 1988. "Law, State and Control of Politics: A Case Study of the Legal Order and the Rule of Law in Contemporary Namibia, 1970-1988." LL.M. thesis, University of Warwick.

Banghart, Peter. 1969. "Migrant Labour in South West Africa and Its Effect on Ovambo Tribal Life." M.A. thesis, University of Stellenbosch.

Emmett, Anthony. 1987. "The Rise of African Nationalism in South West Africa/Namibia, 1915-1966." Ph.D. dissertation, University of the Witwatersrand.

Hartmann, Paul. 1986. "The Role of Mining in the Economy of South West Africa, 1950-1985." M.Sc. thesis, University of Stellenbosch.

Hayes, Patricia. 1992. "A History of the Ovambo of Namibia, 1880-1935." Ph.D. dissertation, Cambridge University.

Katjiuanjo, Steve. 1991. "The Impact of Unionisation in the Mining Industry (CDM): The Case of MUN, 1986-90." Honours B.Soc.Sc. thesis, University of Cape Town.

Kavari, Vitura. 1990. "The Contract Labour System and the Process of Labour Control in Namibia." M.Sc. thesis, University of Manchester.

Loffler, John. 1979. "Labour and Politics in Namibia in the 1970s." M.A. thesis, University of York.

Macfarlane, Alastair. 1990. "Labour Control: Managerial Strategies in the Namibian Mining Sector, 1970-1985." Ph.D. dissertation, Oxford Polytechnic.

Moorsom, Richard. 1973. "Colonisation and Proletarianisation: An Exploratory Investigation of the Formation of the Working Class in Namibia Under German and South African Colonial Rule Until 1945." M.A. thesis, Sussex University.

Ngavirue, Zedekia. 1972. "Political Parties and Interest Groups in South West Africa: A Study of a Plural Society." Ph.D. dissertation, Oxford University.

Olivier, M. J. 1961. "Inboorlingbeleid en Administrasie in die Mandaatgebied van Suidwes Afrika." D.Phil. dissertation, University of Stellenbosch.

Raedel, Fritz. 1947. "Die Wirtschaft und die Arbeiterfrage Suedwest Afrikas." Ph.D. dissertation, University of Stellenbosch.

Werner, Wolfgang. 1989. "An Economic and Social History of the Herero of Namibia, 1915-1946." Ph.D. dissertation, University of Cape Town.

UNPUBLISHED MANUSCRIPTS AND PAPERS

Angulah, Hiskia. 1988. "Legislative Control of Labour in Namibia: A Focus on the Migrant/Contract Labour System, 1910-1987." Mimeo. Warwick: University of Warwick.

Anonymous. 1972. "The Roads to Freedom in Namibia: Strike and Political Protest." Paper presented to the Namibia Fights for Freedom Conference convened by SWAPO, Brussels, 26–28 May.

Barkan, Joel, Gretchen Bauer, and Carol Lynn Martin. July 1994. "The Consolidation of Democracy in Namibia: Assessment and Recommendations." Final report prepared for Associates in Rural Development, Washington, D.C., and the United States Agency for International Development, Windhoek.

Bauer, Gretchen. May 1993. "Research Needs Assessment for the National Union of Namibian Workers (NUNW) and Affiliated Unions." Report prepared for the Friedrich Ebert Foundation, Windhoek.

———. 1996. "Prospects for the Consolidation of Democracy in Namibia." Revised version of paper originally presented at the Thirty-seventh Annual African Studies Association Meeting, Toronto.

Bolton, Brian. 1984. "The Condition of the Namibian Workers." Paper presented at the Seminar on the Activities of Foreign Economic Interests in the Exploitation of Namibia's Natural and Human Resources, Ljubljana, Yugoslavia, 16–20 April.

Chamber of Mines of SWA/Namibia. 1980. "A Working Paper on Labour Law and Labour Practice in SWA/Namibia." Mimeo. Windhoek.

Cheadle, Thompson, and Haysom. 1987. "Preliminary Written Representations Before the Commission of Inquiry into Labour Matters at Windhoek." Mimeo. Windhoek: Legal Assistance Centre.

First, Ruth. 1972. "The Bantustans: The Implementation of the Odendaal Report." Paper presented to the Namibia Fights for Freedom Conference convened by SWAPO, Brussels, 26–28 May.

Girvan, Lori Ann, and Chris Tapscott. 1993. "The Role of Farmers' Associations in Agricultural Policy Formulation and Implementation: A Look at Namibia." Draft of a paper prepared for an International Conference on Governments, Farmers' Organizations, and Food Policy, Kadoma, Zimbabwe, 31 May–3 June 1993.

Kane-Berman, John. 1972. "Contract Labour in South West Africa." Johannesburg: South African Institute of Race Relations.

———. 1973. "The Labour Situation in South West Africa." Johannesburg: South African Institute of Race Relations.

Kauluma, James. 1977. "The Contract Migrant Labor Situation in Namibia and the Response to It." Mimeo. Windhoek.

Koerner-Damman, Marita. 1990. "Labour in Namibia at Independence." Mimeo. Frankfurt: Goethe University.

Kuhrau, Karl. 1992. "The New Labour Act and Labour Relations in Namibia—Prospects for Development." Paper presented to the Namibia Working Group Meeting organized by the Namibian International Business Development Organisation, 30 July 1992, Windhoek.

Louw, Leon. 1982. "Free Enterprise as a Liberation Movement." Mimeo. Windhoek: Private Sector Foundation.

Lubowski, Anton. December 1986 and March 1988. "Progress Reports of the NUNW." Mimeos. Windhoek.

Mbuende, Kaire. 1990. "Social Movements and the Demise of Apartheid Colonialism in Namibia." Mimeo. Windhoek.

Meiring, Bob. 1988. "Industrial Relations in an Impoverished, Politicized and Polarized Society—A Discussion of the Fundamentals." Mimeo. Windhoek: Private Sector Foundation.

Mey, Theo. 1986. "Report: Exploratory Study on Labour Relations in SWA/Namibia." Windhoek: The Academy.

Mwase, Ngila. 1989. "The Manpower Study on Namibia." Paper presented at the UN Council for Namibia Seminar on the Integration of Namibia into the Regional Structures for Economic Cooperation and Development in Southern Africa, Harare, 23–27 October.

Peltola, Pekka. 1993. "The Role of the National Union of Namibian Workers in the Struggle for Independence." Mimeo. Helsinki: University of Helsinki.

Ritter, Rainer. 1992. "Experiences and Perspectives of the Namibian Economy: What Is Achievable?" Paper presented at Conference on Development of Democracy and Social Market Economy in Southern Africa, Windhoek, 2–3 December.

Simons, Ray. 1972. "The Namibian Challenge." Paper presented to Namibia Fights for Freedom Conference convened by SWAPO, Brussels, 26–28 May.

Smuts, David, Clive Thompson, and Halton Cheadle. 1992. "Namibian Labour Code Seminar." Windhoek: Namibia Labour Law Seminars.

Thompson, Cheadle, Jacobus, and Lubowski. 1988. "Before the Commission of Inquiry into Labour Matters at Windhoek: Supplementary Written Representations." Mimeo. Windhoek.

Vesikko, Markku. 1991. "Some Aspects of Trade Unions and Their Situation in Namibia." Mimeo. Windhoek.

Vesikko, Markku, and Bernhard Esau. 1992. "Report to the ICFTU Coordination Committee for Southern Africa, Brussels, October 1992." Mimeo. Windhoek.

CONFERENCE PROCEEDINGS

"A Collection of Papers Presented at the ILO/NIEA Symposium on the Role of Employers' Organisations in Africa." 30–31 August 1990. Windhoek: Namibia Institute for Economic Affairs.

"A Collection of Papers Presented at the Namibia Peace Plan (NPP 435) Symposium on Human Rights." 17–18 November 1989. Windhoek: Namibia Peace Plan.

"A Collection of Papers Presented at the NIEA Symposium on the Report of the Commission of Inquiry into Labour Matters in Namibia." 1–2 June 1989. Windhoek: Namibia Institute for Economic Affairs.

"Decolonization and Transition to a New Namibia: Hopes, Fears, Opinions, Attitudes—

What Do Namibians Expect from Their Future?" Proceedings, 8–10 May 1992. Windhoek: Midgaard Farm.

"Democracy and Trade Unions in Africa: Do We Need a New Orientation of Actions with Regard to Africa Today?" Proceedings and papers from conference sponsored by the ICFTU and Friedrich Ebert Foundation, 9–11 November 1992. Harare, Zimbabwe.

"First Regional Workshop on Labour Law and Industrial Relations in Southern Africa." Papers and proceedings, 13–15 July 1993. Durban, South Africa.

"National Tripartite Seminar on Employment and Development Planning in Namibia Organized by the Ministry of Labour and Manpower Development in Co-operation with the National Planning Commission and the International Labour Organisation." Proceedings, 6–8 April 1992. Safari Hotel, Windhoek.

"National Tripartite Seminar on the Labour Bill Conducted by the Ministry of Labour and Manpower Development." Proceedings, 13–14 February 1992. SKW Hall, Windhoek.

"National Union of Namibian Workers Demarcation Forum Organized by the NUNW and the ICFTU." Proceedings, 13 March 1993. Union Centre, Katutura.

"National Union of Namibian Workers Economic Conference Organized by the Friedrich Ebert Foundation and the NUNW." Proceedings, 2–4 October 1992. Harmony Seminar Centre, Windhoek.

"Prime Minister's Consultative Meeting on Labour Relations in Namibia." Proceedings and papers, 25–26 February 1993. Cabinet Chambers, Windhoek.

"Private Sector Investment Conference Organized by the Ministry of Trade and Industry." Proceedings, 4–6 February 1991. Kalahari Sands Hotel, Windhoek.

"Reconstruction and Reconciliation: Critical Choices for Southern Africa." Proceedings, 15–19 November 1990. Windhoek: Friedrich Ebert Foundation.

Annual Reports

Chamber of Mines of Namibia. 1980–91, 1993. *Annual Reports*. Windhoek: Chamber of Mines of Namibia.

Private Sector Foundation. 1980–91. *Annual Reports*. Windhoek: Private Sector Foundation.

Suidwes Afrikaanse Landbou Unie (SWALU). 1977–86, 1993. *Jaarsverslae*. Windhoek: SWALU.

Books and Articles on Namibia

Adams, Fiona, Wolfgang Werner, and Peter Vale. 1990. "The Land Issue in Namibia: An Inquiry." *Research Report No. 1*. Windhoek: NISER.

Africa. 1972. "The Ovambo Strike." 7:37–38.

Africa Watch. 1992. *Accountability in Namibia: Human Rights and the Transition to Democracy.* New York: Human Rights Watch.

Allison, Caroline, and Reginald Green. 1986. "Political Economy and Structural Change: Namibia at Independence." *IDS Discussion Paper No. 212.* Sussex: IDS.

Amukugo, Elizabeth. 1993. *Education and Politics in Namibia: Past Trends and Future Prospects.* Windhoek: New Namibia Books.

Andersson, Neil, and Shula Marks. 1987. "Work and Health in Namibia: Preliminary Notes." *Journal of Southern African Studies* 13:274–92.

Angula, Helmut Kangulohi. 1990. *The Two Thousand Days of Haimbodi Ya Haufiku.* Windhoek: Gamsberg Macmillan.

Anonymous. N.d. "The Workers Strike Back." *Action on Namibia.*

———. 1981. "Inside Rossing Mine: An Interview with Arthur Pickering." *Action on Namibia.*

———. 1987. "Flowers in the Desert: Trade Unions in Namibia." *Learn and Teach* 6:9–16.

Asante, S. K. B., and W. W. Asombang. 1989. "An Independent Namibia? The Future Facing SWAPO." *Third World Quarterly* 11:1–19.

Balch, Jeffrey, and Jan Nico Scholten. 1990. "Namibian Reconstruction and National Reconciliation: Putting the Horse Before the Cart." *Review of African Political Economy* 40:82–93.

Banghart, Peter. 1972. "The Effects of the Migrant Labour on the Ovambo of South West Africa." *Fort Hare Papers* 5:267–81.

Bauer, Gretchen. 1992. "The New Labour Act: Best Compromise Achievable." *Namibia Review* 1(6):18–24.

———. 1993. "Defining a Role: Trade Unions in Namibia." *Southern Africa Report.* 8(5):8–11.

———. 1993. "Tripartism and Workers in Namibia." *South African Labour Bulletin.* 17(4):64–68.

Becker, Heike. 1995. *Namibian Women's Movement, 1980 to 1992: From Anti-colonial Resistance to Reconstruction.* Frankfurt: Verlag für Interkulturelle Kommunikation.

Beinart, William. 1987. "'Jamani': Cape Workers in German South West Africa, 1904–1912." In *Hidden Struggles in Rural South Africa,* edited by William Beinart and Colin Bundy. Johannesburg: Ravan Press.

Beukes, Erica Thiro, Attie Beukes, and Hewat Beukes. 1986. *Namibia: A Struggle Betrayed.* Rehoboth: Akasia Drukkery.

Bush, Ray. 1989. "The Namibian Election Process: Just About 'Free and Fair.'" *Review of African Political Economy* 45–46:151–57.

Catholic Institute for International Relations. 1983. *A Future for Namibia 3: Mines and Independence.* London: CIIR.

———. 1986. *Namibia in the 1980s.* London: CIIR.

Cawthra, Gavin. 1988. "South Africa at War." In *South Africa in Question*, edited by John Lonsdale. Cambridge: Cambridge University Press.

Cisse, Kene, ed. 1992. *Africa Political Magazine Who Is Who: Namibia Today*. Windhoek.

Clarence-Smith, Gervase, and Richard Moorsom. 1975. "Underdevelopment and Class Formation in Ovamboland, 1845–1915." *Journal of African History* 16:365–81.

Cleaver, Tessa, and Marion Wallace. 1990. *Namibia Women in War*. London: Zed Books.

Cliffe, Lionel. 1989. "Namibia Postscript: The Election Results." *Review of African Political Economy* 45–46:157–58.

Cliffe, Lionel, with Ray Bush, Jenny Lindsay, Brian Mokopakgosi, Donna Pankhurst, and Balefi Tsie. 1993. *The Transition to Independence in Namibia*. Boulder: Lynne Rienner.

Corbett, Andrew. 1993. "Capital, Labour and Government." *Namibia Yearbook, 1992–93*. No. 3:52–55.

Cronje, Gillian, and Suzanne Cronje. 1979. *The Workers of Namibia*. London: International Defence and Aid Fund.

Cullinan, Sue. 1982. "The Namibian Dispute." *Work in Progress* 24:28–39.

———. 1982. "SWAPO and the Anti-Colonial Struggle." *Work in Progress* 23:27–43.

———. 1985. "SWAPO and the Future of Namibia." *South Africa International* 15:141–49.

Curry, Steve, and Colin Stoneman. 1993. "Problems of Industrial Development and Market Integration in Namibia." *Journal of Southern African Studies* 19(1):40–59.

Davidson, Alex. 1991. "Democracy and Development in Namibia: The State of Democracy and Civil Rights, 1988–1991." *Studies in Democracy 2*. Uppsala: University of Uppsala.

———. 1994. "Government and Opposition in Namibia: The State of Democracy Four Years After Independence." *Studies in Democracy 8*. Uppsala: University of Uppsala.

De Beer, David. 1972. "The Ovambo Strike." *South African Outlook* 102:25–27.

———. 1988. "Namibia: Placing Present Developments in Perspective." *Review of African Political Economy* 42:90–100.

Dobell, Lauren. 1992. "The SWAPO Congress." *Southern Africa Report* 7(5):23–26.

———. 1995. "SWAPO in Office." In *Namibia's Liberation Struggle: The Two-Edged Sword*, edited by Colin Leys and John Saul. London: James Currey, Athens: Ohio University Press.

———. 1995. "The SWAPO Sweep." *Southern Africa Report* 10(4):5–9.

Dollie, Na-iem, ed. 1988. *A Political Review of Namibia: Nationalism in Namibia*. Cape Town: Logo Print.

Douwes Dekker, L., D. Hemson, J. S. Kane-Berman, J. Lever, and L. Schlemmer. 1975. "Case Studies in African Labour Action in South Africa and Namibia." In *The Development of an African Working Class*, edited by Richard Sandbrook and Robin Cohen. London: Longman.

Drechsler, Horst. 1980. [1966] *"Let Us Die Fighting": The Struggle of the Herero and Nama Against German Imperialism, 1884–1915*. London: Zed Press.

Du Pisani, Andre. 1982. "Namibia: From Incorporation to Controlled Change." *Journal of Contemporary African Studies* 1:281–305.

———. 1985. "Namibia: A New Transitional Government." *South Africa International* 16:66–73.

———. 1985. *SWA/Namibia: Politics of Continuity and Change.* Johannesburg: Jonathan Ball Publishers.

———. 1989. "Whither Namibia?" In *The Southern Africa Policy Forum.* Queenstown, Md.: Aspen Institute.

———. 1991. "Rumours of Rain: Namibia's Post-Independence Experience." *Africa Insight* 21:171–79.

Du Preez, Max. 1986. "Namibia: A Future Displaced." In South African Research Service, *South African Review III.* Johannesburg: Ravan Press.

Ellis, Justin. 1984. *A Future for Namibia 4: Education, Repression and Liberation, Namibia.* London: Catholic Institute for International Relations.

Eriksen, Tore Linne. 1989. *The Political Economy of Namibia: An Annotated Critical Bibliography.* Uppsala: Scandinavian Institute of African Studies.

Esterhuysen, Pieter. 1991. "The Countdown to Independence." In *Namibia 1990: An Africa Institute Country Survey,* edited by Erich Leistner and Pieter Esterhuysen. Pretoria: Africa Institute of South Africa.

———. 1991. "The Decisive Years." In *Namibia 1990: An Africa Institute Country Survey,* edited by Erich Leistner and Pieter Esterhuysen. Pretoria: Africa Institute of South Africa.

Etukudo, Akanimo. 1992. "From Scepticism to Confidence: African Employers' Organisations as Partners in Development." *Business Spotlight* 2:13–20.

Eze, Osita. 1976. "Labour Regime and the Namibian Worker: Some Reflections on Human Rights." *International and Comparative Law* 9:473–90.

Financial Mail Special Survey. "South West: Calm Amidst the Storm." 20 August 1965. 61 pp.

Financial Mail Special Survey. "South West Africa: Desert Deadlock." 2 March 1973. 68 pp.

Financial Mail Special Survey. "Namibia." 22 July 1983. 40 pp.

First, Ruth. 1963. *South West Africa.* Harmondsworth: Penguin.

Ford, John. 1993. "The Labour Act—How It Affects Your Business." *Namibia Business Journal* 3(1):1–2, 8–9.

Forrest, Joshua. 1992. "A Promising Start: The Inauguration and Consolidation of Democracy in Namibia." *World Policy Journal* 9:739–53.

———. 1994. "Namibia—The First Post Apartheid Democracy." *Journal of Democracy* 5(3):88–100.

Fraenkel, Peter, and Roger Murray. 1985. *The Namibians.* London: Minority Rights Group.

Frayne, Bruce. 1992. *Urbanisation in Post-Independence Windhoek.* Research Report No. 6. Windhoek: NISER.

Freeman, Linda. 1992. "Contradictions of Independence: Namibia in Transition." *Transformation* 17:25–47.

Gebhardt, Bettina. 1978. "The Socioeconomic Status of Farm Labourers in Namibia." *South African Labour Bulletin* 4:145–73.

Gorbunov, Y. 1988. *Namibia—A Struggle for Independence: A Collection of Articles, Documents and Speeches.* Moscow: Progress Publishers.

Gordon, Robert. 1975. "A Note on the History of Labour Action in Namibia." *South African Labour Bulletin* 1:7–17.

———. 1977. *Mines, Masters and Migrants: Life in a Namibian Mine Compound.* Johannesburg: Ravan Press.

———. 1978. "The Celebration of Ethnicity: A 'Tribal Fight' in a Namibian Mine Compound." In *Ethnicity in Modern Africa*, edited by Brian du Toit. Boulder: Westview.

———. 1978. "Some Organisational Aspects of Labour Protest Amongst Contract Workers in Namibia." *South African Labour Bulletin* 4:116–23.

———. 1978. "Variations in Migration Rates: The Ovambo Case." *Journal of Southern African Affairs* 3:261–94.

———. 1993. "The Impact of the Second World War on Namibia." *Journal of Southern African Studies* 19(1):147–65.

Gottschalk, Keith. 1978. "South African Labour Policy in Namibia, 1915–1978." *South African Labour Bulletin* 4:75–106.

———. 1985. "South African Colonial Policy in Namibia." *Namibian Review Publications* 2:36–44.

Green, Pippa. 1987. "Cutting the 'Wire': Labor Control and Worker Resistance in Namibia." *Southern Africa Perspectives No. 2.* New York: Africa Fund.

Green, Reginald, Kimmo Kiljunen, and Marja-Liisa Kiljunen, eds. 1981. *Namibia—The Last Colony.* London: Longman.

Hackland, Brian, Anne Murray-Hudson, and Brian Wood. 1986. "Behind the Diplomacy: Namibia, 1983–85." *Third World Quarterly* 8:51–77.

Hamutenya, Hidipo, and Hage Geingob. 1972. "African Nationalism in Namibia." In *Southern Africa in Perspective: Essays on Regional Politics*, edited by Christian Potholm and Richard Dale. New York: Free Press.

Harding, Jeremy. 1993. *The Fate of Africa: Trial by Fire.* New York: Simon and Schuster.

Hartneit-Sievers, Axel. 1985. *SWAPO of Namibia.* Hamburg: Institut für Afrika-Kunde.

Herbstein, Denis, and John Evenson. 1989. *The Devils Are Among Us: The War for Namibia.* London: Zed Press.

Hishongwa, Ndeutala. 1992. *The Contract Labour System and Its Effect on Family and Social Life in Namibia.* Windhoek: Gamsberg Macmillan.

Horner, Simon. 1991. "Added Value Equals Greater Prosperity: An Interview with Dr. Ben Amathila, Minister for Trade and Industry." *Courier* 127:39–41.

———. 1991. "Partnership with Business to Create Wealth: An Interview with Prime Minister Geingob." *Courier* 127:35–36.

Horrell, Muriel. 1967. *South West Africa.* Johannesburg: South African Institute of Race Relations.

Hubbard, Dianne. 1989. "Ulenga: SWAPO, Unions—One Struggle." *South African Labour Bulletin* 14:101–4.

Hubbard, Dianne, and Colette Solomon. 1995. "The Many Faces of Feminism in Namibia." In *The Challenge of Local Feminisms: Women's Movements in Global Perspective*, edited by Amrita Basu. Boulder: Westview Press.

Innes, Duncan. 1977. "Imperialism and the National Struggle in Namibia." *Review of African Political Economy* 9:44–59.

International Defence and Aid Fund. 1982. "Apartheid's Army in Namibia: South African's Illegal Military Occupation." *Fact Paper on Southern Africa No. 10*. London: IDAF.

———. 1987. "Working Under South African Occupation: Labour in Namibia." *Fact Paper on Southern Africa No. 14*. London: IDAF.

Kaakunga, Elia. 1990. *Problems of Capitalist Development in Namibia: The Dialectics of Progress and Destruction*. Abo: Abo Academy Press.

Kaangueehi, Sondagh. 1986. "From the 'Old Location' to Katutura." In *Katutura Revisited: Essays on a Black Namibian Apartheid Suburb*, edited by Christine Von Garnier. Windhoek: Roman Catholic Church.

Katjavivi, Peter. 1988. *A History of Resistance in Namibia*. Paris: UNESCO.

Katjavivi, Peter, Per Frostin, and Kaire Mbuende. 1989. *Church and Liberation in Namibia*. London: Pluto Press.

Kauraisa, Charles. 1967. "The Labour Force." In *South West Africa: Travesty of Trust*, edited by Charles Segal and Ruth First. London: Andre Deutsch.

Kaure, Alexactus Tukuapi. 1993. "Three Years of Independence: Achievements and Future Challenges." *Namibia Review* 2:2–6.

Kerina, Mburumba. 1981. *The Making of a Nation*. New York: Books in Focus.

Kiljunen, Kimmo. 1980. "Namibia: The Ideology of National Liberation." *IDS Bulletin* 11:65–71.

Koenig, Barbara. 1983. *Namibia: The Ravages of War*. London: International Defence and Aid Fund.

Konrad Adenauer Foundation. 1992. *Namibian Views and Perspectives Since Independence*. Windhoek: Konrad Adenauer Foundation and the Namibian Institute for Democracy.

———. 1992. *Namibian Views: Affirmative Action*. Windhoek: Konrad Adenauer Foundation and the Namibia Institute for Democracy.

Kooy, Marcelle. 1973. "The Contract Labour System and the Ovambo Crisis of 1971 in South West Africa." *African Studies Review* 16:83–106.

Kuhrau, Karl. 1991. "Guidelines for Fair Retrenchment." *Business Spotlight*, October.

———. 1991. "The New Labour Bill and Retrenchment." *Business Spotlight*, November–December.

———. 1992. "The New Labour Act: Preparing for Transition." *Business Spotlight* 2:5–6.

———. 1992. "The New Labour Bill and Conditions of Employment." *Business Spotlight* 1:13–15.

———. 1992. "Trade Unions—To Recognise or Not to Recognise?" *Business Spotlight* 3:9–11.

Landis, Elizabeth. 1985. "Security Legislation in Namibia: Memorandum of the South West Africa (Namibian) Bar Council." *Yale Journal of International Law* 11 (1):48–103.

Leistner, Erich, and Pieter Esterhuysen, eds. 1991. *Namibia 1990: An Africa Institute Country Survey*. Pretoria: Africa Institute of South Africa.

Leistner, Erich, Pieter Esterhuysen, and Theo Malan. 1980. *Namibia/SWA Prospectus*. Pretoria: Africa Institute of South Africa.

Leys, Colin, and John Saul. 1994. "Liberation Without Democracy? The SWAPO Crisis of 1976." *Journal of Southern African Studies* 20(1):123–47.

———. 1995. "SWAPO Inside Namibia." In *Namibia's Liberation Struggle: The Two-Edged Sword*, edited by Colin Leys and John Saul. London: James Currey, Athens: Ohio University Press.

———, eds. 1995. *Namibia's Liberation Struggle: The Two-Edged Sword*. London: James Currey, Athens: Ohio University Press.

Lindeke, William. 1992. "Export Processing Zones: Hidden Thorns and Alternatives." *Namibia Review* 1:11–16.

Lindeke, William, and Winnie Wanzala. 1994. "Regional Elections in Namibia: Deepening Democracy and Gender Inclusion." *Africa Today* 41(3):5–14.

Lindeke, William, Winnie Wanzala, and Victor Tonchi. 1992. "Namibia's Election Revisited." *Politikon* 18(2):121–38.

Lindsay, Jenny. 1990. "Constituting a Nation." *Southern Africa Report* 15(4):5–7.

Longmire, Philip. 1990. "Land and Labour in the Namibian Economy." In *Studies in the Economic History of Southern Africa*, edited by Z. A. Konczacki, Jane Parpart, and Timothy Shaw. Vol. 1. London: Frank Cass.

Lubowski, Molly, and Marita van der Vyver. 1992. *Anton Lubowski: Paradox of a Man*. Strand: Queillerie Publishers.

Lush, David. 1993. *Last Steps to Uhuru: An Eye-Witness Account of Namibia's Transition to Independence*. Windhoek: New Namibia Books.

Magyar, Karl. 1987. "Namibia: Development Problems in a Transitional Context." *South Africa International* 17:153–66.

Mandaza, Ibbo. 1989. "The Namibia Question: Towards the Post-White Settler Colonial Situation." *Southern African Political and Economic Monthly* 3:3–8.

Marcum, John. 1990. "Namibia's Independence and the Transformation of Africa." *SAIS Review* 10:153–65.

Maseko, Sipho. 1995. "The Role and Effects of the Namibian Student Movement." In *Namibia's Liberation Struggle: The Two-Edged Sword*, edited by Colin Leys and John Saul. London: James Currey, Athens: Ohio University Press.

Max, Gerson. 1977. "Die Geestelike en Materiele Situasie van die Kontrakarbeiders." *Afrikanisher Heimatkalender*, 69–74.

Mbako, Simon Zhu. 1988. "Namibia: South Africa's Neo-Colonial Strategy in Crisis." *African Communist* 112:18–37.

Mbuende, Kaire. 1986. *Namibia, the Broken Shield: Anatomy of Imperialism and Revolution*. Malmo: Liber Forlag.

Melber, Henning. 1983. "The National Union of Namibian Workers: Background and Formation." *Journal of Modern African Studies* 21:151–58.

Mineworkers Union of Namibia. 1989. *Shop Steward Training Manual.* Windhoek: MUN.

Moleah, Alfred. 1983. *Namibia: The Struggle for Liberation.* Wilmington: Disa Press.

Moorsom, Richard. 1977. "Underdevelopment and Class Formation: The Origins of Migrant Labour in Namibia, 1815–1915." In *Perspectives on South Africa: A Collection of Working Papers,* edited by Tuffy Adler. Johannesburg: University of the Witwatersrand African Studies Institute.

———. 1977. "Underdevelopment, Contract Labour and Worker Consciousness in Namibia, 1915–1972." *Journal of Southern African Studies* 4:52–87.

———. 1978. "Migrant Workers and the Formation of SWANLA, 1900–1926." *South African Labour Bulletin* 4:107–15.

———. 1979. "Labour Consciousness and the 1971–72 Contract Workers Strike in Namibia." *Development and Change* 10:205–31.

———. 1980. "Namibia in the Frontline: The Political Economy of Decolonisation in South Africa's Colony." *Review of African Political Economy* 17:71–82.

———. 1980. "Underdevelopment and Class Formation: The Birth of the Contract Labour System in Namibia." In *Southern African Research in Progress: Collected Papers 5,* edited by Anne Akeryod and Christopher Hill. York: University of York Centre for Southern African Studies.

———. 1982. *A Future for Namibia 2: Transforming a Wasted Land.* London: Catholic Institute for International Relations.

———. 1984. *A Future for Namibia 5: Exploiting the Sea.* London: Catholic Institute for International Relations.

———. 1990. *Namibia's Economy at Independence: Report on Potential Norwegian-Namibian Cooperation.* Bergen: Chr. Michelsen Institute.

Morris, Jo. 1974. "The Black Workers in Namibia." In *The Role of Foreign Firms in Namibia: Studies on External Investment and Black Workers' Conditions in Namibia,* edited by Roger Murray, Jo Morris, John Dugard, and Neville Rubin. Uppsala: Africa Publications Trust.

Murray, Roger. 1989. "Namibia: Overcoming the Colonial Legacy." *Africa Recovery* 3:17–20.

———. 1990. "Pragmatic Approach May Reap Benefits." *Africa Economic Digest* 11:2–6.

———. 1992. *Namibia Through the 1990s: Turning Rich Resources into Growth.* London: Economist Intelligence Unit.

Murray-Hudson, Anne. 1986. "Mobilisations Grow Inside Namibia: SWAPO Builds Mass Opposition." *Action on Namibia* Autumn:7–10.

Mutjavikua, Cleophas. 1993. "Law to Enhance Labour Relations." *Namibia Review* 2:13–14.

Namibia Foundation. 1990. "Namibia—A Vision of the Future." *Namibia Brief* 12:5–22.

———. 1991. "Namibia Welcomes Investors as Partners." *Namibia Brief* 13:1–11.

Namibia Peace Plan Study and Contact Group (NPP 435). 1987. *The Choice! Namibia Peace Plan 435 or Society Under Siege.* Windhoek: NPP 435.

Namibia Report. 1990. "New Labour Code Proposed." 1:1–8.

Namibia Support Committee. 1991. "Trade Unions in Namibia." *South African Labour Bulletin* 15:70–74.

National Democratic Institute. 1990. *Nation Building: The UN and Namibia.* Washington, D.C.: NDI.

———. 1994. *Comments on the Namibian Presidential and National Assembly Elections.* Washington, D.C.: NDI.

National Union of Namibian Workers. 1992. *Shopsteward Handbook.* Windhoek: NUNW.

National Union of Namibian Workers and COSATU. 1990. *Namibian Workers Organise.* Johannesburg: COSATU.

Ndadi, Vinnia. 1989. [1974] *Breaking Contract.* London: International Defence and Aid Fund.

Nehova, Hinananje Shafodino. 1978. "The Price of Liberation." In *Namibia: SWAPO Fights for Freedom,* edited by Liberation Support Movement. Oakland: LSM.

Ngavirue, Zedekia. 1982. *Manpower Survey '81: A Report on a Survey Conducted by the Private Sector Foundation.* Windhoek: PSF.

Niddrie, David. 1988. "Namibia—Nation-in-Waiting." *Work in Progress* 54:7–12.

———. 1989. "Namibia: The Detentions." *Work in Progress* 61:21–23.

———. 1989. "Namibia: To the Victor the Spoils." *Work in Progress* 61:18–20.

Norval, Dixon, and Rosy Namoya. 1992. *The Informal Sector Within Greater Windhoek.* Windhoek: First National Development Corporation.

Omar, Gasan. 1990. "An Introduction to Namibia's Political Economy." *SALDRU Working Paper No. 78.* Cape Town: SALDRU Labour Research Service.

Overseas Development Institute. 1989. "Economic Prospects for Namibia." *ODI Briefing Paper.* London: ODI.

Pakleppa, Richard. 1988. "40,000 Workers Stay Away in Namibia." *South African Labour Bulletin* 13:15–23.

Peltola, Pekka. 1995. *The Lost May Day: Namibian Workers Struggle for Independence.* Helsinki: Finnish Anthropological Society.

Pendleton, Wade. 1974. *Katutura: A Place Where We Do Not Stay.* San Diego: San Diego University Press.

———. 1994. *Katutura: A Place Where We Stay. Life in a Post-Apartheid Township in Namibia: Katutura Before and Now.* Windhoek: Gamsberg Macmillan.

Pieters, David, and Cathy Blatt. 1992. "Namibia: Guided by the Politics of Reconciliation." *Namibia Brief* 14:5–15.

Potgieter, P. J. J. S. 1991. "The Resolution 435 Election in Namibia." *Politikon* 18:26–48.

Private Sector Foundation. 1981. *Labour Relations in SWA/Namibia: A First Assessment.* Windhoek: PSF.

———. 1986. *Works Councils.* Windhoek: PSF.

Puetz, Joachim, Heidi Von Egidy, and Perri Caplan. 1989. *Namibia Handbook and Political Who's Who*. Windhoek: Magus.

Ridgway, Dawn, Milly Jafta, Nicky Kautja, Magda Oliphant, and Kapofi Shipingana. 1991. *An Investigation into the Shooting at the Old Location on 10 December 1959.* Windhoek: University of Namibia.

Ritter, Rainer. 1992. "Is Government Too Big in Namibia?" *Business Spotlight* 2:10–12.

Rogers, Barbara. 1972. "Namibia's General Strike." *Africa Today* 19:3–8.

———. 1978. "Notes on the Labour Conditions at the Rossing Mine." *South African Labour Bulletin* 4:140–44.

Rotberg, Robert, ed. 1983. *Namibia: Political and Economic Prospects*. Cape Town: David Philip.

Rukoro, Vekuii. 1986. "Legal Aid and Community Advice Bureau." In *Katutura Revisited: Essays on a Black Namibian Apartheid Suburb*, edited by Christine Von Garnier. Windhoek: Roman Catholic Church.

Ruppel, Hartmut. 1987. "Namibia: Security Legislation and Its Consequences." In *Namibia in Perspective*, edited by Gerhard Toetemeyer, Vezera Kandetu, and Wolfgang Werner. Windhoek: Council of Churches of Namibia.

Saul, John, and Colin Leys. 1995. "SWAPO: The Politics of Exile." In *Namibia's Liberation Struggle: The Two Edged Sword*, edited by Colin Leys and John Saul. London: James Currey, Athens: Ohio University Press.

Saunders, Christopher. 1983. "Towards the Decolonisation of Namibian History: Notes on Some Recent Work in English." *Namibian Review* 27:29–36.

———. 1992. "Transition in Namibia, 1989–1990: And the South African Case." *Transformation* 17:12–24.

Schmokel, Wolfe. 1985. "The Myth of the White Farmer: Commercial Agriculture in Namibia, 1900–1983." *International Journal of African Historical Studies* 18:93–108.

Sechaba. 1972. "The Great Namibian Strike." 6(4):19–24.

Segal, Ronald, and Ruth First, eds. 1967. *South West Africa: Travesty of Trust*. London: Andre Deutsch.

Seiler, John. 1982. "South Africa in Namibia: Persistence, Misperception, and Ultimate Failure." *Journal of Modern African Studies* 20:689–712.

Serfontein, J. H. P. 1976. "South West Africa/Namibia: The Domestic Scene." In *SWA/Namibia: A Symposium*, edited by J. D. Van der Vyver. Braamfontein: South African Institute of International Affairs.

Shipanga, Andreas. 1989. *In Search of Freedom: The Andreas Shipanga Story*. Gibraltar: Ashanti Publishing.

Shityuwete, Helao. 1990. *Never Follow the Wolf: The Autobiography of a Namibian Freedom Fighter*. London: Kliptown Books.

Siiskonen, Harri. 1990. *Trade and Socioeconomic Change in Ovamboland, 1850–1906*. Helsinki: Societas Historica Fennica.

Simon, David. 1985. "Decolonisation and Local Government in Namibia: The Neo-Apartheid Plan, 1977–83." *Journal of Modern African Studies* 23:507–26.

———. 1990–91. "A Democratic Charter." *Namibia Yearbook*. No. 1:62–64.

Soggot, David. 1986. *Namibia: The Violent Heritage*. London: Rex Collings.

South African Labour Bulletin. 1978. "Focus on Namibia." 4:1–194.

Stals, Ernst, and Pieter Esterhuysen. 1991. "From Pre-Colonial Obscurity to International Prominence." In *Namibia 1990: An Africa Institute Country Survey*, edited by Erich Leistner and Pieter Esterhuysen. Pretoria: Africa Institute of South Africa.

Steenkamp, Philip. 1994. "The Church and the Liberation of Namibia." In *Christianity and Democratization in Africa*, edited by Paul Gifford. London: James Currey.

———. 1995. "The Churches." In *Namibia's Liberation Struggle: The Two Edged Sword*, edited by Colin Leys and John Saul. London: James Currey, Athens: Ohio University Press.

Strand, Per. 1991. "SWAPO and Nation Building in Namibia, Transfer of Power in a Post-Communist Era." *Discussion Paper No. 8*. Windhoek: NISER.

Strauss, Andre. 1986. "Community Based Organisations (CBOs) in Katutura." In *Katutura Revisited: Essays on a Black Namibian Apartheid Suburb*, edited by Christine Von Garnier. Windhoek: Roman Catholic Church.

———. 1987. "Community Organisations in Namibia." In *Namibia in Perspective*, edited by Gerhard Toetemeyer, Vezera Kandetu, and Wolfgang Werner. Windhoek: Council of Churches of Namibia.

Streek, Barry. 1984. "Unions in Namibia." *South African Labour Bulletin* 9:14–16.

Tamas, Kristof. 1992. "After Return—Repatriated Exiles in Independent Namibia." *Discussion Paper No. 15*. Windhoek: NISER.

Tapscott, Chris. 1991. "Namibia: A Class Act?" *Southern Africa Report* 6:3–6.

———. 1993. "National Reconciliation, Social Equity and Class Formation in Independent Namibia." *Journal of Southern African Studies* 19(1):29–39.

———. 1994. "Land Reform in Namibia: Why Not?" *Southern Africa Report* 9(3):12–15.

Tapscott, Chris, and Ben Mulongeni. 1990. *An Evaluation of the Welfare and Future Prospects of Repatriated Namibians in Northern Namibia*. Research Report No. 3. Windhoek: NISER.

Terreblanche, Christelle. 1993. "Namibian Trade Unions in Tatters." *South*, 29 October– 2 November.

Thomas, Wolfgang. 1978. *Economic Development in Namibia: Towards Acceptable Development Strategies for Independent Namibia*. Munich: Kaiser Verlag.

Tjingaete, Fanuel. 1989. "Set the Market Free." *Optima* 37:71–78.

Tjitendero, Sandra. 1992. "Export Processing Zones: A Strategy for Industrial Development." *Namibia Review* 1:5–10.

Toetemeyer, Gerhard. 1977. *South West Africa/Namibia: Facts, Attitudes, Assessment, and Prospects*. Randburg: Fokus Suid.

———. 1978. *Namibia Old and New: Traditional and Modern Leaders in Ovamboland*. London: Hurst.

———. 1990. "The Prospects for Democracy and Development in an Independent Namibia." *IDASA Occasional Paper No. 28*. Johannesburg: IDASA.

————. 1991. "The Regional Reconstruction of the State—The Namibian Case." *Politikon* 19(1):66–82.

Toetemeyer, Gerhard, Vezera Kandetu, and Wolfgang Werner, eds. 1987. *Namibia in Perspective.* Windhoek: Council of Churches of Namibia.

Toetemeyer, Gerhard, Victor Tonchi, and Andre du Pisani. 1994. *Namibia Regional Resources Manual.* Windhoek: Friedrich Ebert Stiftung.

Ulenga, Ben. 1987. "The Exploited Worker in Namibia—A Testimony." In *Namibia in Perspective,* edited by Gerhard Toetemeyer, Vezera Kandetu and Wolfgang Werner. Windhoek: Council of Churches of Namibia.

Uys, Stanley. 1982. "Namibia: The Socialist Dilemma." *African Affairs* 81:569–76.

Vale, Peter. 1988. "Beyond the Bend: South Africa, Southern Africa and Namibian Independence." *IDASA Occasional Paper No. 13.* Johannesburg: IDASA.

Verbaan, Mark. 1990. "Namibian Unions: Not Quite There." *Work in Progress* 64:34–35.

Vigne, Randolph. 1983. "The Namibia File." *Third World Quarterly* 5:345–60.

————. 1987. "SWAPO of Namibia: A Movement in Exile." *Third World Quarterly* 9:85–107.

Voipio, Rauha. 1972. *Kontrak Soos die Owambo Dit Sien.* Windhoek: Evangelical Lutheran Ovambo-Kavango Church.

Von Garnier, Christine, ed. 1986. *Katutura Revisited: Essays on a Black Namibian Apartheid Suburb.* Windhoek: Roman Catholic Church.

Weaver, Tony. 1984. "Namibian Review." In South African Research Service, *South African Review II.* Johannesburg: Ravan Press.

————. 1987. "The War in Namibia." In *Namibia in Perspective,* edited by Gerhard Toetemeyer, Vezera Kandetu, and Wolfgang Werner. Windhoek: Council of Churches of Namibia.

————. 1989. "The South African Defence Force in Namibia." In *War and Society: The Militarisation of South Africa,* edited by Jacklyn Cock and Laurie Nathan. Cape Town: David Philip.

Wellmer, Gottfried. 1990. "Notes on Namibia's Transition to Independence." *Southern Africa Dossier.* Maputo: Eduardo Mondlane University.

Werner, Wolfgang. 1987. "Namibia Update: Trade Unions and Labour Action, May–August 1987." *South African Labour Bulletin* 12:60–73.

————. 1987. "Namibia Update: Trade Unions and Labour Action, September–October 1987." *South African Labour Bulletin* 13:94–101.

————. 1988. "Namibia Update: Namibian Mineworkers' Congress." *South African Labour Bulletin* 13:114–16.

————. 1990. " 'Playing Soldiers': The Truppenspieler Movement Among the Herero of Namibia, 1915 to ca. 1945." *Journal of Southern African Studies* 16:476–502.

Wiehahn, Nic. 1989. "Industrial Relations in Namibia." *Optima* 37:57–63.

Winter, Colin. 1977. *Namibia: The Story of a Bishop in Exile.* London: Lutterworth Press.

Wood, Brian. 1984. "The Militarisation of Namibia's Economy." *Review of African Political Economy* 29:138–43.

———. 1987. "The Battle for Trade Unions in Namibia." *South African Labour Bulletin* 12(4):56–61.

———. 1987. "Ben Ulenga Interview Part II." *Action on Namibia* Summer:10–14.

———. 1987. "Interview with Ben Ulenga." *Action on Namibia* Spring:7–10.

———. 1987. "The Making of a Trade Unionist: An Interview with Ben Ulenga, 19 March 1987." *Review of African Political Economy* 39:86–102.

———. 1991. "Preventing the Vacuum: Determinants of the Namibia Settlement." *Journal of Southern African Studies* 17:742–69.

Wood, Brian, ed. 1988. *Namibia, 1884–1984: Readings on Namibia's History and Society.* London: Namibia Support Committee in cooperation with the United Nations Institute for Namibia.

World Bank. 1991. *Namibia: Poverty Alleviation with Sustainable Growth.* Washington, D.C.: World Bank.

Ya Otto, John. 1981. *Battlefront Namibia.* Westport: Lawrence Hill.

OTHER BOOKS AND ARTICLES

Adesina, Jimi. 1992. "Labour Movements and Policy Making in Africa." *Working Paper 1/1992.* Dakar: CODESRIA.

Adler, Glenn, and Eddie Webster. 1995. "Challenging Transition Theory: The Labor Movement, Radical Reform, and the Transition to Democracy in South Africa." *Politics and Society* 23:75–106.

Ake, Claude. 1991. "Rethinking African Democracy." *Journal of Democracy* 2(1):32–44.

Akwetey, Emmanuel Obliteifo. 1994. *Trade Unions and Democratization: A Comparative Study of Zambia and Ghana.* Stockholm Studies in Politics No. 50. University of Stockholm.

Allen, Victor. 1969. "The Study of African Trade Unionism." *Journal of Modern African Studies* 7:289–307.

———. 1972. "The Meaning of the Working Class in Africa." *Journal of Modern African Studies* 10:169–89.

Ananaba, Wogu. 1979. *The Trade Union Movement in Africa: Promise and Performance.* London: Hurst.

Anyang' Nyong'o, Peter. 1992. "Democratization Processes in Africa." *Review of African Political Economy* 54:97–105.

———. 1992. "The One-Party State and Its Apologists: The Democratic Alternative." In *30 Years of Independence in Africa: The Lost Decades?*, edited by Peter Anyang' Nyong'o. Nairobi: African Association of Political Science.

Anyang' Nyong'o, Peter, ed. 1987. *Popular Struggles for Democracy in Africa.* London: Zed Books.

Atkinson, Doreen. 1992. "State and Civil Society in Flux: Parameters of a Changing Debate." *Theoria* 79:1–28.

Bangura, Yusuf, and Bjorn Beckman. 1991. "African Workers and Structural Adjustment: The Nigerian Case." In *The IMF and the South: The Social Impact of Crisis and Adjustment*, edited by Dharam Ghai. London: Zed Books.

Baskin, Jeremy. 1991. *Striking Back: A History of COSATU*. Johannesburg: Ravan Press.

Bates, Robert. 1971. *Unions, Parties and Political Development: A Study of Mineworkers in Zambia*. New Haven: Yale University Press.

Bayart, Jean-Francois. 1986. "Civil Society in Africa." In *Political Domination in Africa: Reflections on the Limits of Power*, edited by Patrick Chabal. Cambridge: Cambridge University Press.

Berg, Elliot, and Jeffrey Butler. 1966. "Trade Unions." In *Political Parties and National Integration in Tropical Africa*, edited by James Coleman and Carl Rosberg. Berkeley: University of California Press.

Bergquist, Charles. 1986. *Labor in Latin America: Comparative Essays on Chile, Argentina, Venezuela, and Colombia*. Stanford: Stanford University Press.

Bienefeld, Manfred. 1979. "Trade Unions, the Labour Process and the Tanzanian State." *Journal of Modern African Studies* 17(4):553–93.

Botha, Thozamile. 1992. "Civic Associations as Autonomous Organs of Grassroots Participation." *Theoria* 79:57–74.

Bratton, Michael. 1989. "Beyond the State: Civil Society and Associational Life in Africa." *World Politics* 42:407–30.

———. 1992. "Zambia Starts Over." *Journal of Democracy* 3(2):81–94.

———. 1995. "Testing Competing Explanations for Regime Transitions in Africa." Paper presented at the Thirty-eighth Annual African Studies Association Meeting, Orlando.

Bratton, Michael, and Nicolas van de Walle. 1992. "Popular Protest and Political Reform in Africa." *Comparative Politics* 24(4):419–42.

———. 1997. *Democratic Experiments in Africa: Regime Transitions in Comparative Perspective*. Cambridge: Cambridge University Press.

Callaghy, Thomas. 1993. "Political Passions and Economic Interests: Economic Reform and Political Structure in Africa." In *Hemmed In: Responses to Africa's Economic Decline*, edited by Thomas Callaghy and John Ravenhill. New York: Columbia University Press.

Chazan, Naomi. 1982. "The New Politics of Participation in Tropical Africa." *Comparative Politics* 14(2):169–89.

Chege, Michael. 1987. "The State and Labour in Kenya." In *Popular Struggles for Democracy in Africa*, edited by Peter Anyang' Nyong'o. London: Zed Press.

Cohen, Robin. 1976. "From Peasants to Workers in Africa." In *The Political Economy of Contemporary Africa*, edited by Peter Gutkind and Immanuel Wallerstein. Beverly Hills: Sage.

———. 1980. "Resistance and Hidden Forms of Consciousness Amongst African Workers." *Review of African Political Economy* 19:8–22.

———. 1991. *Contested Domains: Debates in International Labour Studies*. London: Zed Books.

Cohen, Robin, Jean Copans, and Peter Gutkind. 1978. "Introduction." In *African Labour History*, edited by Peter Gutkind, Robin Cohen, and Jean Copans. London: Sage.

Cohen, Robin, Peter Gutkind, and Phyllis Brazier, eds. 1979. *Peasants and Proletarians: The Struggles of Third World Workers.* New York: Monthly Review Press.

Coleman, James. 1954. "Nationalism in Tropical Africa." *American Political Science Review* 48(2):404–26.

Collier, Ruth Berins, and David Collier. 1991. *Shaping the Political Arena: Critical Junctures, the Labor Movement and Regime Dynamics in Latin America.* Princeton: Princeton University Press.

Cooper, David. 1978. "The State, Mineworkers and Multinationals: The Selebi Phikwe Strike, Botswana, 1975." In *African Labour History*, edited by Peter Gutkind, Robin Cohen, and Jean Copans. London: Sage.

Crisp, Jeff. 1984. *The Story of an African Working Class.* London: Zed Books.

Damachi, Ukandi, Dieter Seibel, and Lester Trachtman, eds. 1979. *Industrial Relations in Africa.* London: Macmillan.

Davies, Ioan. 1966. *African Trade Unions.* Harmondsworth: Penguin.

Deyo, Frederic. 1990. "Economic Policy and the Popular Sector." In *Manufacturing Miracles: Paths of Industrialization in Latin America and East Asia,* edited by Gary Gereffi and Donald Wyman. Princeton: Princeton University Press.

Diamond, Larry. 1996. "Is the Third Wave Over?" *Journal of Democracy* 7(3):20–37.

Diamond, Larry, Juan Linz, and Seymour Martin Lipset, eds. 1988. *Democracy in Developing Countries: Africa.* Vol. 2. Boulder: Lynne Rienner.

Fanon, Frantz. 1968. [1961] *The Wretched of the Earth.* New York: Grove Press.

Fatton, Robert. 1990. "Liberal Democracy in Africa." *Political Science Quarterly* 105(3):455–73.

———. 1991. "Democracy and Civil Society in Africa." *Mediterranean Quarterly* 2(4):83–95.

Fine, Bob, Francine de Clerq, and Duncan Innes. 1981. "Trade Unions and the State: The Question of Legality." *South African Labour Bulletin* 7:39–68.

Fine, Robert. 1992. "Civil Society Theory and the Politics of Transition in South Africa." *Review of African Political Economy* 55:71–83.

Fischer, Georges. 1961. "Trade Unions and Decolonisation." *Presence Africaine* 6–7(34–35):121–69.

Freund, Bill. 1984. "Labor and Labor History in Africa: A Review of the Literature." *African Studies Review* 27:1–58.

———. 1988. *The African Worker.* Cambridge: Cambridge University Press.

———. 1992. "The Unions of South Africa." *Dissent* Summer:378–85.

Friedland, William. 1974. "African Trade Union Studies: Analysis of Two Decades." *Cahiers d'Etudes Africaines* 14(3):575–93.

Friedman, Steve. 1987. *Building Tomorrow Today: African Workers in Trade Unions, 1970–1984.* Johannesburg: Ravan Press.

Gertzel, Cherry. 1974. "Labour and the State: The Case of Zambia's Mineworkers' Union." *Journal of Commonwealth and Comparative Studies,* No. 13.

Gutkind, Peter. 1975. "The View from Below: Political Consciousness of the Urban Poor in Ibadan." *Cahiers d'Etudes Africaines* 15(1):5–35.

Gyimah-Boadi, E. 1996. "Civil Society in Africa." *Journal of Democracy* 7(2):118–32.

Harbeson, John, Donald Rothchild, and Naomi Chazan, eds. 1994. *Civil Society and the State in Africa.* Boulder: Lynne Rienner.

Hodgkin, Thomas. 1957. *Nationalism in Colonial Africa.* New York: New York University Press.

Huntington, Samuel. 1996. "Democracy for the Long Haul." *Journal of Democracy* 7(2):3–13.

Hyden, Goran, and Walter Bgoya. 1987. "The State and the Crisis in Africa: In Search of a Second Liberation." *Development Dialogue* 2:5–29.

Hyman, Richard. 1979. "Third World Strikes in International Perspective." *Development and Change* 10:321–37.

Ihonvbere, Julius. 1996. "On the Threshold of Another False Start? A Critical Evaluation of Prodemocracy Movements in Africa." *Journal of Asian and African Studies* 33(1–2):125–42.

Imam, Ayesha. 1992. "Democratization Processes in Africa: Problems and Prospects." *Review of African Political Economy* 54:102–5.

Issue: A Journal of Opinion. 1991. "Focus: Challenges to and Transition from Authoritarianism in Africa." 20(1):1–64.

Issue: A Journal of Opinion. 1993. "Focus: Toward a New African Political Order: African Perspectives on Democratization Processes, Regional Conflict Management." 21(1–2):1–91.

Jeffries, Richard. 1975. "The Labour Aristocracy? Ghana Case Study." *Review of African Political Economy* 3:59–70.

Joseph, Richard. 1991. "Africa: The Rebirth of Political Freedom." *Journal of Democracy* 2(4):11–24.

Kante, Babacar. 1994. "Senegal's Empty Elections." *Journal of Democracy* 5(1):96–108.

Karl, Terry Lynn. 1990. "Dilemmas of Democratization in Latin America." *Comparative Politics* 23(1):1–21.

Katznelson, Ira, and Aristide Zolberg, eds. 1986. *Working Class Formation: Nineteenth Century Patterns in Western Europe and the United States.* Princeton: Princeton University Press.

Keck, Margaret. 1989. "The New Unionism in the Brazilian Transition." In *Democratizing Brazil: Problems of Transition and Consolidation,* edited by Alfred Stepan. New York: Oxford University Press.

Keet, Dot. 1991. "ICFTU Conference for African Trade Unionists: International Solidarity or Paternalism?" *South African Labour Bulletin* 16:70–82.

———. 1992. "Zimbabwe Trade Unions: From 'Corporatist Brokers' Towards an 'Independent Labour Movement'?" *South African Labour Bulletin* 16:56–62.

Kraus, Jon. 1976. "African Trade Unions: Progress or Poverty?" *African Studies Review* 19:95–108.

———. 1979. "Strikes and Labour Power in Ghana." *Development and Change* 10: 259–86.

———. 1988. "The Political Economy of Trade Union–State Relations in Radical and Populist Regimes in Africa." In *Labour and Unions in Asia and Africa,* edited by Roger Southall. New York: St. Martin's Press.

Loxley, John. 1987. "Labour Migration and the Liberation Struggle in Southern Africa." In *International Labour and the Third World: The Making of a New Working Class,* edited by Rosalind Boyd, Robin Cohen, and Peter Gutkind. Aldershot: Gower Publishing.

Loxley, John, and John Saul. 1975. "Multinationals, Workers and the Parastatals in Tanzania." *Review of African Political Economy* 2:54–88.

Malaba, Luke. 1980. "Supply, Control and Organization of African Labour in Rhodesia." *Review of African Political Economy* 18:7–28.

Mamdani, Mahmood. 1987. "Contradictory Class Perspectives on the Question of Democracy: The Case of Uganda." In *Popular Struggles for Democracy in Africa,* edited by Peter Anyang' Nyong'o. London: Zed Books.

———. 1992. "Africa: Democratic Theory and Democratic Struggles." *Dissent* Summer:312–18.

Mamdani, Mahmood, Thandika Mkandawire, and Ernest Wamba-dia-Wamba. 1988. "Social Movements, Social Transformation and Struggle for Democracy in Africa." *Economic and Political Weekly* 23(19):973–81.

Mann, Michael. 1988. "The Giant Stirs: South African Business in the Age of Reform." In *State, Resistance and Change in South Africa,* edited by Philip Frankel, Noam Pines, and Mark Swilling. London: Croom Helm.

Marks, Gary. 1989. *Unions in Politics: Britain, Germany and the United States in the Nineteenth and Early Twentieth Centuries.* Princeton: Princeton University Press.

Marx, Anthony. 1989. "South African Black Trade Unions as an Emerging Working Class Movement." *Journal of Modern African Studies* 27:383–400.

Massey, David. 1980. "The Changing Political Economy of Migrant Labour in Botswana." *South African Labour Bulletin* 5:4–26.

Mbembe, Achille. 1991. "Democratization and Social Movements in Africa." *Africa Demos* 1(1): 4.

Mihyo, Paschal. 1975. "The Struggle for Workers' Control in Tanzania." *Review of African Political Economy* 4:62–85.

Monga, Celestin. 1995. "Civil Society and Democratisation in Francophone Africa." *Journal of Modern African Studies* 33:359–79.

Munck, Ronaldo. 1988. *The New International Labour Studies: An Introduction.* London: Zed Press.

Nyang'oro, Julius. 1994. "Reform Politics and the Democratization Process in Africa." *African Studies Review* 37(1):133–49.

———. 1996. "Critical Notes on Political Liberalization in Africa." *Journal of Asian and African Studies* 33(1–2):112–24.

O'Donnell, Guillermo. 1996. "What Makes Democracies Endure?" *Journal of Democracy* 7(1):39–55.

Orr, Charles. 1966. "Trade Unionism in Colonial Africa." *Journal of Modern African Studies* 4:65–81.

Panford, Kwamina. 1988. "State–Trade Union Relations: The Dilemmas of Single Trade Union Systems in Ghana and Nigeria." *Labour and Society* 13(1):37–53.

Parpart, Jane. 1987. "Class Consciousness Among the Zambian Copper Miners, 1950–1968." *Canadian Journal of African Studies* 21:54–77.

Parson, Jack. 1980. "The Working Class, the State and Social Change in Botswana." *South African Labour Bulletin* 5:44–55.

Payne, Leigh. 1991. "Working Class Strategies in the Transition to Democracy in Brazil." *Comparative Politics* 23:221–38.

Peace, Adrian. 1975. "The Lagos Proletariat: Labour Aristocrats or Populist Militants?" In *The Development of an African Working Class,* edited by Richard Sandbrook and Robin Cohen. London: Longman.

Plaut, Martin. 1992. "Debates in a Shark Tank—The Politics of South Africa's Non-Racial Trade Unions." *African Affairs* 91:389–403.

Richer, Pete. 1992. "Zimbabwean Unions: From State Partners to Outcasts." *South African Labour Bulletin* 16:66–69.

Rueschemeyer, Dietrich, Evelyne Huber Stephens, and John Stephens. 1992. *Capitalist Development and Democracy.* Chicago: University of Chicago Press.

Sachikonye, Lloyd. 1987. "State, Capital and Trade Unions." In *Zimbabwe: The Political Economy of Transition, 1980–1986,* edited by Ibbo Mandaza. Dakar: CODESRIA.

———. 1989. "The Debate on Democratization in Contemporary Zimbabwe." *Review of African Political Economy* 45–46:117–25.

Sandbrook, Richard. 1972. "Patrons, Clients, and Unions: The Labour Movement and Political Conflict in Kenya." *Journal of Commonwealth Political Studies* 10:3–27.

———. 1977. "The Political Potential of African Urban Workers." *Canadian Journal of African Studies* 11:411–33.

Sandbrook, Richard, and Robin Cohen, eds. 1975. *The Development of an African Working Class.* London: Longman.

Saul, John. 1975. "The 'Labour Aristocracy' Thesis Reconsidered." In *The Development of an African Working Class,* edited by Richard Sandbrook and Robin Cohen. London: Longman.

Scipes, Kim. 1992. "Understanding the New Labor Movements in the 'Third World': The Emergence of Social Movement Unionism." *Critical Sociology* 19(2):81–101.

Seidman, Gay. 1994. *Manufacturing Militance: Workers' Movements in Brazil and South Africa, 1970–1985.* Berkeley: University of California Press.

Shivji, Issa. 1976. *Class Struggles in Tanzania.* New York: Monthly Review Press.

Simons, Jack, and Ray Simons. 1983. *Class and Colour in South Africa, 1850–1950.* London: International Defence and Aid Fund.

Sithole, Masipula. 1990. "Zimbabwe: In Search of a Stable Democracy." In *Politics in Developing Countries: Comparing Experiences with Democracy,* edited by Larry Diamond, Juan Linz, and Seymour Martin Lipset. Boulder: Lynne Rienner.

Sklar, Richard. 1975. *Corporate Power in an African State: The Political Impact of Multinational Mining Companies in Zambia.* Berkeley: University of California Press.

————. 1979. "The Nature of Class Domination in Africa." *Journal of Modern African Studies* 17:531–52.

South African Labour Bulletin. 1979. "Focus on Wiehahn." 5:1–126.

Southall, Roger, ed. 1988. *Labour and Unions in Asia and Africa.* New York: St. Martin's Press.

————. 1988. *Trade Unions and the New Industrialization of the Third World.* Pittsburgh: University of Pittsburgh Press.

Stichter, Sharon. 1975. "Workers, Trade Unions, and the Mau Mau Rebellion." *Canadian Journal of African Studies* 9:259–75.

————. 1985. *Migrant Laborers.* Cambridge: Cambridge University Press.

Thomas, Henk, ed. 1995. *Globalization and Third World Trade Unions: The Challenge of Rapid Economic Change.* London: Zed Books.

Valenzuela, Samuel. 1989. "Labor Movements in Transitions to Democracy: A Framework for Analysis." *Comparative Politics* 21:445–72.

Van Onselen, Charles. 1976. *Chibaro: African Mine Labour in Southern Rhodesia, 1900–1933.* London: Pluto Press.

Von Freyhold, Michaela. 1987. "Labour Movements or Popular Struggles in Africa." *Review of African Political Economy* 39:23–32.

Wallerstein, Immanuel. 1961. *Africa: The Politics of Independence.* New York: Vintage Books.

Wanyande, Peter. 1988. "Democracy and the One-Party State: The African Experience." In *Democratic Theory and Practice in Africa,* edited by Walter Oyugi, Atieno Odhiambo, Michael Chege, and Afrifa Gitonga. London: James Currey.

Waterman, Peter. 1975. "The 'Labour Aristocracy' in Africa: Introduction to a Debate." *Development and Change* 6:57–73.

————. 1978. "Consciousness, Organisation and Action Amongst Lagos Portworkers." *Review of African Political Economy* 13:47–62.

————. 1979. "Strikes in the Third World: Introduction." *Development and Change* 10:177–80.

Webster, Eddie. 1988. "The Rise of Social-Movement Unionism: The Two Faces of the Black Trade Union Movement in South Africa." In *State, Resistance and Change in South Africa,* edited by Philip Frankel, Noam Pines, and Mark Swilling. London: Croom Helm.

Woddis, Jack. 1961. *Africa: The Lion Awakes.* London: Lawrence and Wishart.

Young, Crawford. 1988. "The African Colonial State and Its Political Legacy." In *The Precarious Balance: State and Society in Africa,* edited by Donald Rothchild and Naomi Chazan. Boulder: Westview Press.

————. 1994. *The African Colonial State in Comparative Perspective*. New Haven: Yale University Press.

————. 1994. "Democratization in Africa: The Contradictions of a Political Imperative." In *Economic Change and Political Liberalization in Sub-Saharan Africa*, edited by Jennifer Widner. Baltimore: Johns Hopkins University Press.

INDEX

An *n* after a page number indicates a note.